FREEDOM TO BUILD

Dweller Control of the Housing Process

Edited by JOHN F.C. TURNER
and ROBERT FICHTER

The Macmillan Company, New York, New York
Collier-Macmillan Limited, London

The Macmillan Company
866 Third Avenue, New York, N.Y. 10022
Collier-Macmillan Canada Ltd., Toronto, Ontario
Library of Congress Catalog Card Number: 72–80906
First Printing
Printed in the United States of America

Acknowledgments

THE AUTHORS are indebted to many people and it is impossible to recognize them all by name. The following, however, have made personal contributions without which the book, or certain chapters, could never have been written and published:

Bertha Berry
Abigail Collins
Cora du Bois
Barrie Grenell
Susan Grindley
Ivan Illich
Sascha Illich
David Judelson
Michael Kuhn
Aprodicio Laquian
Hal Levin
Robert Ledogar
Anthony Leeds
James Morton
Welton Myers
Lisa Peattie
Donald Schon
Peggy Spohn
David Suskind
Maxine Terner

The directors and staff of the

American Institute of Indian Studies
Centro Interamericano de Documentación
Joint Center for Urban Studies of M.I.T. and Harvard University
Ministerio de la Vivienda, Peru, and its predecessors
Olivetti Foundation
Organization for Social and Technical Innovation
Town Planning Organization of the State of Orissa, India
Urban Institute
Weizmann Institute

Preface

THIS IS A BOOK concerned with the activity called housing. From a variety of perspectives, the authors examine the participation or lack of participation of dwellers themselves in that activity. Their conclusions, in brief, are that as dwellers lose control over their living environments, shelter becomes a commodity of reduced value to the individual and often an inordinate expense to society.

When housing is seen as a physical product, it will be judged by physical criteria alone. Conventional housing standards, for instance, measure acceptability in terms of occupant-area ratios, air circulation, plumbing facilities, and so forth, calculated on the needs of some hypothetical standardized inhabitant.

The authors contend that such measures of value are based on false premises. They contend that genuine housing values lie in the ability of dwellers to create and maintain environments which serve both their material and their psychological needs—not in buildings as such.

The urgency of a basic shelter problem cannot be ignored; but neither the shelter problem nor the manifold social problems of which it is a part can be solved by bureaucratically administered, politically imposed programs.

The needs of the poor are most vivid. The situation of many poor people, who must depend on contractor-oriented bureaucratic systems for a roof over their heads, dramatizes the exorbitant costs, in human and money terms, of taking a fundamental life activity out of the users' hands. But this is not just a book about the poor. It is, rather, an exploration into the complex modes of housing supply in our contemporary world.

Approximately a third of the world's people house themselves with their own hands, sometimes in the absence of government and professional intervention, sometimes in spite of it. And while simple, primitive modes of housing are not to be praised just for these qualities, the authors again and again note an opposition between what individuals can do for themselves, given minimally sympathetic conditions, and what centralized, hierarchic authorities will not, cannot, or should not do for them.

In a sense this book is part of a breaking wave of reaction against authoritarian solutions to technocratically posed problems. It is the work of professionals who, like so many professionals today, have become extremely skeptical of the values into which they were initiated at the beginning of their careers.

One might well read the book as a collective autobiography turning on a common conversion experience. The essence of that experience is that much of what has been done in the name of human well-being has been arrogantly and ignorantly done at the expense of human well-being; that those who have been trained to support and enhance such fundamental human efforts as housing, education, and health care have claimed possession of those activities, forgetting that a basic human right is the right to do for one's self what one is quite able to do.

The call for restored or increased autonomy may not, in any event, lead to greater autonomy. Yet the evidence of the following papers suggests that the costs of our present courses of action are very high indeed, and that if societies possess any degree of free will whatever, it is in their interests to alter the prevailing drift toward excessive freedom for the few and constraints on the freedom of the many.

It must be said at the beginning, and very emphatically, that none of the authors conceives of housing in isolation from the many other basic activities of life. A poor family, which may have been victimized by miserable schooling, inadequate health care, and sparse job opportunities, will not be rescued by any small increments of freedom in the area of housing alone. And it must also be said that much of the case material in this book that suggests the possibilities of greater autonomy in housing is based on relatively strong, upwardly mobile families. The hopeless poor, therefore, may well remain just as much a dilemma after this book as before it.

The concepts offered here are not a panacea, but they point the way to improved living conditions for an indeterminately large population in both the industrialized and transitional economies of the world. The authors are emphatic in their contention that millions of households could do for themselves in housing, with certain minimal aids, what is either not being done for them at all or being done badly for them, and at an extravagant price in wasted public resources.

The authors of the following papers have an extensive experience in the field of housing to draw on. *William C. Grindley* worked in Peru, both as a Peace Corps volunteer and as a field architect for a labor-banking alliance, before he undertook a detailed study of the owner-builder phenomenon in the United States. He has recently completed a policy study for the World Bank, focusing on site and service programs. *Richard Spohn,* a lawyer, served as program director of an adult education program for migrant workers in upstate New York, directed a community action program which cooperated with Self Help Housing Inc. in California, and is presently associate director of the Ralph Nader Congress Project. *Rolf Goetze* served as a Peace Corps architect in Nepal, worked in Appalachia, and then conducted a comparative study of housing rehabilitation experiments as a fellow of the Harvard-M.I.T. Joint Center for Urban Studies before joining the Mayor's staff in Boston as a housing specialist. He is also presently teaching at Boston University. *Hans H. Harms* studied architecture in Germany, after working as a bricklayer in the postwar period, later took postgraduate studies in architecture and urban planning in the United

States, worked on housing in France and Latin America (Peru and Colombia), taught in Germany, and is presently director of the Community Projects Laboratory at the Massachusetts Institute of Technology.

Peter Grenell lived in India for three years, two of them as an American Institute of Indian Studies fellow and the third as a Ford Foundation consultant in Calcutta, later assisted in the preparation of a self-help demonstration project presented to the Department of Housing and Urban Development, and most recently has been with urban planning teams in Fall River, Mass., and Dallas, Tex. *John F. C. Turner* trained as an architect in London, spent eight years in Peru, during which time he became intimately familiar with squatter settlements, and for the past six years has lived in the United States, writing, teaching at M.I.T., and working as a consultant to national and international housing and urban development agencies. *Ian Donald Terner* has been an officer in a private housing firm, has done work with self-help and industrialized housing in Asia, Latin America, and the United States, has been an assistant professor of urban planning at Harvard, and in the past year has coauthored an analysis, with John Turner, of industrialized housing experiments in several Third World nations.

These six have assisted one another and learned from one another on a number of occasions. And while they do not represent an ideological unity, they have found themselves again and again in agreement on certain fundamental points which are the substance of this book.

They agree, for instance, that the provision of housing for low-income people through direct government action has generally been a failure. It has been their experience, as much in the United States as in India or Peru, that governments have neither the will nor often the resources to provide sufficient shelter, haven't the flexibility to provide the right kinds of shelter, and haven't the wisdom to recognize the amount of social damage they have done when they have tried to make up the so-called housing deficit through massive project planning.

They also agree that a great unused resource exists in the desire, energy, and initiative of families to house themselves. In Peru, for example, John Turner gradually learned how squatter settlements manifest a natural ordering of household priorities which government housing projects only manage to distort. In India, Peter Grenell saw the growth of a planned city which ignored some basic life patterns of its inhabitants, as well as its impact on the lives of older neighboring communities. And in the United States, Rolf Goetze observed, at close range and over a considerable period of time, the way in which federal housing programs tend to derange traditional housing incentives that apparently can, with the right sort of help, produce shelter more cheaply and more satisfactorily than any government program in existence.

The authors have varying preoccupations and some differences of opinion. One stresses the housing problems of the poor; another asserts a universal problem of housing quality. They differ on the ability of our present "free market system" to serve pressing shelter needs, and they are far from complete agreement on the consequences of technology and high levels of consumption on the natural environment. But whatever arguments they have had among themselves, they commonly subscribe to the need for greater autonomy and the potential of greater user autonomy in the provision of housing.

Their thoughts have matured together during the past few years through shared experience, joint research, and, most recently, the discipline of writing the chapters of this book. Some of the material comes out of research Rolf Goetze and John Turner carried out together at the Joint Center for Urban Studies of M.I.T. and Harvard University. At the request of Ernest Weissman and Wilson Garcés of the United Nations Centre for Housing, Building and Planning, they prepared a working paper on the problems of and policies for uncontrolled urban settlements.[1] In 1968, these two, together with Hans Harms, Peter Grenell, and Donald Terner, pre-

[1] This paper, which continues to have a worldwide influence on attitudes and policies with regard to low-income housing and squatter settlements, has been reprinted in various abridged forms and in several languages. The most accessible are the articles in the *International Social Development Review No. 1, Urbanization: Development Policies and Planning,* United Nations, New York, 1968, and in Gerald Breese, editor, *The City in Newly Developing Countries,* Prentice-Hall, 1969.

pared *Architecture of Democracy,* a special issue of the British magazine *Architectural Design.*[2]

In 1969 and 1970, with Peggy and Richard Spohn, the authors were contracted by Donald Schon for the preparation of a major study on self-help housing in the United States for the U.S. Department of Housing and Urban Development.[3] In addition to being the Executive President of the Organization for Social and Technical Innovation (OSTI), Schon played an active part in the direction and formulation of the work and subsequently chaired the discussions for which the papers of this book were originally prepared—the symposium on User-Controlled Housing at the 135th meeting of the American Association for the Advancement of Science, organized by Anthony Leeds.[4]

The last stage in the development of the authors' ideas, before the final writing, took place at the Centro Interamericano de Documentación (CIDOC) in Cuernavaca, Mexico, at the Invitation of Ivan and Sascha Illich. For a week in September 1971, the authors met with fifteen seminar participants to discuss the issues and implications of user-control in housing. These discussions contributed to the development of the themes introduced in the last three chapters of this book.

The authors are aware of the tentative nature of their thinking. They have discussed the issues presented here too many times among themselves not to be conscious of the research and analysis still to be done. Yet for all of that, they are not timid about the broad outlines of their conclusions. They are quite willing to say that what they have observed and what they have recommended deserves the most serious consideration by those who are in positions of power

[2] Vol. XXXIII No. 8, August 1968.

[3] An unpublished twelve-volume study based on extensive field observations throughout the continental United States, Alaska, and Puerto Rico. Four of these volumes dealt with the technological aspect of self-help construction and were prepared under subcontract by Building Systems Development, now of New York, whose Executive President is Ezra Ehrencrantz.

[4] Anthony Leeds is Professor of Social Anthropology at the University of Texas, Austin. He and Elizabeth Leeds have written extensively on the *favelas* of Brazil and on the counter-productive consequences of conventional public housing policies.

and by those who can influence men and women in positions of power. To the extent that a book can affect the course of national action, it is their hope that this book may contribute in some considerable way to the decisions which will determine our national housing policy, and our many local housing policies, in the years to come.

R. F.
December 1971

Contents

PART ONE

Autonomy in Housing: Cases and Issues

1

WILLIAM C. GRINDLEY

Owner-Builders: Survivors with a Future

EVERY YEAR some 160,000 families in the United States build their own homes. To be more precise, they act as general contractors who oversee design and financing as well as construction. Many owner-builders put in months of hard labor, from pouring the foundations to nailing on the shingles; others work along with men they have hired to help them; still others merely supervise men they have hired. Yet these are not distinctions that count in the present study. In this paper we are concerned with some broad aspects of control within the single-family housing market; and whether the owner-builder puts just a little "administrative equity" and "sweat equity" into the project or a great deal, he is preeminently *the person who controls* the planning and building of his own home.

It is easy to understand why more people do not become owner-builders. Restrictive codes, discriminatory federal mortgage insuring practices, and the general trend toward specialization of construction tasks have all contributed to a climate unfavorable to the man who may have thought about building his own home. Owner-building also requires time. Generally this time is taken from family recreation or from career-advancement activity such as night school.

Consequently there are opportunity costs to spending time building as opposed to presently earning more or seeking a better future income. But the startling fact is the number of people who persist in the face of so many obstacles and inhibitions.

Census figures tell the story—a story no one has paid much attention to. Owner-builders are presently responsible for approximately 20 percent of the new single-family dwellings constructed annually in the United States and 12 percent of *all* housing begun each year.

One might try to explain away the phenomenon as an anachronism, as a holdover from the days of the frontier, as a kind of log-cabin nostalgia which must be rapidly disappearing. And in fact there has been a decline since 1949, when one out of three single-family dwellings was built by its owner.[1] But over the past decade there seems to have been a leveling off at 17 to 20 percent of new single-family home construction.[2] Furthermore, the number of mortgages granted owner-builders by banks and savings and loan associations has even increased to some extent in recent years, in spite of a nation-wide credit squeeze.

One might also guess that owner-builders are confined to rural areas. It is true that they account for a very important share of all new housing in rural areas—some 40 percent. Yet in the suburbs surrounding the Standard Metropolitan Statistical Areas (SMSAs) they are also formidable contributors to the new housing stock. In the suburban belts around the SMSAs, 50,000 units—10 percent of all single-family dwellings—are constructed by owner-builders every year. This is nearly a third of all owner-built units erected annually.

One reason for the neglect of the owner-builder phenomenon has been the statistical context in which it has been placed. When they are lumped in with housing units provided by multi-family apartment houses, owner-built, single-family dwellings tend to be overlooked. But in the following table, *only* single-family construction

[1] Housing and Home Finance Agency, Department of Housing and Urban Development, *Ideas and Methods Exchange Bulletin*, no. 54 (Washington, D.C.: U.S. Government Printing Office, January 1959).

[2] Bureau of the Census, Department of Commerce, with the Department of Housing and Urban Development, *Construction Reports C-25 Series* (Washington, D.C.: U.S. Government Printing Office, 1963–69).

is considered; and placed beside the two other major contributors to that stock—contractors working on commission, the so-called custom builders, and developers, who build houses for the market—the owner-builder resumes his place as an important actor in housing production.

Table 1. Characteristics of Single-Family Dwellings (1968)

	Owner-Built	*Contractor-Built*	*Developer-Built*
Number	158,000	178,000	536,000
Location:			
Inside SMSA	27%	43%	66%
Outside SMSA	73	57	34
Units by region (per thousand families):			
Northeast	1.8	2.6	5.6
Northcentral	3.6	2.5	7.7
South	4.6	6.0	11.4
West	1.8	2.5	14.2
Median size (sq. ft.):	1,270	1,480	1,605
Type of financing:			
Conventional	53%	67%	62%
FHA/VA	6	11	33
Cash	41	22	5

One statistic seems particularly significant, since it reflects the role the federal government plays in guiding national energies. While the Federal Housing Administration (FHA) and the Veterans Administration (VA) assist the purchase of one out of every three developer-built homes by offering mortgage insurance, they perform this service for only *one out of seventeen owner-built homes.*

If there were no other long-term financing alternatives, this sort of discrimination might well reduce owner-building to the negligible level of activity it is often assumed to be. Yet commercial banks and savings and loan associations have supported owner-builders when the federal government would not. One is compelled to ask why, if private commercial lending institutions do not consider the owner-builder an inordinate risk, the major public servant of housing need apparently does.

There is no certain answer, though it does seem that considerations of scale rather than of risk are paramount. The FHA and the VA certainly have no declared policy of favoring developers over custom-builders and owner-builders, but because developers deal with numerous standardized units which can be "fed" into the application processing mechanisms with maximum efficiency, the developer has a visibility which the single owner-builder does not have.

It appears to be in the interest of FHA and VA administrative procedure to ignore the owner-builder because his single application will require, in all likelihood, as much work as the fifty or one hundred proposed by the developer. This observation is supported by the fact that only one out of nine custom-built, individually processed houses is insured by the FHA and VA. A short-sighted view of economy might suggest that this makes perfect sense: that with a chronic housing shortage, the public interest is better served by federal support, formal and informal, of developers who are willing to build many houses at a time rather than individuals who have nothing more ambitious in mind than building houses for themselves.

But this is just the point, in a longer view of economy and the public interest. The resources of labor and talent and time individuals seem ready to expend to house themselves are no burden on the society at large. Formally stated, the opportunity costs to the public sector of utilizing the administrative and construction labor talents of the owner-builder are zero. And the research upon which this paper is based suggests that those talents and the corresponding willingness of individuals to make some sacrifices for their own good are not rare and are not unique in the sense that they might have been confined to architects or other professionals of the building trades. In fact, even more impressive than the number of owner-builders who annually contribute to housing production was the variety of people who undertook a project which many of us think we could never carry through.

Figure 1 gives a statistical profile of owner-builders by income in comparison with home buyers by income.

A rule of thumb says that a family can afford a house priced at no more than two times its annual income. According to this rule, the minimum income necessary to buy the median-priced, new single-family house for sale in 1968 was $12,500. Only 20 percent of the below median income population could have afforded to buy the median-priced new single-family house. Viewed another way this statistic tells us that only 3 percent of the new houses for sale could have been purchased by families with income less than $6,000 a year, a sector of the population which accounts for over 20 percent of *all* families.

Quite evidently, the owner-builder is economically *less* well off than home buyers, yet *equal* to the population as a whole. A glance at the graph shows that 23.5 percent of those who undertook their own construction had incomes of less than $6,000 per year. In other words, it seems that many rural families compensate for their relatively lower income as they achieve home ownership through the owner-builder process. These are attainments which are denied to persons of exactly equivalent incomes trying to purchase new homes in the suburbs or smaller cities.

Owner-building is thus making a substantial contribution to the housing of lower-income families. This becomes especially significant when one considers that it is the lower-middle and lower classes, as defined by income, who should be the clientele of public agencies charged with facilitating a more equitable housing situation. Owner-building warrants further attention by both the market and housing assistance agencies. And some important lessons for these agents derive from this study.

The first major lesson seems to be clear: lower-income families have more capacity to satisfy their housing needs than public agencies have assumed. Or, to put it another way, our public resources have seemed so insufficient because we have completely overlooked one of the greatest resources of all—individual initiative.

There are other implications to be derived from this graph. Housing economists have long been perplexed by the fact that over 45 percent of families with income under $6,000 (in 1969 dollars) own

Fig. 1. *Annual Incomes of Families Buying and Owner-Building New Single-Family Houses (1968)*

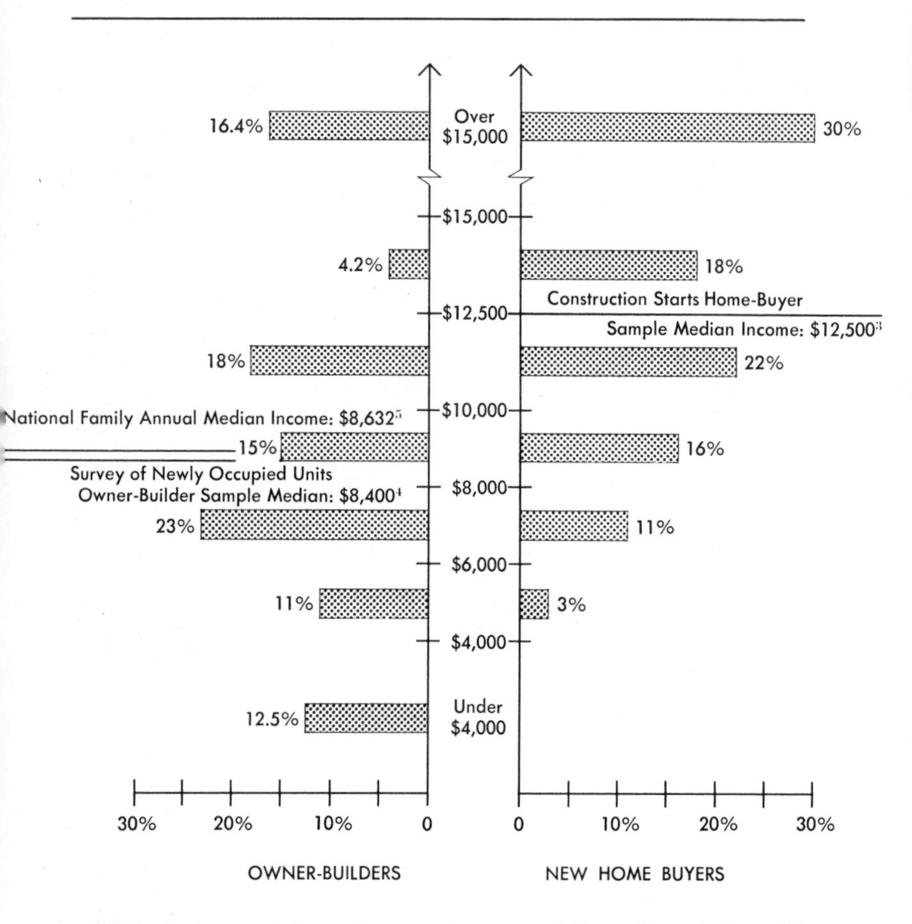

[3] U.S. Savings and Loan League, *Savings and Loan Fact Book, 1968* (Chicago, 1968).

[4] Bureau of the Census, Department of Commerce, with the Department of Housing and Urban Development, *Housing Surveys, Parts 1 and 2, Part 1—Occupants of New Housing Units; Part 2—Mobile Homes and the Housing Supply* (Washington, D.C.: U.S. Government Printing Office, 1968).

[5] Bureau of the Census, Department of Commerce, *Consumer Income, Series P-60, no. 66* (Washington, D.C.: U.S. Government Printing Office, 1968), p. 71.

their own homes. To explain such a statistic, which runs counter to the conventional wisdom about the poor, the economists have suggested that either they own old houses; that they have financed the purchase for the new ones through profits on the sale of a previous house; that financing came out of accumulated capital; or that the low-income family must have had a higher income at the time of purchase.[6]

There is no reason to repudiate these explanations, but they overlook the economies implicit in the owner-builder form of self-help. The reason perhaps is that the owner-builder is thought of as a rare and decreasing species. In fact, owner-builders are not such strange creatures. The great majority are families with children under the age of eighteen. According to the statistical profile, the head of an owner-builder family is five to ten years younger than his home-buying counterpart and has a strong inclination to stay in the area where he builds his house. In our survey more than half of the owner-builders appear to have owned their own homes previously. They gave as their reasons for becoming owner-builders such things as the desire to improve their living conditions, to settle in a better neighborhood, or, in the case of former renters, the desire to have a more secure housing tenancy.

If these seem prosaic reasons for undertaking such an ambitious project, it must be stressed that the owner-builders are, on the whole, very ordinary people. It is only in the exceptional case that the owner-builder, by anybody's measure, could be called an eccentric or could be said to have talents beyond the average. It remains to be seen whether some obscure set of social or psychological circumstances prompts owner-building, but numerous case studies suggest there is no reason why a far greater percentage of the population could not own homes through owner-building.

Field work tells us that the owner-builder method of planning, construction, and maintenance is efficient. The first major saving—a conversion from money to time—occurs in administration and management. Since an owner-builder is, by definition, one who adminis-

[6] Maisel, Sherman J., "Rates of Ownership, Mobility, and Purchase," in *Essays in Urban Land Economics,* University of California Real Estate Research Program (Los Angeles: 1966), p. 92.

ters and manages the construction of his house, this very heavy financial liability is transferred into a demand on leisure time, which the owner-builder will happily give up (if in fact he does not view building his own house as recreation or therapy) for the saving in cash it will mean to him.

An owner-builder's saving on construction costs range from 22 to 53 percent of the construction cost of developer-built houses. It should be emphasized that these savings do not include the equity earned on the actual labor an owner-builder may invest in his house. Selective purchasing of materials and favorable arrangements for construction help (donations of time by friends, use of moonlighting craftsmen, and so forth) also significantly reduce costs. On the average, an owner-builder's output performance is comparable to fully professional work: an average of 1.2 to 1.3 man-hours per square foot against one man-hour per square foot for professional work.

Before going to case material, some statistical generalizations ought to be made about the house the owner-builder produces. Typically it is 10 to 20 percent smaller than developer-built homes. It has as many bedrooms as one would find in a house built by a custom builder or a contractor, though it may not have a second or a third bathroom. The owner-builder provides an adequate heating system, but does without central air conditioning. A garage is often postponed, but in cold-weather areas, there will be a basement. And where appliances are concerned, the owner-built house is quite comparable to any other type. The quality of the owner-built home is generally as high as those which surround it. In fact the owner-built home is indistinguishable from the developer-built or custom-built home of approximate market value.

In short the owner-builder adjusts his priorities to his needs, spends time in place of money, and calls upon resources of material and labor that the custom builder and the developer either may not know about or may be unable to use because of their particular systems.

The first of these factors is of utmost importance. Casework tells us that all of the respondents thought of their homes in terms of their own lives rather than in terms of the dwelling as a discrete entity. This is an awkward consideration for statisticians to handle, for models of supply and demand cannot very well take into account the immense variability of perceived human needs. The owner-builder, on the other hand, is an expert—*the* expert—in determining his mix of needs, resources, and priorities. He can do what no one can do for him: he can call on his time, energy, and talent and a network of friends and contacts to create for himself a living environment which is both feasible and desirable. Some examples follow.

Case I

Tim Johnston lives outside Widener, Georgia. He came originally from Theobald, which is seventy miles away. One of five children, he was raised in the back room of the small store his father still owns in Theobald.

When he was sixteen and legally able to do so, Tim quit school and went to work in the local gas station. Within a year he was married and eager to find a home. Tim had an aunt who owned a house trailer, and he lived with her while he was looking for a better job in a larger town nearby. Once he and his wife almost moved to Atlanta, but they decided against it, mainly because Tim liked to hunt and fish. Finally he found a job in an auto repair shop, and eventually learned quite a lot about auto mechanics.

Three years ago, when Tim was twenty and a second child was due, he and his wife began to think about getting their own home. They had moved, by then, from the trailer to a former mill-owned house, but it was in bad shape and "the wind blew through the windows like there was no glass in them."

With less than $700 in the bank, buying a house was out of the question, so Tim began to think about building for himself. He was determined to put up something better than "a 2 x 4 shack."

As soon as it got around that he was looking for land, his aunt came to the rescue. For $100, she sold him an acre of land from a small farm she had inherited from her husband.

With an income of $3,600 a year, Tim decided it really wasn't any use trying to get a mortgage loan. But he did have one resource. Because of some painting and repairs he had done on the mill house, he had established credit with a small building supplier. The building supplier also helped him select a three-bedroom plan from some books that had come with brick samples.

Tim wanted a brick veneer home similar to the home owned by his boss at the auto repair shop, though practical considerations made him settle for a cement block shell, which he intends to veneer as soon as he gets the money.

It took nearly a year to work out all the details. Once Tim almost gave up and bought a mobile home, but the experience of living cramped up in his aunt's trailer was too vivid. So he stayed at it.

Construction began with the floor slab and footings. Tim subcontracted this part of the job, but he did all the block work himself, getting visibly better from one course of blocks to the next.

It took six weeks to finish the shell. Tim spent every evening and all of his weekends on it, sometimes with the help of a teen-ager who mixed the mortar and carried the blocks. After the shell was done, Tim ordered a set of precut trusses of a type which had been recommended to him by a high school friend from Theobald. He spent his week of summer vacation putting them in place as well as roofing, shingling, and matching the gabled ends.

By the fall, he and his wife moved in, "to save the $13 a week rent." The septic tank hadn't been finished since the concrete company wouldn't extend him the ninety days' credit his friend, the material supplier, had allowed. But with running water and electricity taken care of, the house was fit to live in. He put aside the money that would have gone for rent in order to buy a space heater. It was to be a small one—only enough to heat one room for the first winter—but the heating facilities hadn't been any better in the rented house.

At the time of the interview, all the interior, except for one bedroom, had been finished and painted. In what he calls "a moment of madness," Tim put in a gravel driveway, and his wife bought some box hedges from the supermarket to go on either side of the front stoop. Tim says they need screens, an outside light, and a fan for the summer. He still intends to cover the cinder block walls with a brick veneer, but he has decided that improvement will have to be postponed for awhile. The main thing, Tim says, is that they are free from rent payments, and he is looking forward to "adding on a garage as soon as we save enough to start a repair business."

Case II

Daniel Shore is a postman in the suburban community of Danvers outside Boston. Shore has carried mail on a number of routes in the last twelve years. As a result he has a keen sense of how families live and what their financial situations are. He notes that the mail people receive tells a lot about them; and he adds, with a wry expression, that his own mail never brings overdue payment letters or invitations to sign up for credit cards.

Shore was raised on a dairy farm near Danvers and finished high school in that city at the end of World War II. His wife, also in her forties, is a lifetime resident of Danvers. She has never seriously thought of living anywhere else. The Shores have three children, two boys, aged nineteen and eleven, and a fourteen-year-old daughter. Dan Shore is very proud of his older son, now studying architecture in a well-known school out of state. The boy has worked as a draftsman during school vacations since the age of sixteen and, according to his father, "knows where he is going."

Shore built his own home in 1958, but he had been a home owner twice before. In 1948, shortly after their first child was born, he and his wife bought a thirty-year-old Dutch colonial with two bedrooms and a very small lot. After they had been in the house for awhile, Shore realized that some major repairs were overdue, and since he wasn't satisfied enough with the neighborhood to put a lot of money into the place, he commissioned a friend to build him a three-bedroom ranch-style house. At that time the Shores planned on having at least one more child, and since they already felt cramped in the Dutch colonial, they had one more reason to move.

Shore helped with the weather boarding, the landscaping, and the interior painting and wallpapering, though he now feels he didn't save much money that way. However, he did learn a lot about the costs of a mixed utilities system. His contractor friend had persuaded him to put in a hot air heating system, which turned out to be much cheaper to install than to operate. Shore was and is very sensitive to the costs of operating a home.

The family moved into their contractor-built ranch home in 1951. It was certainly an improvement over their first house; yet over the years Shore began to think he might be able to build himself a house that suited the family better and also was cheaper to operate. He had worked closely with his contractor friend in 1951 and he felt confident that he had learned enough to become his own general contractor.

In 1958, therefore, Shore sold the ranch-style house for $18,900, realizing a profit of $3,600 over his construction costs. Shortly before the sale, he had bought a lot from an elderly lady to whom he had delivered mail some years before. When Mrs. Shore first saw the lot, she was aghast. It was a steep site overlooking the river with a dump at the bottom of the hill and the nearest house 300 yards away. Shore says that he had no trouble visualizing how a house might be set on the 11,250 square foot lot. At that time Mrs. Shore saw only an unpaved road and a dumping ground, but since she was expecting a third child and also had to think about settling her family in an apartment, she left it to her husband to do the best he could.

Shore planned their two-story, full-basement, four-bedroom Cape Cod house "with an eye to the future." A large downstairs room, for instance, can be used as a bedroom for the children during those interim years when they are likely to be home separately and only for a short time, so that a part of the upstairs can be closed off and money saved on fuel costs. When the children are gone, Shore sees the possibility of making the lower level into a self-contained apartment for himself and his wife, thus freeing the house itself for tenants who would be a major source of income for the Shores in their old age.

After his problems with hot air heating, Shore opted for a three-zone hot water system. He has been very pleased with the results: his heating and hot water bills now run to less than $200 a year. He also decided that one large bathroom on the main floor with a double vanity would be enough for his family, a decision he hasn't regretted. And once more with an eye to operating costs, he built the furnace room beneath the bathroom so that needed extra warmth is provided at no extra expense. Mrs. Shore particularly appreciates such details as the chute from the master bedroom to the laundry room in the basement, which Shore himself passes off as "something just as easy to do as not."

Since Shore had already established mortgage credit in Danvers, he had no problem getting a loan. When he took out his $10,500 loan in 1958, Dan Shore earned $6,400 a year. His wife has never worked outside of the home, a fact that both of them are proud of.

Within a month after choosing his lot, Shore had it cleared and had contracted for foundation work. He also contracted out the framing and the electrical, heating, and plumbing systems, the last of which he helped install.

The schedule called for the family to be in by the winter. Shore worked hard, therefore, through the summer and fall of 1958, doing his own roofing and shingling. On a couple of occasions he hired men to help him, but he thinks now he might have gotten along just as well without them. As he puts it, "with too many people around, nothing gets done."

The winter was spent installing the heating system, insulation, wiring, and flooring. Since the contractors worked in the daytime while Shore himself worked at night, he could keep a close check on their progress without getting in their way.

By the spring of 1959, the house was built, a little behind his proposed schedule, but Shore insisted that all the painting and wallpapering be completed before his family moved in. This meant an additional few months of rent, but Shore felt it was worth it so that his wife, with the responsibility of a new son, would not have to live in the midst of confusion. On the whole, Shore says he has never been more relaxed than during the period of building his house. He describes it, a little self-consciously, as a "feeling of accomplishment." He says he wouldn't do it again because of his age, but he has few reservations about recommending the building of one's own house to other people. "You don't have to be an Albert Einstein to build your own home," he says. "All you need are patience and sharp tools."

On the lower side of their lot, the Shores have recently added a two-car garage-workshop which they built from $500 worth of scrap materials. They have also put in a swimming pool, an amenity very popular among the neighborhood children.

The garage-workshop was added so that Shore could store the tools he uses in his "moonlight" asphalt business. With his present $8,400 salary from the post office and income from his "hot topping" and snow removal business, Shore presently earns about $10,400 a year. In 1965, six years after his house was built, the town assessed the full market value of the Shores' property at $27,000. Shore protested, and when it turned out that the assessor had mistakenly assumed the house had two bathrooms and a fireplace, the market value was adjusted downward to $22,000. Shore was naturally pleased, though he confided that, "You can't put dollars and cents on it when you have what you want in a house. I wouldn't sell this place for $40,000."

Case III

Nine years ago the textile research firm John Outman worked for decided to move south from Massachusetts. Outman followed his job, settling his family in the town of Hardly, South Carolina. Outman had been a mechanical engineering draftsman for seven years when his company announced its move. At that point he was thirty-three, his wife twenty-nine. They had three children, two boys aged eleven and nine, and a five-year-old girl. They had also owned a house in Massachusetts, and had the ambition one day to buy and renovate a barn somewhere in Vermont. But Outman had only a fourth-grade education, not the best credentials for getting another job. Furthermore, he was well respected by his firm, felt capable in what he was doing, and liked the people he had been working with. So the family gave up the dream of Vermont and went South.

About a year after moving to Hardly, Outman "picked up" 5 acres on the edge of town, "from someone I got to know through a friend." He bought the land for $100 an acre, and a year later he bought two more adjoining acres.

In the meantime, he had been trying out some house designs in his spare moments at work. He admits that some of them were not very practical. One was to be of poured concrete with a swimming pool on the roof; another featured plywood vaulting. He tried to get a loan to build the poured concrete extravaganza, but no bank would touch it. So he went back to his drawing board, laid out the plans for a 40-by-80-foot three-story shell, got an engineer at the plant to do a final structural design and calculate its cost for a $75 fee; then, with surprising ease, Outman persuaded a bank to grant him a $16,000 twenty-year mortgage at 6 percent. His income at that time was $5,500, while his wife earned another $2,600 working full time at a dress shop in the local shopping center.

As soon as he had the loan in hand, he hired a bulldozer operator to clear the site. Next he brought in a contractor to put down the foundations and erect cinder block walls. Outman himself helped out as much as he could in his spare time. In November 1962, some six months from the time of site clearing, he took ten days of vacation, and with two assistants did the entire framing and roofing job. He attributes this phenomenal speed to the engineer's design which standardized all vertical and horizontal members and eliminated difficult joinery problems.

From then on, until he and his family moved into the house in March 1963, Outman merely supervised the work of two full-time carpenters. At one point, however, he did score a coup: he discovered a railroad salvage sale in a nearby city and managed to get all of his plywood and steel reinforcing at less than half the market price.

Of all the houses in the survey, Outman's is the most unusual, and it would appear more unusual if it were not set off by itself. The first thing that strikes the eye is its size: it looks more like a warehouse than a conventional dwelling. Inside, only the middle floor would be considered finished; yet every one of the nearly ten thousand square feet are in use or show evidence of having been used. In one corner of the middle floor, there is a work table and dozens of model airplanes that apparently were a family hobby some years ago. Another corner has been enclosed to make a darkroom for one of the boys who has become very interested in photography. The other son has taken up painting, and a generous space has been set aside on the top floor for his studio. Outman's wife has a sewing area, another area for canning, and she plans to help her children install an interior finish on the north side of the lower floor for a recreation and dancing area. Outman himself took up wine and beer making as a hobby, and it hasn't inconvenienced the rest of the family that he has set aside a 20-by-80-foot space as his personal, legalized brewery.

In a sense, the house and its occupants are the more remarkable because they do not think of themselves as at all remarkable. The most that Outman will say about the environment he has created for himself and his family is that, "this house is not just a place to eat and sleep in—it is a way of life."

The three cases cited are representative of many more. The first owner-builder had no other way to home ownership; the second wanted a house to fit special, long-term desires and with the least cost for those specifications; the third wanted an intangible quality which only his "barn" could give him in terms of his resources. While Tim Johnston is probably representative of many low-income, small-town families, John Outman, who earns not much more, is an atypical case requiring a special match between needs and means which the market probably could not package for him.

The owner-builders described were at different stages of the family life cycle and knew how to coordinate resources and needs with varying degrees of sophistication; yet all of them sought to maximize their administrative and labor resources to accomplish *their* views of what *their* housing should do for *their families.* The three suggest a range of uses for housing and ways of getting houses and perhaps a way out of our housing shortage. Certainly they indicate the need for much more research.

Owner-builder families are very much like their home-buying counterparts. On the other hand, the *need* to build one's own house in a society dominated by commercial suppliers of housing seems to imply some fundamentally different set of values and energies among the owner-builder population. This will take much more study to explain.

If the owner-builder is no more than a holdover from an individualistic age, then, in the long run, he must be declared irrelevant to the housing needs of present society. But our evidence strongly suggests that the owner-builder is alive and well in the United States; that with the proper encouragement the number of owner-builders can be substantially increased; and that owner-building represents a national resource which has been neglected because of housing policies based on models of aggregate demand.

Is housing an object merely for consumption and/or investment, and is owner-building just another means to attain those ends? No one can give a simple answer to that question; yet our research suggests that a man who builds his house gains something more than shelter and equity.

If this is true, and if owner-building taps dormant energy and enthusiasm, it should be encouraged on at least two counts. It represents, first of all, perhaps the best hope for housing thousands of lower-income families. And second, it should be encouraged because it represents participation—the basic human desire to exercise control over the making of one's environment—which may be especially important both to those who have relatively fewer economic options in life and to those who wish greater personal fulfillment. This is a point which especially needs to be stressed since the supply and demand criteria upon which so much current housing policy has been based neglects individual need and individual ability to set goals, to adjust resources to needs, to learn in the course of doing and, in a word, to be independent through control of daily activities.

The Owner-Builder Network: Some Problems and Possibilities

Every owner-builder is a nodal point in an informal network of supply and information. Owner-builders give each other advice; lumberyard dealers and plumbing suppliers often become teachers; and experienced owner-builders are an important check on the honesty and competence of both suppliers and craftsmen. The system is informal, yet it is efficient and extensive.

In contrast to the owner-builder, who can make so many fine adjustments as he goes along and who is almost bound to get a comprehensive education in housing as he grows into the network, the home-buyer must either take the product offered him, or leave it. As a rule the home buyer enters the planning and construction cycle at such a late stage that most of the decisions affecting the life cost of the house will already have been made.

He can, of course, remodel his house or add to it, so that the line between the owner-builder and the home buyer needn't be hard and fast. Yet in general, the home buyer is just that, the recipient of a product assembled for him. He may be as devoted to his home as the owner-builder, but he simply cannot know it as well, and he certainly has not exercised his *potential* for making decisions and assuming responsibilities to anything like the same degree as the owner-builder. Of course, many home buyers may not want to make such decisions, but we are speaking here of the need to increase options for those who *are* interested, especially those who presently have little or no choice.

The owner-builder information and supply network offers so many possibilities that one would like to see it extended to other tenure and dwelling modes beyond the single-family home if an information and supply network could be formalized. A formalized network on the owner-builder model could both increase the number of housing units constructed each year and bring about a more appropriate match between the needs of housing users and the ability of suppliers to meet them. Yet this suggestion raises a number of questions.

First, can this informal network be enlarged and to some extent institutionalized without killing it in the process? There is a danger that the helpful lumberyard dealer may not give his tips so freely to five or ten or twenty times the number of people represented by present owner-builders—especially when those people may be socially or racially different from him. And if that problem is met by introducing professionals, paid for their advice, some elusive but basic quality may be lost.

Second, can the federal government alter its present role sufficiently to promote a system in which it would not be a dominant actor, making decisions "in the best interests of" abstract clients? The FHA and the VA have been key figures in the single-family housing market; yet their interest in owner-building has been lukewarm at best. The real estate and home building associations, another pair of key figures, would have to be convinced that a greater client role in housing would be to their advantage—no easy task.

Third, can some form of user control without the degree of user responsibility found among owner-builders be developed? This is a particularly crucial issue if a client-centered rather than supplier-centered system is to be viable in an urban context. The user must take some responsibility; otherwise the present establishment, with suppliers the prime beneficiaries, would simply reassert itself.

It would be dishonest to minimize these difficulties, and one might be tempted to give up and say that the obstacles are too great were it not for the fact that the owner-builder phenomenon suggests such an enormous potential. Tentative studies show that more than 70 percent of the population is capable, thanks to their education, of the kind of responsibility required for owner-building. If non-central city families could save 22 to 53 percent of construction costs, as some owner-builders do, somewhere between 5 and 9 million families could own housing presently unavailable to them.

In summary, the survival of so many owner-builders should suggest to public authorities that there may be other, perhaps less-entangled ways for lower-income households to satisfy housing needs than those generally available. Thousands of low-income families have found a way through their own ingenuity and a local information and supply network. Potential owner-builders should be encouraged to do the same, to do what they are capable of doing—housing themselves by virtue of their own energy, economy, and whatever minimum support structures may be necessary.

2

RICHARD B. SPOHN
with the assistance of William Grindley and Peter Grenell

The Owner-Builder: Legislative Analysis and Recommendation

Self-Help and Owner-Building

AMISH BARN-RAISINGS are part of American folklore, as are various other forms of practical group charity and cooperation. However, the first significant mutual self-help housing effort by a public body or social agency was conducted by the County Relief Board of Westmoreland County, Pennsylvania, organized in 1933. It sought to get unemployed coal miners "back to the farm," by forming a self-sufficient community. The participants were paid for one quarter of their labor, and by 1940 approximately 250 homes had been built.[1] The American Friends Service Committee sponsored another coal miners project in 1937 in western Pennsylvania, producing fifty homes. In 1938, some coal miners in Nova Scotia were organized by a local university to build the first Canadian mutual-help cooperative.[2] Puerto Rico was the next site for organ-

This chapter is a shortened version of an article published in the Harvard Journal on Legislation, v. 9, number 3, March, 1972.

[1] ORGANIZATION FOR SOCIAL AND TECHNICAL INNOVATION, SELF-HELP HOUSING IN THE U.S.A., A PRELIMINARY REPORT 28 (1969) (cited hereinafter as OSTI REPORT).

[2] R. MARGOLIS, SOMETHING TO BUILD ON 19 (Washington, D.C.: International Self-Help Housing Association, 1967).

ized mutual-help housing, and since 1949 has been responsible for housing over 30,000 rural families, making it by far the largest organized mutual- or self-help housing effort in this country.[3] In the early 1950s, Flanner House, an Indianapolis settlement house, initiated a mutual-help program that stands as a demonstration of the viability of mutual-help as a technique of home construction for moderate-income people. In the 1960s, programs for migrant and seasonal agricultural workers sprouted in various places, most notably in Florida and California. A California program, Self-Help Enterprises, Inc., was an outgrowth of another American Friends Service Committee project, and is today the largest and most successful mutual-help housing program in the continental U.S., having produced over 1000 homes.

Money for these efforts has come from two major sources, the Department of Agriculture's Farmers Home Administration (FmHA) and the Office of Economic Opportunity. The FHA provides insured loans to individual low-income families for thirty-three years at sliding interest rates,[4] and OEO provides funds for project organization and technical assistance.[5] FmHA assistance is limited to localities with populations of 10,000[6] or less, although until recently it was 5,500, and before 1965, 2,500.

In 1961, the Congress authorized HUD's predecessor, the Housing and Home Finance Agency, to make grants for the purposes of "developing and demonstrating new or improved means . . . of providing housing for low-income persons and families."[7] In 1968, this was amended to call for "the study of self-help in the construction, rehabilitation, and maintenance of housing for low income persons and families and the methods of selecting, involving, and directing such persons and families in

[3] OSTI Report 28–29.
[4] 42 U.S.C. § 1472 (1970).
[5] 42 U.S.C. § 2861 (1970).
[6] 42 U.S.C. § 1490 (1970).
[7] Housing Act of 1961, Pub. L. No. 87–70, § 207, 75 Stat. 149, 165; § 207 was repealed by The Housing and Urban Development Act of 1970, Pub. L. No. 91–609, 503, 84 Stat. 1770.

self-help activities."[8] The Secretary of HUD was charged with making a report to Congress setting forth the results of self-help studies and demonstrations, "with such recommendations as he deems appropriate." This report was made by HUD to the Congress on August 15, 1969,[9] on the basis of a study of twenty-seven housing programs, nine of which were self-help or mutual-help programs. It was found that mutual- and self-help housing had been successfully constructed in all climates, in both rural and urban areas, by both sexes, and by people of various racial origins and socio-economic statuses. The principal difference between commercial and self-help construction was in the speed rather than the quality of the work; mutual-help participants achieved an unusually high equity-to-income ratio; and there was a substantial reduction of costs to both the participants and the public, even though opportunity costs to the individual were high. It also pointed out that these costs varied enormously depending on a complex set of circumstances: "It is evident that self-help methods, properly applied, increase housing production, decrease costs to the user and to the public, and contribute to the elimination of the symptoms and causes of poverty."[10]

However, the statutory authority for the self-help demonstration projects was repealed by the HUD Act of 1970,[11] and since the appointment of Eugene R. Gulledge, Assistant Secretary for Production, HUD has been maintaining a very low profile in the business of fostering self-help.[12] Despite provisions in the

[8] The Housing and Urban Development Act of 1968, Pub. L. No. 90–448, § 1714(a), 82 Stat. 476, 607.

[9] Department of Housing and Urban Development, Summary Report on a Study of Self-Help Housing in the United States (unpublished August 15, 1969 report by Secretary George W. Romney to the House Banking and Currency Committee, copy received from the Office of the Assistant Secretary for Research and Technology, HUD, October 26, 1971) 27, *citing* S. Maisel, House Building in Transition 344 (1953). *See also* Housing and Home Finance Agency, Housing in the United States 57 (1949) (26 percent) and *Id.*, Ideas and Methods Exchange Bulletin, No. 54 (1959) (35 percent in 1949).

[10] *Id.* 36.

[11] Pub L. No. 91–609, § 503, 84 Stat. 1770.

[12] Conversation with several professionals involved in self-help housing in various roles revealed a uniform conviction of Mr. Gulledge's decided lack of enthusiasm toward self-help. Cited were his pre-HUD position in the hous-

1968 HUD act that call for the Secretary of HUD to provide technical assistance and seed money to nonprofit organizations involved in self-help and other programs,[13] the Department has not sought appropriations to do so. The 1970 Act strengthened these provisions,[14] and HUD is reportedly requesting, as the result of Congressional prodding, a one million dollar budget allocation from the Office of Management and Budget.[15] The Department hopes that this will "signify tacit approval of the self-help housing approach by the present administration."[16] There is also currently a Departmental Task Force studying self-help housing, and it is to make recommendations to the Secretary on its findings.

Individual officials are not entirely responsible for the situation, however. An experienced observer of HUD's self-help policy feels that

> HUD's hostility to self-help is not so much a matter of deliberate policy as it is program structure. HUD is programmed to serve real-

ing industry, speeches he had made, and actions he had or had not taken. Mr. Gulledge felt he had to allay fears about his attitude towards nonprofit sponsors of housing in a speech noted in Keyes, *The Role of Nonprofit Sponsors in the Production of Housing,* in HOUSE BANKING & CURRENCY COMMITTEE, PAPERS SUBMITTED TO SUBCOMMITTEE ON HOUSING PANELS ON HOUSING PRODUCTION, HOUSING DEMAND, AND DEVELOPING A SUITABLE LIVING ENVIRONMENT, 92nd Cong., 1st Sess., 173 (1971).

[13] Pub. L. No. 90–448, § 106(a), (b), 82 Stat. 476, 490.

[14] Pub. L. No. 91–609, § 903(a), 84 Stat. 1770, 12 U.S.C. § 1701x (1971).

[15] Letter to author from Mr. Mark Sullivan for Mr. Harold B. Finger, Ass't Sec. of HUD for Research and Technology, undated but received Oct. 24, 1971.

[16] *Id.* This "tacit approval" is a somewhat weaker commitment to self-help than the advisory service the Office of Research and Technology promised in its FY 1972 budget justification and program description. HEARINGS ON HUD-SPACE-SCIENCE APPROPRIATIONS FOR 1972 BEFORE THE SUBCOMMITTEE ON HUD-SPACE-SCIENCE OF THE HOUSE COMMITTEE ON APPROPRIATIONS, PART 2, DEPARTMENT OF HOUSING AND URBAN DEVELOPMENT, 92nd Cong., 1st Sess., at 960. Mr. Sullivan failed to mention it in response to author's inquiries regarding HUD's intentions for self-help; Mr. Finger failed to mention it in his testimony at the Hearings, *id.,* 1022–23; and a reliable confidential source in HUD indicated in a Jan. 11, 1972 telephone conversation that the Department is not committed to implementing it. The program appears broader than the one proposed in this paper, although there are similar components.

> tors, builders, title searchers, appraisers and consultants . . . it's surrounded by an industry. . . . [M]ost self-help sponsors simply are not large enough to support the scale HUD prefers. . . . HUD would rather be making 235 commitments in blocks of hundreds. Some HUD field people say frankly that they do not wish to be bothered with fewer than 70 units at a time.[17]

Whether as a result of policy or program structure, however, organized self-help housing programs get little help or encouragement from HUD. The HUD Act of 1968 authorized the Farmers Home Administration of the Department of Agriculture to administer a program of technical assistance grants to mutual self-help sponsor organizations and to establish and operate a land loan revolving fund.[18] The regulations for this program were slow in being written and released—a delay some felt to be deliberate.[19] Although the FmHA can produce no current statistics,[20] sources close to the scene indicate that somewhere between ten to twenty projects are now operating with funds from this program.[21]

Within the general context of self-help housing, individual owner-builders are inconspicuous, and therefore are neglected by the powers which might assist them. While the mutual self-help programs described above are notable, they do not begin to compare—as William Grindley has shown in the preceding chapter—with the production achieved by individuals and families working on their own. Therefore, though this paper is addressed to the potentialities of all self-help housing efforts, its emphasis is on the individual owner-builder, who has had fewer advocates even than those groups willing to participate in mutual housing aid.

[17] Letter to author from Mr. Clay L. Cochran, Executive Director, Rural Housing Alliance, Nov. 16, 1971.

[18] Pub. L. No. 90–448, § 1005, 82 Stat. 476, 553, adding § 523 to the Housing Act of 1949, 42 U.S.C. § 1490c (1970).

[19] Letter from Mr. Clay L. Cochran, *supra* note 17.

[20] Letter from Mr. Robert E. Nipp, Acting Director of Information, FmHA, U.S. Dept. of Agriculture, Dec. 1, 1971.

[21] Letter from Mr. Clay L. Cochran, *supra* note 17.

Current Legislative and Administrative Problems

Little official assistance is given to the owner-builder, and there is much that gets in his way. If he participates in an organized, mutual self-help program, he receives aid as outlined above. But if he is an independent owner-builder, he is left mostly to his own devices.

PROBLEMS AT THE FEDERAL LEVEL

Only one federal program offers financial assistance to low- and moderate-income owner-builders: the Department of Agriculture's Section 502 program.[22] It provides loans that can be used to purchase a site and construct a dwelling, at a current interest rate of 7¼ percent for thirty-three years.[23] Families with annual incomes of less than $5,000, with some exceptions for families with higher incomes, can qualify for an "interest credit" that will reduce the rate to as low as 1 percent.[24] The use of the interest subsidy, and also the size of the loans, has been steadily increasing, although there are indications that the Section 502 interest credit analog in HUD, the Section 235 program, provides a larger subsidy.[25] If a family has an income considered to be insufficient to repay the loan, a person with adequate repayment ability may cosign.[26] The authorization of funds for 1972 under this program requires that at least 50 percent of the loans be made to low-income families.[27] However, the FmHA is unable to say how many owner-builders have been assisted under Section 502.[28]

Although the introductory sections to the 1968 Act establishing the Section 235 program emphasize self-help techniques,[29] there

[22] Housing Act of 1949, § 502, 42 U.S.C. § 1472 (1970).

[23] *FmHA Instruction 440.1*, Exhibit B; 7 C.F.R. § 1822.8(c).

[24] 42 U.S.C. § 1490a (1970).

[25] Rural Housing Alliance, Farmers Home's Interest Credit Program: The First Two Years (1971).

[26] 42 U.S.C. § 1472(a) (1970).

[27] Administration Letter 68 (444) (1971).

[28] Letter from Mr. Robert E. Nipp, see *supra* note 20.

[29] "The Congress declares that in the administration of those housing programs authorized by this Act which are designed to assist families with in-

is no mention of a provision for them in the section itself. The traditional FHA "203" mortgage insurance programs likewise make no mention of owner-builders or self-help,[30] although loans are made under it, as testified to by statistics[31] and federal officials.[32] This is apparently a matter of accommodation, since there is nothing in the statutes or regulations[33] authorizing such loans. The owner-builder is therefore at the mercy of the local FHA office.

There are two insured loan programs[34] to assist the poor rural owner-occupant in carrying out minor repairs on his house to make it safe and sanitary. These programs are specifically aimed at low-income people who do not qualify for the full Section 502 loan program, and they are unusual because they permit less-than-complete finishing or full amenities and equipment.

The only program (FmHA 523) of technical and financial assistance to self-help housing is limited to organized rural self-help groups—the individual owner-builder acting on his own does not qualify.[35] As for technical assistance to self-help efforts to be provided by HUD, we have seen that the Department has been unwilling or unable to follow Congressional directives.

There are a number of restrictions on the major FmHA pro-

---

comes so low that they could not otherwise decently house themselves, and of other Government programs designed to assist in the provision of housing for such families, the highest priority and emphasis should be given to meeting the housing needs of those families for which the national goal has not become a reality; *and in carrying out of such programs there should be the fullest practicable utilization of the resources and capabilities of private enterprise and of individual self-help techniques."* [Emphasis added.] 42 U.S.C. § 1701t (1970).

[30] 12 U.S.C. § 1709 (1970).

[31] Materials provided by Mr. William F. Shaw, Chief, Statistics Branch, FHA, HUD, in Dec. 8, 1971 letter to author.

[32] Mr. William F. Shaw, *see supra* note 31; telephone conversation with Public Information Officer, HUD Boston Area Office, Dec. 10, 1971; interview with Public Information Officer, HUD San Francisco Regional Office, Dec. 28, 1971.

[33] 24 C.F.R. § 203 (1971).

[34] 42 U.S.C. § 1474 (1970); Administration Letter 921 (444) (1967); 7 C.F.R. § 1822.18 (1971).

[35] 42 U.S.C. § 1490c (1970).

grams. A key one is the definition of "rural," which now applies to communities of not more than 10,000[36] (leaving a gap between the FmHA and the FHA, which does little in communities of under 25,000[37]). An applicant who is not a farmer must be of low or moderate income, must be without "decent, safe, and sanitary housing for his own use," and must be working in, if not living in, the rural area.[38] He must also be "without sufficient resources to provide on his own account the necessary housing, buildings, or related facilities, and be unable to secure the necessary credit from other sources upon terms and conditions which he reasonably could be expected to fulfill, including a Federal Housing Administration (HUD) section 235 insured mortgage."[39] Although he should be able to meet his operating and family expenses and his debts, including the proposed loan, if his income is not sufficient to meet the loan payments he may be able to qualify for interest credit assistance.[40] These credits are supposed to be made to those with adjusted annual family incomes of less than $5,000, and in no case are they to be made with such income over $8,000.[41]

A recent administrative order terminated the power of the FmHA to handle Section 235 interest subsidies,[42] in direct conflict with the Section 235 legislation, by which the Secretary of HUD is to allocate to the Secretary of Agriculture, for use in rural areas and small towns, "a reasonable portion of the total authority to contract to make assistance payments" as approved in the rele-

[36] 42 U.S.C. § 1490 (1970).

[37] HUD/USDA Interagency Task Force, Report on Rural Housing. 115 Cong. Rec. 28, 724 (1969); *see also* letter of July 1, 1969 from Rep. Patman to Secretary George W. Romney, *Id.;* Clay L. Cochran, Chairman, National Rural Housing Coalition, Statement on Major 1971 Housing Legislation before the Senate Committee on Banking, Housing, and Urban Affairs, 92d Cong., 1st Sess., Sept. 17, 1971 (mimeographed copy 10).

[38] 7 C.F.R. § 1822.4(a) (1971).

[39] *Id.*, § 1822.4(a) (2).

[40] *Id.*, § 1822.4(a) (4). Of course the eligible applicant must "possess the character, ability, and experience to carry out the undertakings and obligations required of him in connection with the loan." *Id.*, § 1822.4(a) (5).

[41] *Id.*, § 1822.7(n) (i) (a).

[42] Administration Letter 68(444), June 30, 1971.

vant annual appropriations acts.[43] Congress's intent that the Secretary of Agriculture deal in 235 was underscored by the authorization of funds to cover the expenses of doing so,[44] yet this intent has been ignored.

There are other impediments, of an administrative nature, which have kept all but a very few owner-builders from using 235.[45] Aside from lack of information about the program, many potential owner-builders are denied access to Section 235 subsidies by the HUD procedure of reserving them only for commercial contractors[46] who build many units at a time. This eases the paperwork burden, for such applications can be processed in a single package, and commercial builders are usually familiar with FHA procedures. This practice allows field personnel to avoid dealing with owner-builders, who are often considered to be unreliable and time-consuming clients.

Some commercial builders have seriously abused the 235 program and the purchasers of their very shoddy products, as a recent Congressional investigation has shown.[47] So far, only one

[43] 12 U.S.C. § 1715 (k) (1971).

[44] 42 U.S.C. § 1483 (1971).

[45] Letter from Mr. William F. Shaw, Chief, Statistics Branch, FHA/HUD, December 8, 1971. The closest he could come was to say that 0.9 percent of all section 235 loans in the first nine months of 1970 had been for the purpose of "financing new construction," and that his estimate was that owner-builders did not comprise the bulk of the recipients. Officials in two Regional Offices indicated that the chances of an owner-builder's getting any aid under section 235 were virtually nil, and that in any event he would have to build before he could qualify. Telephone conversations with Mr. Andrews, Boston Area Office 235 Specialist, Dec. 16, 1971, and with Mr. Segaguchi, San Francisco Regional Office 235 Specialist, December 29, 1971. This estimate would appear to conflict with the regulation which states that ". . . a mortgagor eligible under Section 235 will, to the maximum extent feasible, be given opportunity to contribute the value of his labor as equity in his property." HUD, HOMEOWNERSHIP FOR LOWER INCOME FAMILIES (SECTION 235), Bulletin HPMC-FHA 4441.1A, September, 1971, No. 21. However, the procedure noted in note 46 *infra.* indicates that the owner-builder probably would not get the opportunity to do so, or at least that he would have to make advance arrangements with the builder with the Section 235 reservations to so contribute his labor. *Id.*, no. 17.

[46] *Id.*, no. 38.

[47] HOUSE COMMITTEE ON BANKING AND CURRENCY, INVESTIGATIONS AND HEARING OF ABUSES IN FEDERAL LOW- AND MODERATE-INCOME HOUSING PROGRAMS, 91st Cong., 2nd Sess. (1970).

HUD Regional Office (San Francisco) has begun to experiment with the granting of Section 235 funds to single households, although they are not owner-builders.

As for the Farmers Home Administration program, it might be noted that until recently local agents were required to be graduates in agriculture, even though they may have had nothing to do with it after joining FmHA. These agents often have less experience in housing and housing-related concerns than the job demands. This leads to a bias against owner-builders, who are a possible source of difficulty. More crucial to FmHA's local reluctance to support owner-builders is the requirement that the local agent countersign all checks drawn on supervised bank accounts containing loan funds for building in process. He is thus even more wary of owner-builders.

A third FmHA obstacle to owner-builders is derived from the program's greatest strength, its decentralized form of administration. According to the American Friends Service Committee:

> Discretionary power at the disposal of the County Supervisor can be a real asset if the supervisor is motivated to use the regulations to make the maximum use of available funds to serve the poor. One would hesitate to urge strict regulations and procedures where no step can be taken without checking the regulations or where every deviation from the norm had to be referred to a higher bureaucratic level. The great advantage of the FmHA loan program is the *potential* for humane consideration of each individual client, as opposed to the bureaucratic procedures of the Federal Housing Administration, where the client never sees or deals with the bureaucrat who turns him down. However, this same discretionary power can totally undermine the purpose of the program when in the hands of one not sympathetic to the poor, the blacks or those needing special consideration.[48]

Abuses of this discretionary power have recently been documented, including numerous incidents of racial discrimination against black and Spanish-speaking families,[49] especially in the South. Agents have withheld or distorted important information,

[48] Studies in Bad Housing in America: Abuse of Power 20 (1971).
[49] *Id.*

refused to process owner-builder applications or discouraged the seeking of assistance, and refused to approve loan applications for trumped-up reasons.[50]

The FmHA Washington headquarters is seriously understaffed to administer the $800 million loan program,[51] and in the field offices, the local agents have a range of responsibilities that spreads them very thin. The amount of paper work required by the FmHA has often been criticized. One commentator refers to "the paper jungle involved in getting an FmHA mortgage" and charges that "this extraordinarily complex wall of forms and documents has isolated the FmHA from much contact with the poor —except for impecunious lawyers."[52]

Finally, charges have been made that the FmHA field offices "skim off" many clients who could get credit at commercial institutions by sending them to banks and savings-and-loan associations, where they are sure to be refused. In this way the FmHA office is able to maintain a good "track record" for itself.[53] Thus, needy would-be owner-builders are crowded out by those who would not be eligible under the original intent of the program.

PROBLEMS AT THE STATE LEVEL

A survey of state agencies which might provide assistance to owner-builders reveals that few actually are doing so, and none provide it in any comprehensive fashion. The California Department of Housing and Community Development provides "technical assistance to 'self-help' housing groups" of "families working together to build their own homes."[54] Under the California Department of Veteran Affairs Cal-Vet housing program, a veteran can secure financial assistance to build his own home.[55] The

[50] *Id.*

[51] Cochran, *Statement on Items in the 1971 Budget Concerning the Rural Housing Program of the Farmers Home Administration* before the Senate Appropriations Subcommittee 91st Cong., 2nd Sess. (1970).

[52] Troy, "An Evaluation: Self-Help Projects Have Special Virtues and Pains," 2 SOUTH TODAY 11 (March, 1971).

[53] "The Battle Over Rural Housing," *Savings and Loan News* (June, 1971).

[54] Letter from Mr. Donald R. Crow, Administrative Assistant, Department of Housing and Community Development, Dec. 9, 1971.

[55] *Id.*

Maine Housing Authority will assist the owner-builder "in locating plans or contacting precutting firms or modular firms," and will also buy mortgages on owner-built homes from a lending institution.[56] The new Minnesota Housing Finance Agency expects procedures to be developed to permit the financing of owner-built housing.[57] The North Carolina Housing Corporation indicated it would like to purchase low-income mortgages but has been unable to do so "due to conditions in the bond market"; however, the North Carolina State University Extension Service renders "a great deal" of technical assistance to owner-builders.[58] The Florida Department of Community Affairs, Division of Economic Opportunity, provides technical assistance "to groups and organizations seeking to help bring decent housing to the poor," yet, while apparently most sympathetic to the owner-builder approach, has no specific programs to facilitate it.[59] The Michigan State Housing Development Authority will provide "complete financial and technical assistance," including mortgages and site inspections, and will recommend appropriate blueprints, but the state requires that an owner have a builder's license before he can do his own general contracting. No owner-built home has yet been erected under the program.[60] The Maryland Department of Economic and Community Development will provide mortgage insurance to owner-builders, as well as assistance in learning about helpful programs, grants, and other financing opportunities, and how to apply for them.[61] In addition, the Department is establishing a "housing information system," which it expects will include information pertinent to owner-building.[62] The Hawaii Housing

[56] Letter from Mr. Eben L. Elwell, Director, Maine Housing Authority, Dec. 8, 1971.

[57] Letter from Mr. James J. Solem, Director, Office of Local and Urban Affairs, Minnesota State Planning Agency, Dec. 20, 1971.

[58] Letter from Mr. Luther C. Hodges, Associate Director, North Carolina Housing Corporation, Dec. 13, 1971.

[59] Letter from Mr. Hubert D. Thomas, STAP Housing Specialist, Division of Economic Opportunity, Dept. of Community Affairs, Dec. 30, 1971.

[60] Letter from Mr. Doug Smith, Housing Development Officer, Michigan State Housing Development Authority, Jan. 14, 1972.

[61] Letter from Mr. Louis Peddicord, Executive Assistant, Dept. of Economic and Community Development, Dec. 23, 1971.

[62] *Id.*

Authority is empowered to provide long-term mortgages for owner-builders, but has no program of technical assistance.[63] Delaware, Massachusetts, New Jersey, New York, Ohio, Pennsylvania, Vermont, and West Virginia give no technical or financial assistance to owner-builders. No replies were forthcoming from Alaska, Connecticut, Illinois, or Missouri.

OTHER DIFFICULTIES

Other "legal" impediments to owner-building may be grouped into three main categories: zoning and subdivision regulations; building codes and standards; and housing codes and standards. (These have been described elsewhere in this book, especially in the Conclusion pp. 269–271.) The owner-builder is also frustrated by the practices of private financing institutions: interim financing is usually given for a one-year period, and then only after the foundation has been laid. Construction loans are often given only to commercial contractors; and insurance companies frequently will insure only licensed builders.

Proposed: A Housing Advisory Service

The Housing Advisory Service proposed below will not solve all the problems facing owner-builders, either in the short or the long run, but it can make a good start. A significant number of people currently engage in owner-building in spite of the obstacles. Broad technical and financial assistance to owner-builders should therefore produce significant growth in this method of meeting the housing crisis.

THE NETWORK

The owner-builder can draw on a network of resources. Materials and equipment suppliers are obviously part of the network, as are general contractors, subcontractors, hired professionals, experienced friends, and friends with little more than energy and good will. A housing module or component manufacturer may

[63] Letter from Mr. Robert E. Cooper, Development Administrator, Hawaii Housing Authority, Department of Social Services and Housing, December 16, 1971.

be accessible. Credit and finance sources will most likely be part of the network, be they banks, savings-and-loan institutions, credit unions, friends, or government agencies. The owner-builder may also wish to hire or consult an architect, a surveyor, a lawyer, an engineer, a land broker, and other technical advisors. A most fruitful source of aid is often other owner-builders.

The network is at once an opportunity and a constraint. It exists independently of the owner-builder and will respond to him according to the experience it has had with other owner-builders. Other factors—race and income, for example—will also color this response. It is important to note that these factors of bias not only limit the access of the potential owner-builder to the network, but can prevent him from even considering it as a resource.

The network is necessarily a local phenomenon, and can be either formal or informal, often depending on the size of the community, its cohesiveness, and its patterns of interaction. It will be diversified, option-laden, and sophisticated in relation to the community it serves.

The key aspect of the network is that through it the owner-builder can exercise great control over his own housing. Through use and manipulation of the network, his housing becomes not just a finished product thrust upon him from outside, with perhaps a few standardized options, but rather a process into which he enters as the determinant, exercising responsible autonomy, and drawing upon a network that offers a wide variety of choices. He is free to combine the services and goods of the network as his own desires, capabilities, and, to some extent, norms permit. The network provides many different ways of achieving the desired end—satisfactory shelter—which otherwise might be either unavailable or not subject to personal choice or control.

THE HOUSING ADVISORY SERVICE

Information is the key to the network. At present in the U.S., there is no institutional source of information for the would-be owner-builder, who must depend on chance and persistence.

The following proposal could be described as profoundly conservative, in that it is based on maintaining and expanding an existing system. Yet in stressing development of this system as an option for housing production, it is a radical departure from current practices because it is demand/user/dweller-oriented. It also differs from the housing allowance. A housing allowance might open up more housing choices, but these choices would nevertheless be defined and determined by the supplier. In addition, housing costs would probably rise, as in the comparable case of Medicare. The proposal would, in sum, be a departure from the present symbiotic relationship between the government and producers-for-profit, emphasizing instead a joining of the demand and the supply/production functions by minimal government facilitation.

There have been a number of attempts to deal with the informational needs of owner-builders. In Melbourne, Australia, the Royal Australian Institute of Architects has operated the Architects' Housing Service since 1946. During the 1949–1951 Australian building boom, it was responsible for more than 12 percent of the homes built. For $50 the Service provides architectural consultation, construction advice, and inexpensive, high quality plans and specifications which are constantly upgraded through architectural and model homes competitions sponsored by the Gas and Fuel Corporation of Victoria.

In this country, Community Design Centers (CDCs) have been established in sixty-five cities to make architectural, engineering, and planning services available to inner-city low-income people. The first of the CDCs was the Architects Renewal Committee for Harlem (ARCH), established in 1964. Another CDC is operated in Philadelphia by the Architects workshop, which has been funded by HUD with its "701" planning funds. The Community Services Department of the American Institute of Architects serves as a clearinghouse of information for CDCs around the country. In Detroit, a branch of the building department gives advice to "do-it-yourselfers." In Milwaukee there is a Housing Clinic which offers advice and design and plan assistance on repairs and helps select contractors. In San Francisco, the Federally Assisted Code Enforcement (FACE) program supplies similar assistance from architects and architecture students. While none of these programs, with the exception of the Australian Architect's Housing Service, provides comprehensive assistance to the individual owner-builder, they are illustrative of the proposal made here.

We propose a Housing Advisory Service (HAS), either state or federally funded. It would operate in designated areas, providing free advice, information, and technical assistance to potential owner-builders of low- and moderate-incomes, helping them manipulate the network (and also external sources of finance) and providing advice and technical assistance during construction. A formal organizational unit would thus be established to assist owner-builders as needed, especially in the difficult phases of planning and construction; help them decide what they should do themselves and what to give to subcontractors; help them do what they choose to do themselves; and advise them of the options and criteria for choosing among alternatives —in short, to help them get the most out of the network and themselves.

The HAS office would be the focal point for owner-builder interests, and all members of the network would be familiarized with it, so that an owner-builder who contacted the network at any point would be made aware of the HAS services.

The staff of the HAS would be chosen in part because of their familiarity with both the owner-builder process and the network, and in part for their interest in and capacity for assisting low- and moderate-income families. In addition to counseling owner-builders and facilitating the functioning of the network in their behalf, a major task of the HAS would be to work toward the elimination of the barriers and obstacles discussed above. These impediments are not necessarily part of an integrated conspiracy against owner-builders, so considerable adjustment and compromise might be possible if a concerted and informed effort were made. However, the complex of public and private special interests, jurisdictional jealousies, and bureaucratic inertia will not yield to a random and unorganized awareness of the problems facing owner-builders. Leadership for the significant institutional and legal changes required to unleash the potential of owner-building, requires an instrument such as the HAS. The state or federal office responsible for the coordination and direction of the HAS field offices would work for broad and permanent change.

It is important to avoid the sort of "demonstration program" that turns out to be a one-shot, underfunded, and poorly supported operation meant primarily as a sop to some pressure group. The first HASs should be established as prototypes—instruments not only to carry out the projected tasks, but also to test the concept informing them and to gauge the environment in which they are to operate. A preliminary step to establishment of the pilot HASs would be the necessary program planning and administrative designations, especially the probing, analysis, and selection of appropriate network areas and the design of program-monitoring and evaluation instruments. During the pilot phase, the front office should conduct a comprehensive market survey and analysis in order to gauge the potential for owner-building within its jurisdiction. During the planning phase it should be determined whether the HAS field operations could best be carried out through a government agency or through publicly funded nonprofit organizations.

The HAS would be authorized to receive advance commitments of interest subsidy reservations under appropriate programs. A federal revolving performance insurance fund would be established, as a support to the federal HAS, to assure lenders that the units will be completed. The costs for this insurance could be added to the mortgage.

The HAS would be part of the Department of Agriculture's Farmers Home Administration. As noted earlier, 70 percent of the owner-built homes are outside of SMSAs (Standard Metropolitan Statistical Areas), and FmHA is already involved in mutual and self-help housing under the 1968 HUD Act, although only on an organized group basis. (In addition, the 1970 census found that 61 percent of occupied substandard housing is in non-SMSA areas, although the allocations of federal subsidized housing programs do not proportionally match this percentage.)

If the HAS approach proves successful, then HUD could be given authority to set up an equivalent program in the cities, if at that time the split in responsibility for housing between HUD and the Department of Agriculture has not yet been resolved. To cover a wider target population, and to serve communities presently ignored by both the FHA and FmHA, the FmHA population limitation should be raised to 25,000.[64] In addition, authority to make 235 assistance payments should be given to the Secretary of Agriculture as Congress intended, and the HAS offices should be authorized to contract for them.

PRECURSORS

There are precedents for these proposals in existing legislation. These include the umbrella endorsement of self-help in section 235, the Congressional intent articulated in section 106, and the FmHA Section 523 program. In addition, there is section 506 of the Housing Act of 1949,[65] which authorizes the Secretary of Agriculture to carry out programs of research and technical studies of problems and innovations in housing materials and construction methods.

> [*I*]n addition to the financial assistance authorized in this title [which includes the 502, 504, and 523 programs] the Secretary is authorized to furnish, through such agencies as he may determine, to any person, including a person eligible for financial assistance under this title, without charge or at such charges as the Secretary may determine, technical services such as building plans, specifications, construction supervision and inspection, and advice and information regarding farm dwellings and other buildings.[66]

(The definition of "farm dwellings" could cover houses being constructed by owner-builders.[67]) It seems arguable that the

[64] This has been suggested by, among others, The National Housing Conference, *see 1971 Resolutions,* 117 CONG. REC. E3108 (daily ed. April 4, 1971) (extension of remarks of Senator Humphrey); and The National Rural Housing Coalition, People Have a Right to Decent Housing, 1971 Resolutions 12–13.

[65] 42 U.S.C. § 1476 (1970).

[66] *Id.*, § 1476(a).

[67] 42 U.S.C. § 1471(b) (1971).

Secretary has the authority to set up an HAS system under these provisions. Farmers have long received such assistance, but individual owner-builders, especially those with low incomes, have not fared as well, mainly because of the discretion lodged with the local agents, their heavy work loads, and other factors discussed above. It is unlikely that anything short of legislative mandate will break the pattern.

The proposed federal legislation could easily be adapted to state use. While the great balance of housing programs over the years have been instituted or paid for at the federal and local levels, a number of states have initiated such programs in recent years, particularly in the areas of public housing, mortgage financing, and research. If federal revenue-sharing becomes a significant reality, this activity is likely to increase. There are several states with legislative provisions under which an HAS might arguably be initiated—for the benefit of owner-builders neglected by existing state agencies—or which at least could open the door for discussion and supplemental authorizing legislation. For instance, the Maine State Housing Authority is authorized to serve as a clearinghouse for housing information—to conduct research and demonstration model housing programs dealing with, among other things, planning, types of building design, and techniques of construction; to provide or coordinate technical assistance and consultation about housing to individuals; to prepare, publish, and disseminate educational materials dealing with housing matters; and to encourage and coordinate effective use of existing and new resources and services for housing.[68] These powers could easily form the legislative base for an HAS program. The West Virginia Housing Development Fund is involved in both planning and production; it has been described as "a particularly effective and broad-gauged instrument,"[69] which, while concerned mostly with projects and sponsors, is nevertheless backed by legisla-

[68] 30 ME. REV. STAT. ANN. § 4601-A (Supp. 1970).

[69] Schechter and Schlefer, *Housing Needs and National Goals,* in HOUSE BANKING & CURRENCY COMMITTEE, PAPERS SUBMITTED TO SUBCOMMITTEE ON HOUSING PANELS ON HOUSING PRODUCTION, HOUSING DEMAND, AND DEVELOPING A SUITABLE LIVING ENVIRONMENT, 92nd Cong., 1st Sess., 84 (1971).

tive authority that permits research into and demonstration of a program of technical assistance similar to the program proposed here.[70] Missouri's new State Housing Development Commission has similar authority,[71] as does the Illinois Housing Development Authority.[72] Michigan's State Housing Development Authority can set up research and demonstration projects.[73] In addition, there is a provision in the state mortgage assistance plan whereby an owner-builder uses his labor to add "sweat equity" to his interest in the house.[74] North Carolina's Low-Income Housing Development Corporation is involved in an OEO-financed program of technical and financial assistance to nonprofit sponsors of housing,[75] and the new North Carolina Housing Corporation and Housing Development Fund might be used to provide loans to low-income families with closing cost funds for construction loans that are not federally insured.[76] Other states, including New York,[77] New Jersey,[78] Delaware,[79] Pennsylvania,[80] Alaska,[81] and Vermont,[82] have programs of financial assistance which might be made available to owner-builders, were an HAS to spur such involvement.

Legislative Draft

The draft that follows does not deal with many of the obstacles to owner-building discussed in this chapter. It would authorize a Housing Advisory Service, a major responsibility of which would be to work at all levels to eliminate the myriad statutory, organ-

[70] W. VA. CODE ANN. § 31–18–6(22,23,24) (1971).
[71] MO. ANN. STAT. § 215.030(23) and (24) (Supp. 1970).
[72] ILL. ANN. STAT. ch. 67 1/2, § 307.5 (Supp. 1971).
[73] MICH. COMP. LAWS ANN. § 125.1422(h) (Supp. 1969).
[74] *Id.*, § 125.1444(2) (e)–(f).
[75] Schecter and Schlefer, *supra* note 69, at 83–84.
[76] N.C. GEN. STAT. § 122A–7 (Supp. 1971).
[77] N.Y. PRIV. HOUS. FIN. LAW § 11–36(a) (McKinney Supp. 1971).
[78] N.J. REV. STAT. § 55:14J (Supp. 1970).
[79] DEL. CODE ANN. tit. 31 § 4066(b) (1) (Supp. 1970).
[80] PA. STAT. ANN., tit. 35, §§ 1664(d), 1680 (Supp. 1970).
[81] ALASKA STAT. § 18.56.090 (Supp. 1971).
[82] VT. STAT. ANN. tit. 24, § 4004a (Supp. 1971).

izational, and systemic roadblocks to owner-building. Perhaps the areas most in need of reform are financing and official codes and standards. Clearly the advocacy role assigned to the HAS must be aimed not only at officially sanctioned and established obstacles, but also at commercial markets and at broad-based popular attitudes and myths, not the least of which is that people cannot build their own homes.

Following the draft of the proposed legislation is an illustration of what Section 523 of the Housing Act of 1949 would look like as amended. This is the current statutory provision which would be most affected by the proposed legislation.

AN ACT

To assist low- and moderate-income owner-builders by the establishment of a Housing Advisory Service, as defined herein.

Be it enacted by the Senate and House of Representatives of the United States of America in Congress assembled, That this Act may be cited as the "Housing Advisory Service Act of 197–."

Declaration of Policy

SEC. 2 The Congress reaffirms the national goal of a "decent home and a suitable living environment for every American family." The Congress finds that this goal has not been fully realized for many of the Nation's families; that this is a matter of grave national concern; and that there exist in the public and private sectors of the economy the resources and capabilities necessary to the full realization of this goal.

The Congress reaffirms its policy, stated in the Housing and Urban Development Act of 1968, that in the carrying out of housing programs for low income families "there should be the fullest practicable utilization of the resources and capabilities of private enterprise and of individual self-help techniques." The Congress declares that this policy should be extended to all housing programs.

The Congress finds that a significant number of low- and moderate-income families are capable and desirous of building their own homes in whole or in part, with considerable savings to themselves and benefits to the public, and declares that undertakings of this nature should be encouraged and fostered to the greatest extent practicable.

Comment: The language herein reiterates earlier policy pronouncements regarding housing goals and the stress the Congress intended to be placed on self-help techniques.[83] Specific notice is taken of owner-building, and the Congress declares that the method should be supported.

Definitions

SEC. 3(a) As used in this title, the term "owner-builder" means any noncorporate person who acts, on his own and without the aid of a formally established mutual-help group program, as the general contractor for and/or provides part or all of the labor necessary to build his own dwelling.

(b) "Owner-building" is the process engaged in by owner-builders in the construction of their dwellings.

Comment: The definitions closely follow that of the Bureau of the Census,[84] with the qualification distinguishing the "owner-builder" from the participant in a mutual self-help program.

Existing Programs

SEC. 4 In the administration of the programs authorized by sections 106, 203, 235, and 237 and other relevant sections of the National Housing Act, the Secretary of Housing and Urban Development shall to the greatest extent practicable make available to owner-builders the full assistance and benefits of these pro-

[83] 12 U.S.C. § 1701t (1970).

[84] *See* BUREAU OF THE CENSUS, DEP'T. OF COMMERCE/HUD, CONSTRUCTION REPORTS, C-25 SERIES, ONE-FAMILY HOMES, 1968 104 (1969).

grams. The Secretary of Agriculture shall do likewise in the administration of the programs authorized by sections 502, 503, 504, 506, 523, 524, and other relevant sections of the Housing Act of 1949. To this end, both Secretaries shall conduct a thorough review of existing regulations, procedures, and practices to uncover and eliminate all obstacles to the realization by owner-builders of such assistance and benefits.

> *Comment:* A specific Congressional directive is made to the Secretaries to make available to owner-builders the benefits of the housing assistance programs which they respectively administer. Full reviews of the programs are to be made with this goal in mind.

Reform of Existing Obstacles

SEC. 5 The Secretary of the Department of Housing and Urban Development and the Secretary of the Department of Agriculture shall initiate a joint review and study of the existing obstacles to owner-building found in local building and housing codes and standards, property taxation provisions, zoning practices, commercial financing and insurance practices, housing materials supply practices, housing industry labor union practices, and in such other related areas as each Secretary shall deem appropriate. Upon the results of these studies they shall make recommendations for reforms which would facilitate the owner-building process. Such recommendations shall be made known to the Congress not later than one year after the date of enactment of this Act.

> *Comment:* The Secretaries are to conduct a joint study of the myriad obstacles to owner-building which now exist at all levels of governmental regulations and in the private sector. This investigation and analysis should provide the groundwork for the HAS' performing its informational and educational roles as well as its advocacy and facilitating roles. Recommendations are also to be made to the Congress, which should relate not only to federal action, but should also include suggestions for state, local, and private action and reform.

Owner-Builders and the Housing Advisory Service

SEC. 6 Section 523(a) of the Housing Act of 1949 is amended as follows:

(a) by changing the period at the end of subsection (2) to a comma and adding a new subsection as follows: "and (3) to make financial and technical assistance available on reasonable terms and conditions in rural areas and small towns to individuals and families who meet the requirements of section 501 of this Act and who are owner-builders or prospective owner-builders, such assistance to be provided through a Housing Advisory Service as herein established."

(b) by changing subsection (b)(2) to subsection (b)(3), and by adding the following new subsection (b)(2):

"(2) to establish a Housing Advisory Service to facilitate the process of owner-building. This Service shall operate in such localities as the Secretary shall deem appropriate, on the basis of present and potential owner-building activity. The responsibilities of the Housing Advisory Service shall include:

(A) at the national level, to engage in research regarding, to disseminate information on, and to actively promote the method and techniques of, owner-building; to seek the elimination of obstacles to owner-building, from whatever source; and to provide such supportive services to the field offices of the Service as the Secretary shall deem appropriate and necessary;

(B) at the local level, to provide to owner-builders and to potential owner-builders information, advice, and technical assistance regarding construction materials, costs, and methods, and the availability and identity of local sources and resources; regarding financing opportunities and requirements, site acquisition, construction performance insurance, legal requirements and constraints, other available housing alternatives, and all other assistance as shall be deemed useful to facilitating the process of owner-building in the locality to foster the approach. The Housing Advisory Service is authorized to receive applications for and make commitments on behalf of the Secretary regarding financial assistance available under this section and title, and under section 235 of the National Housing Act."

(c) by adding the following sentence to new subsection (b) (3): "Such loans shall be available to owner-builders receiving assistance from a Housing Advisory Service, subject to the same limitations."

(d) by replacing the "or" after "(i)" in subsection (c) with a comma, and adding, "or (3)" after "(2)" in the same subsection.

(e) by changing subsection (f) to (g) and subsection (g) to (h) and by adding the following new subsection (f):

"(f) There is hereby created an Owner-Builder Performance Insurance Fund (hereinafter referred to as 'the Fund') which shall be used by the Secretary as a revolving fund for carrying out all the mortgage insurance obligations incurred under this section. There is hereby authorized to be appropriated to the Secretary such sums as may be necessary for the purposes of the Fund. Premium charges, adjusted premium charges, and other fees and service charges received on account of any mortgage or loan which is the obligation of the Fund, the receipts derived from the property covered by such mortgages and loans and from the claims, debts, contracts, property, and security assigned to the Secretary in connection therewith, and all earnings on the assets of the Fund shall be credited to the Fund. All payments made pursuant to claims of mortgagees with respect to mortgages insured under this section, cash adjustments, the principal of and interest paid on debentures which are the obligation of the fund, expenses incurred in connection with or as a consequence of the acquisition and disposal of property acquired under this section, and all administrative expenses in connection with the mortgage insurance operations under this section shall be paid out of the Fund. There is authorized to be appropriated such sums as may be needed from time to time to cover losses sustained by the Fund in carrying out its obligations. Moneys in the Fund not needed for current operations of the Fund shall be deposited with the Treasurer of the United States to the credit of the Fund or invested in bonds or other obligations guaranteed by the United States. The Secretary, with the approval of the Secretary of the Treasury, may purchase in the open market debentures which are the obligation of the Fund. Such purchases shall be made at a price which will provide an investment yield of not less than the yield obtained from other investments authorized by this section. Debentures so purchased shall be cancelled and not reissued."

(f) by amending new subsection 523(g) by changing "$5,000,000" to "$20,000,000," and by changing "July 1, 1973" to "July 1, 1977," and by changing "June 30, 1973" to "June 30, 1977."

Comment: This is the heart of the bill, adding the owner-builder concept to and establishing the Housing Advisory Service within the existing self-help provisions of the Department of Agriculture housing legislation, specifically within section 523 of the Housing Act of 1949.[85] Owner-builders who fit within the requirements of eligibility for FmHA housing assistance, basically those of low- and moderate-income in rural areas,[86] are to be assisted both financially and technically, through the instrumentality of the Housing Advisory Service. The HAS is to operate at the national and local levels, as information-disseminator, educator, advocate, and facilitator of the owner-building method. The local level responsibilities especially are facilitating ones, to fully assist the owner-builder in his task by helping him utilize and manipulate the network of resources available, including financial assistance he might get from the federal government, and to provide technical assistance in the actual building process.

The performance insurance fund is modeled on the "Special Risk Fund" set up for certain HUD housing programs.[87] The insurance of mortgages should ensure that the HAS will provide quality technical assistance, and this fund provides the back-up that should make financial institutions more willing to deal with owner-builders.

The increase in authorized funding is to cover the substantial increase in activity foreseen by the initiation of the Housing Advisory Service. [This is a very tentative figure which should

[85] 42 U.S.C. § 1490(c) (1970).
[86] *See* 42 U.S.C. § 1471 (1970).
[87] 12 U.S.C. § 1715z–3(b) (1970).

be more carefully calculated before final consideration of this bill.]

Population Limit

SEC. 7 Section 520 of the Housing Act of 1949 is amended by changing "10,000" to "25,000."

Comment: The population increase is to cover the current gap between the areas in which FHA offices actually operate, and the current statutory limit on FmHA jurisdiction. This change and figure has been advocated already.

The following is the text of Section 523 as it would be affected by the proposed legislation. The added provisions are in italics.

Mutual and Self-Help Housing

SEC. 523(a) The purposes of this section are (1) to make financial assistance available on reasonable terms and conditions in rural areas and small towns to needy low-income individuals and their families who, with the benefit of technical assistance and overall guidance and supervision, participate in approved programs of mutual or self-help housing by acquiring and developing necessary land, acquiring building materials, providing their own labor, and working cooperatively with others for the provision of decent, safe, and sanitary dwellings for themselves, their families, and others in the area or town involved, (2) to facilitate the efforts of both public and private nonprofit organizations providing assistance to such individuals to contribute their technical and supervisory skills toward more effective and comprehensive programs of mutual or self-help housing in rural areas and small towns wherever necessary, *and (3) to make financial and technical assistance available on reasonable terms and conditions in rural areas and small towns to individuals and families who meet the requirements of section 501 of this Act and who are owner-builders or prospective owner-builders, such assistance to be provided through a Housing Advisory Service as herein established.*

(b) In order to carry out the purpose of this section, the Secretary of Agriculture (in this section referred to as the "Secretary") is authorized—

(1)(A) to make grants to, or contract with, public or private nonprofit corporations, agencies, institutions, organizations, and other associations approved by him, to pay part or all of the costs of developing, conducting, administering, or coordinating effective and comprehensive programs of technical and supervisory assistance which will aid needy low-income individuals and their families in carrying out mutual or self-help housing efforts; and (B) to establish the Self-Help Housing Land Development Fund, referred to herein as the Self-Help Fund, to be used by the Secretary as a revolving fund for making loans, on such terms and conditions and in such amounts as he deems necessary, to public or private nonprofit organizations for the acquisition and development of land as building sites to be subdivided and sold to families, nonprofit organizations, and cooperatives eligible for assistance under section 235 or 236 of the National Housing Act or section 521 of this Act. Such a loan, with interest at a rate not to exceed 3 percent per annum, shall be repaid within a period not to exceed two years from the making of the loan, or within such additional period as may be authorized by the Secretary in any case as being necessary to carry out the purposes hereof;

(2) *to establish a Housing Advisory Service to facilitate the process of owner-building. This Service shall operate in such localities as the Secretary shall deem appropriate, on the basis of present and potential owner-building activity. The responsibilities of the Housing Advisory Service shall include:*

(A) *at the national level, to engage in research regarding, to disseminate information on, and to actively promote the method and techniques of owner-building; to seek the elimination of obstacles to owner-building, from whatever source; and to provide such supportive services to the field offices of the Service as the Secretary shall deem appropriate and necessary;*

(B) *at the local level, to provide to owner-builders and to potential owner-builders information, advice, and technical assistance regarding construction materials, costs, and methods, and the availability and identity of local sources and resources;*

regarding financing opportunities and requirements, site acquisition, construction performance insurance, legal requirements and constraints, other available housing alternatives, and all other assistance as shall be deemed useful to facilitating the process of owner-building in the locality to foster the approach. The Housing Advisory Service is authorized to receive applications for and make commitments on behalf of the Secretary regarding financial assistance available under this section and title, and under section 235 of the National Housing Act; and

(3) to make loans, on such terms and conditions and in such amounts as he deems necessary, to needy low-income individuals participating in the programs of mutual or self-help housing approved by him, for the acquisition and development of land and for the purchase of such other building materials as may be necessary in order to enable them, by providing substantially all of their own labor, and by cooperating with others participating in such programs, to carry out to completion the construction of decent, safe, and sanitary dwellings for such individuals and their families, subject to the following limitations:

(A) there is reasonable assurance of repayment of the loan;

(B) the amount of the loan, together with other funds which may be available, is adequate to achieve the purpose for which the loan is made;

(C) the credit assistance is not otherwise available on like terms or conditions from private sources or through other Federal, State, or local programs;

(D) the loan bears interest at a rate not to exceed 3 per centum per annum on the unpaid balance of principal, plus such additional charge, if any, toward covering other costs of the loan program as the Secretary may determine to be consistent with its purposes; and

(E) the loan is repayable within not more than thirty-three years.

Such loans shall be available to owner-builders receiving assistance from a Housing Advisory Service, subject to the same limitations.

(c) In determining whether to extend financial assistance under paragraph (1), (2), *or* (3) of subsection (b), the Secretary shall take into consideration, among other factors, the suitability of the area within which construction will be carried out to the type of dwelling which can be provided under mutual or self-help housing programs, the extent to which the assistance will facilitate the provision of more decent, safe, and sanitary housing conditions than presently exist in the area, the extent to which the assistance will be utilized efficiently and expeditiously, the extent to which the assistance will effect an increase in the standard of living of low-income individuals participating in the mutual or self-help housing program, and whether the assistance will fulfill a need in the area which is not otherwise being met through other programs, including those carried out by other Federal, State, or local agencies.

(d) As used in this section, the term "construction" includes the erection of new dwellings, and the rehabilitation, alteration, conversion, or improvement of existing structures.

(e) The Secretary is authorized to establish appropriate criteria and procedures in order to determine the eligibility of applicants for the financial assistance provided under this section, including criteria and procedures with respect to the periodic review of any construction carried out with such financial assistance.

(f) *There is hereby created an Owner-Builder Performance Insurance Fund (hereinafter referred to as "the Fund") which shall be used by the Secretary as a revolving fund for carrying out all the mortgage insurance obligations incurred under this section. There is hereby authorized to be appropriated to the Secretary such sums as may be necessary for the purposes of the Fund. Premium charges, adjusted premium charges, and other fees and service charges received on account of any mortgage or loan which is the obligation of the Fund, the receipts derived from the property covered by such mortgages and loans and from the claims, debts, contracts, property, and security assigned to the Secretary in connection therewith, and all earnings on the assets of the Fund shall be credited to the Fund. All payments made pursuant to claims of mortgagees with respect to mortgages insured under this section, cash adjustments, the principal of and interest paid on debentures which are the obligation of the fund, expenses incurred in connection with or as a conse-*

quence of the acquisition and disposal of property acquired under this section, and all administrative expenses in connection with the mortgage insurance operations under this section shall be paid out of the Fund. There is authorized to be appropriated such sums as may be needed from time to time to cover losses sustained by the Fund in carrying out its obligations. Moneys in the Fund not needed for current operations of the Fund shall be deposited with the Treasurer of the United States to the credit of the Fund or invested in bonds or other obligations guaranteed by the United States. The Secretary, with the approval of the Secretary of the Treasury, may purchase in the open market debentures which are the obligation of the Fund. Such purchases shall be made at a price which will provide an investment yield of not less than the yield obtained from other investments authorized by this section. Debentures so purchased shall be cancelled and not reissued.

(g) There are hereby authorized to be appropriated for each fiscal year commencing after June 30, 1968, and ending prior to *July 1, 1977*, such sums, not in excess of *$20,000,000* for any such fiscal year, as may be necessary to carry out the provisions of this section. No grant or loan may be made or contract entered into under the authority of this section after *June 30, 1977*, except pursuant to a commitment or other obligation entered into pursuant to this section before that date.

(h) There are hereby authorized to be appropriated for the purposes of subsection (b)(1)(B) not to exceed $1,000,000 for the fiscal year ending June 30, 1969, and not to exceed $2,000,000 for the fiscal year ending June 30, 1970. Any amount so authorized to be appropriated for any fiscal year which is not appropriated may be appropriated for any succeeding fiscal year or years. Amounts appropriated under this subsection shall be deposited in the Self-Help Fund, which shall be available without fiscal year limitation for making loans under subsection (b)(1)(B). Instruments and property acquired by the Secretary in or as a result of making such loans shall be assets of the Self-Help Fund. Sums received from the repayment of such loans shall be deposited in and be a part of the Self-Help Fund.

3

ROLF GOETZE

Urban Housing Rehabilitation: Two Approaches Contrasted to Illustrate Productive and Meaningful Dweller Participation

HOME OWNERSHIP through the process of owner-building still thrives in rural and suburban areas of the United States. It is also a feature of cities in the so-called Third World, even though land tenure in squatter settlements may be legally precarious. But opportunities for home ownership through owner-building are rare in the cities of the industrialized world and a virtual impossibility for the lower-income populations of those cities.

There are many reasons for this state of affairs, among them the strength of institutions guarding property rights which serve both to underpin high urban land costs and to prevent "have-nots" from seizing opportunities; restrictive building and sanitary codes which call for instant high initial standards, but are useless in attaining or holding a standard over time; an apparently inevitable trend favoring the building trades and their increasing specialization; and, of course, the world-wide tendency to do things for have-nots, instead of helping them to help themselves and offering complementary resources.

As a result, the principal suppliers of new housing inside urban boundaries are subsidized developers and public agencies, while the have-nots largely wait in vain and in substandard quarters. Under current federal laws the poor are expected to rent where the government chooses to subsidize, and the scantier their resources, the more dependent they are.

Yet if home ownership through owner-building is practically out of the question for lower-income central city residents, a potential still exists for home ownership through occupant-rehabilitation of deteriorated dwelling units. The following study details an impressive experiment in rehabilitation leading to home ownership, which warrants careful attention by those concerned with the supply and maintenance of an adequate inner-city housing stock.

A reasonable objective for a housing policy is to ensure the delivery of housing services which are both acceptable to the consumer and priced within his ability to pay. To explore the inability of present U.S. housing policy to attain this objective, this chapter contrasts two different approaches to housing rehabilitation, as shown in programs carried out in Rochester, New York. The two programs were carried out in the same neighborhood and for comparable income groups. Both were completed to FHA standards under federal programs. (The information presented below reflects the situation through 1970.)

Rochester is the central city in a metropolitan area of 700,000 inhabitants in upper New York State. This city has an extremely tight housing market, with a vacancy rate under 1 percent. Dominant in this inner-city housing stock are single-family frame houses, suffering from the results of deferred maintenance which were in turn due to high service costs in the area.

Both the CPT Housing Corp. and Better Rochester Living, Inc. set out to rehabilitate a number of these deteriorated but not abandoned dwellings. The houses selected were generally single-family, detached, nine-room frame houses on tight lots. They cluster into several neighborhoods in Rochester which are both physically and socially gray areas adjoining sounder sections.

While the houses which were rehabilitated were of the same type, the two organizations approached their task in vastly dissimilar ways. CPT, set up by the Third Presbyterian Church of Rochester, is typical of nonprofit rehabilitation for rental to lower-income families; BRL, largely the creation of one man, Welton Myers, is quite unconventional in guiding the efforts of families at the same income level so that they are able to become owners of their own homes.

The approach developed by Better Rochester Living (BRL) made dweller participation and "sweat equity" a cornerstone in a social program facilitating home ownership. Families eagerly self-selected themselves into this program because they saw it offered them ownership rather than just rental of rehabilitated houses. The other approach, followed by the CPT Housing Corp., rehabilitated houses under conventional contracting procedures. These houses were shown to the applicants only after completion, and then only for rental. The CPT method attained physical results which were substantially similar to those of BRL at the outset, but showed less durability as poor tenant living practices hastened the deterioration of the units.

The findings in Tables 2 and 3 present initial cost comparisons for comparable CPT and BRL houses, which in some instances are on the same streets. The amortization and rental payments under the two alternative approaches are compared, and the subsequent maintenance history is evaluated.

Table 2 presents the cost breakdown on the nine CPT houses rehabilitated. Below it are the costs for the nearby BRL houses.

The CPT average purchase price of $8,630 was $1,743 higher than BRL's average. This could either have been due to inexperience in purchasing or to CPT's reluctance to push previous owners too hard, but it does not, on the basis of first-hand inspection appear to reflect substantially larger or better houses.

CPT's average rehabilitation expenditure of $8,030 per unit was more than double BRL's average direct expenditure of $3,457. In addition, CPT incurred outside architect and lawyer fees and financing costs averaging $1,940 per unit, while BRL provided comparable services out of an average of $630 in overhead. Cumulatively CPT spent over $7,600 more per unit on initial rehabilitation costs, without achieving significantly more

Table 2 CPT Housing Corp.

	Address	Purchase Price	Rehabilitation Costs	Pro Rata Professional Expense	Pro Rata Financing Expense	Total Cost per House
A	Arch St.	$10,500	$12,500	$570	$1,370	$24,940
B	Second St.	8,500	8,953	570	1,370	19,393
C	Fourth St.	8,900	6,245	570	1,370	17,085
D	Magnolia St.	7,500	9,292	570	1,370	18,732
E	Garson Ave.	9,900	5,225	570	1,370	17,065
F	Flint St.	9,500	10,910	570	1,370	22,350
G	Lenox St.	6,900	6,711	570	1,370	15,550
H	Gladstone St.	6,000	7,951	570	1,370	15,891
I	Flint St.	10,000	4,213	570	1,370	16,150
	Average per unit	$ 8,630	$ 8,030	$570	$1,370	$18,600

rehabilitation. There is no evidence of higher "maintainability" having been purchased through CPT's rehabilitation procedure.

The CPT approach is a good example of nonprofit, church-sponsored efforts. It reveals the conventional pattern of rehabilitation presently fostered by the federal subsidy system. CPT bought the houses and contracted out the rehabilitation. Not only was there a separate contractor, but other professionals such as architects and lawyers played a role in the rehabilitation.

CPT placed families in the houses upon completion, but market rents were inadequate to cover initial costs. The program, therefore, required a substantial subsidy. Through influence, CPT obtained Section 221(d)(3) Below Market Interest Rate (BMIR) financing to cover initial costs. Further subsidies to cover operating costs, provided under the leased-housing program, finally enabled families to occupy the units.

The BRL operation is quite different. Trained volunteers counsel the applicant families in budgeting and refer them to other agencies, such as employment or homemaker services, where appropriate. Budgeting is the key, however. Although the typical

Table 3 Comparable BRL Houses in CPT Neighborhoods

Address		Price Purchase	Rehabilitation Costs	Pro Rata Overhead	Sales Price
J	Arch St.	$6,800	$3,500	$600	$10,900
K	Arch St.	7,500	3,400	600	11,500
L	Fourth St.	6,700	5,409	700	12,809
M	Garson Ave.	6,900	3,500	700	11,100
N	Garson Ave.	7,200	3,500	700	11,400
O	Garson Ave.	7,000	3,110	600	10,710
P	Flint St.	5,000	4,650	600	10,250
Q	Flint St.	7,000	2,165	600	9,765
R	Flint St.	7,500	3,375	600	11,475
S	Lenox St.	7,000	3,250	600	10,850
T	Lenox St.	7,500	2,850	600	10,950
U	Lenox St.	6,500	4,874	700	10,074
V	Lenox St.	7,020	2,075	600	9,695
W	Lenox St.	6,800	2,755	600	10,155
	Average per unit	$6,887	$3,457	$630	$10,974

Note: Actual street addresses are masked to hide identity of the owners, but all are comparable, single-family houses.

applicant family has a dependable yearly income of $4,500 or better, it is overextended because of installment buying and the husband's pay has often been garnisheed.

As soon as BRL feels a family is ready for home ownership by demonstrating that it can live within its income (a process which may take a few or many months), the applicant family selects a suitable house through a realtor familiar with BRL's criteria. BRL then carries out an inspection, does cost estimates and work writeups, and buys the house from the previous owner on behalf of the family.

In the next step, the family subcontracts with BRL to do a certain portion of the rehabilitation work (painting, refinishing, planting, etc.) as sweat equity to cover closing costs and down payment. Other subcontractors handle major rehabilitation under BRL's supervision as interim owner. This might include upgrading or replacing the heating system, plumbing, and the like. With BRL's experience, the productivity of each rehabilitation dollar is more than doubled. This is evident from the cost figures in Table 3 and is examined more closely below.

First, a parenthetical note about financing. BRL obtains interim financing in its own name from local banks. It also negotiates mortgage and insurance commitments to run between the family and the FHA under the Section 221(h) or 235(j) programs.

During the rehabilitation process which takes place between these events, BRL seeks to minimize costs for professional services, such as those of architects, builders, and contractors. These skills are largely provided from the in-house staff. Even legal matters are prepared by the BRL staff for a retained attorney. Instead of using outside professionals with their concomitant overhead costs, BRL itself furnishes specialized help and guidance whenever it can, and even sets up charge accounts for participating families with local building materials suppliers.

A comparison of amortization payments under BRL with rental payments under CPT suggests that CPT families forgo the opportunity for building up equity without saving on their housing costs. For a BRL house with an $11,400 sales price, the total monthly mortgage payment was $100.64. The owner-family paid 20 percent of its monthly adjusted income, in this case $71. The monthly federal assistance payment of $29.64 to the bank on its behalf reduced the mortgage interest rate borne by the family to 3 percent.

The CPT financial picture is more complex. Each family similarly paid 20 percent of its monthly adjusted income toward rent, but this did not begin to cover debt service on the higher initial cost plus operating expenses. CPT obtained a 3 percent 35-year mortgage on the package under the Section 221(d)(3) program which is similar in impact to 221(h), but further leased-housing subsidies were required to cover ongoing operat-

Fig. 2. *Amortization Payments Under BRL*

For a $4,800 per year family of three, we find:

adjusted annual income =	$4,260.00
One-twelfth of 20 percent of annual income =	71.00

For the
BRL house: $11,400, 6¾ percent, thirty-five year mortgage

Total monthly payment on mortgage:	$ 100.64[1]
Principal and interest:	70.91
+ mortgage insurance premiums:	4.73
	75.64
+ taxes and insurance (estimated):	25.00
	100.64
— 20 percent of mortgagor's monthly income:	—71.00
Leaves monthly federal assistance payment:	$ 29.64
(in effect the family holds a 3 percent mortgage).	

ing costs. Under 221(d)(3) the tenants acquire no equity, and in addition, the taxpayers have to support the continuing burden of leased-housing payments as well as the subsidized mortgage.

The BRL approach brings out homeowner attitudes which accept normal maintenance in stride. Families interviewed revealed that they found ordinary maintenance and improvement problems easy to cope with after participating in rehabilitation.

Some families which had been indifferent to their rented homes became fastidious and resourceful as homeowners. They typically began to do their own painting, hang storm windows, fix

[1] Calculations are based on the HUD 235(j) *Handbook*, November 1968, FHA 4400.9, pp. 21–26. This program has replaced 221(h), but in this instance, the results are equivalent.

and putty panes, and put in shrubs. They also learned to know when to call skilled repairmen.

There have been isolated cases of replacing hot water heaters and equivalent repairs. Professionals in Rochester charge $165 for a new water heater including installation; under BRL, the family obtains the heater for $65 plus $30 for the professional labor supplied by BRL in installing it. In one instance a family decided to install a new furnace to gain space in its basement—normally an $800 operation for materials and labor. Furnishing some of its own labor under the BRL arrangement, the family obtained a new furnace and installation for under $500. When dwellers are faced with such major repairs, BRL is always on hand to offer advice.

A developing self-confidence seems to explain, in part, improved attitudes toward maintenance. One owner, who was using his BRL-acquired skill to insulate and panel his attic, told how he would deal with the tax assessor if the assessor came to give him any trouble. And the owner's whole manner showed that he had learned more than how to handle a staple gun; he had acquired a self-assurance which is as invaluable in dealing with authorities as it is in approaching the day-to-day problems of home upkeep.

Figures on actual maintenance expenditures, after title transfer, are as difficult to obtain from BRL families as they would be from any home owners. They may recall some specific bills, but countless tasks are performed and never thought of as labor costs. In sum, the BRL owner does not perceive maintenance as a problem. He accepts routine repairs, even enjoys them, as part of owning his own home. From a policy-maker's point of view, BRL projects can be called self-maintaining. CPT tenants, on the other hand, expect maintenance to be performed by building management. CPT's former director and the Rochester Housing Authority's director both concede that scattered site leased housing to tenants under the CPT approach is economically prohibitive under present cost limits.

BRL homeowner-dwellers, in the role of housing suppliers to themselves as consumers, perform services automatically that

CPT tenants demand from the Housing Authority. Under BRL, maintenance costs do not just appear to be smaller; they are not a *problem* in the same sense. Whether BRL families self-select themselves into the program that suits their inclinations, or whether they are educated by their participation in the rehabilitation process is not certain. Most observers are convinced the latter occurs, but formal proof would require a long-term, complex sociological study.

Many actors are involved in the delivery of housing services. Owner, manager, tenant, financier, and various service suppliers each have separate roles and act to obtain their own benefits. In principle, markets handle the complex interrelationships among these many roles and interests. But where market processes fail to meet the needs of the low-income consumer, intervention is called for.

The possible forms of such interventions must be carefully considered to avoid upsetting useful market mechanisms; otherwise, costs of delivering housing services may inflate without substantially increasing their quantity or quality. The BRL approach rationally combines several roles in the housing rehabilitation process—owner, manager, contractor, financier—to unify objectives, and this integration results in lower initial costs. The CPT effort, on the other hand, allows the proliferation of uncoordinated interests, multiplying initial costs.

To understand more fully how lower costs are reached through the BRL approach, it is useful to examine the interrelationship among the roles in the process. BRL has carefully orchestrated these roles so they result in minimum costs; CPT, following the pattern set by federal legislation for conventional nonprofits, has left the roles to chance, resulting in inefficiencies—particularly in comparison with BRL.

1. *Distinct and potentially separate roles are simplified by combining them in one actor.* BRL is sponsor, developer-contractor, and interim owner of the dwelling; it largely assumes the conventional role of architect and lawyer as well. The dweller is nightwatchman, subcontractor, trainee, and future owner; yet he

sees himself as present owner because he selected the building. Through this interlocking of roles, potentially divergent interests are held together, and friction from possible conflicts of interest is minimized.

2. *The total number of actors engaged in the overall process is minimized.* Many of the typical services of architect, lawyer, and other professional or middlemen are provided by the BRL staff. These services lower total costs to the family and the project.

3. *The number of actors engaged in any particular operation is minimized.* Where too many actors would jeopardize a given operation, it is broken into discrete steps. For example, in acquiring the property, the prospective dweller, previous owner, realtor, and BRL each have distinctly defined roles. In selecting the property, the dweller deals with the realtor; in acquiring it, BRL negotiates with the previous owner. (Under CPT the roles were not so carefully defined.)

4. *A given BRL staff member stays with a client family and its house from beginning to end.* The same man who evaluates the property does the work writeups and provides the technical assistance to the family. BRL follows this procedure to a much greater extent than is customary in more bureaucratized organizations. (CPT does not provide for ongoing counseling and follow-through.)

5. *The families willingly occupy substandard housing in the interim.* Interim holding costs (mortgage interest, insurance, taxes, utilities, watchman) are a major item in the conventional rehabilitation budget. Insurance and surveillance costs mount rapidly when a building is vacant. BRL minimizes these costs by allowing the future owners to move into their new home as tenants as soon as possible after the time of purchase. Reconstruction work, which would severely inconvenience the family, is performed before occupancy (usually in less than two weeks). Even when a dwelling is still substandard, the new inhabitants are usually eager to move in since their previous quarters were no better. Instead of paying rent to the previous landlord, the families make payments to BRL, and act as watchmen at the same time. By projecting themselves into an ownership role, BRL families are willing to tolerate housing defects and inconveniences

which would lead to a confrontation in other circumstances. Under the CPT approach, no one would think of letting families move in while code violations remain.

6. *The dweller carries out many of the tasks.* Since each operation involves effort and time costs that must be borne by someone, be it owner, taxpayer, or unwitting subsidizer, it may seem logical to let the dweller do all that he wishes and is able to do. Although strict cost-effectiveness considerations argue for subcontracting many of the tasks to professionals, BRL argues for extensive dweller participation on the grounds of immediate savings, psychological benefits, and long-range consequences.

a. *Immediate Savings.* In certain operations it is simply cheaper to train the dweller and provide him with the tools than to rely on existing trades. In rehabilitation there are many minor jobs that must get done, and in subsequent maintenance, most are minor. Other more major tasks, such as redoing the heating system, are sensibly delegated to professionals. The know-how and judgment to enable the dweller to decide when to call the specialist, whether to trust his word, and what to do himself must be developed, however. BRL's approach does this; CPT's does not.

b. *Psychological Benefits.* Contractors do not do some things the way dwellers want them done. Often they will just "rip it out" or "board it up," because to them the simplest, quickest way is the "rational" way to get things done. Would-be owners, on the other hand, may devote many leisure hours to tasks they undertake as a hobby. For example, BRL owners have saved such features as a fireplace and mantel or a stained glass window, which a contractor might have eliminated without a thought. BRL offers the future owner the freedom either to choose immediate efficiencies or to spend more of his spare time indulging his fancies.

Herein may lie a critical difference between two kinds of tenure: low-income home ownership and the rental of completely predetermined housing units for low-income dwellers. The dweller's sense of having a choice—reinforced at every point by the BRL program—may be a key factor in determining living patterns once he moves in.

c. *Long-Range Consequences.* Even when a future owner's participation in a given task cannot be justified within the initial cost, his participation is frequently rational when seen as "education." In the long run, the dweller copes with countless recurring situations that professional maintenance or management services cannot handle at reasonable cost. The BRL dweller's role as trainee and subcontractor helps him make future entrepreneurial decisions. This "education" can affect him profoundly.

For his efforts, the dweller benefits in a variety of ways. As a subcontractor he is credited at the time of closing with the cash equivalent of the labor inputs he furnished (approximately $800–$1,000 of the rehabilitation costs represent earnings for his labor); as a future owner he will benefit from his extra efforts; as a trainee he has learned skills that will save him money in the long run, and that he may even be able to market. He is largely recompensed in ultimate benefits rather than immediate pay—a situation analogous to education.

The BRL dweller, in selecting his own property, makes personal trade-offs within such complex parameters as size, style, number of rooms, neighborhood, and access to transportation, which are difficult for anyone else to make on his behalf. More importantly, even if the identical selection were reached by another process, the situation would be different because the dweller would not have experienced the trading-off among alternatives. With BRL support, he participates broadly in the decision-making process.

The dweller's main benefits from the BRL process are intangible. The altering of lifelong habits and the acquiring of a new outlook is not usually directly apparent to him. This educational process clearly takes time and develops from the dweller's participation in various phases of the entire process. It neither can be sped up radically, nor can there be shortcuts. Indeed, to deal with applicants with more problems probably would take longer. We will return to this later.

The roles played by the greater number of actors involved in the CPT approach were not so carefully orchestrated. Owner, manager, financier, architect, lawyer, contractor, subcontractors, tenant, and volunteer counsellor all had separate interests that were less effectively brought together to control costs. Each service supplier, such as contractor, architect, or lawyer, asked a fair price for his services, but the aggregate total was no longer limited by the market value of the result or by the consumer's ability to pay. Cost inflation was only limited by the available subsidies. It seems likely that were subsidies to increase, so would costs.

CPT made isolated attempts to counsel the dwellers toward better living habits. These were offered on a take-it-or-leave-it basis and most tenants failed to take them seriously. "Why go once a week to 'learn better living habits?' " one remarked. BRL's counselling was successful because it was tied to a salient goal of the dwellers: home ownership. Qualifying for house hunting—a prominent objective of the BRL families—was made contingent upon successful counselling. Success was defined as bringing debts down to a reasonable proportion of income.

In summary, if one were to draw a comparison over the long run, under the BRL process home-ownership mediates between the interests of consumer and housing supplier, resulting in "acceptable" housing costs; under the CPT process, all aspects of housing services are scattered among diverging interest groups, and the price of insufficient co-ordination is increased housing costs to be borne by ongoing tax-payer subsidies.

Limitations of the BRL Approach

If BRL has been so successful for over a hundred families, one might quite naturally ask what constraints inhibit it from operating on a much larger scale. First, it is important to realize that the program at its present scale and rate of production can be considered self-sustaining. The $600–$700 required for helping each family is expended out of BRL seed money (locally raised contributions) but are recovered from the FHA mortgage when the family becomes owner of its home. BRL also has a line of credit with local banks for construction financing, but it is dependent on the government mortgage programs, FNMA and GNMA (the Federal National Mortgage Association and the Government National Mortgage Association, known as Fannie Mae and Ginnie Mae), as well as the FHA programs for mortgage subsidies, as elaborated below.

It is hard to estimate the potential of the BRL approach. In its present form, the program does seem to depend on the critical manipulation of actors and elements which are not all in abundant supply. BRL must have a stock of deteriorated yet structurally sound houses available at prices the organization can afford. Greatly increased scale might inflate prices. BRL is further limited to lower-income families ($5,000–$9,000) who respond to counselling and who are willing and able to invest time in rehabilitation work. Single-headed households and those with severe problems are out of reach of BRL because BRL functions in the guise of a regular FHA contractor, whose budget is merely expected to provide the overhead of a normal contracting business, not social services.

What takes place when the family itself becomes the recipient of a federally subsidized, below-market interest mortgage must be reemphasized. Previously the FHA has simply made a commitment to BRL as a contractor and housing supplier. BRL assumes all responsibility for seeing rehabilitation through. When the family has learned to budget, has consolidated debts, and has improved its financial situation so that it is no longer a credit risk, and when the unit has been brought up to standard, only then does the FHA officially recognize the prospective owners—the people around whom BRL has pivoted the whole process. And it is commendable that BRL has found a way to manipulate bureaucratic practices to everyone's advantage. But for BRL to reach more families would require the redesigning of FHA programs; HUD-FHA policies and practices are presently the limiting constraints.

Before examining specific ways in which federal programs handicap an operation such as BRL's, some remarks are necessary about contradictions built into our national housing effort. As Charles Abrams brought out in his book *The City is the Fron-*

tier, the FHA was created during the Depression as a means of stimulating the economy through the building sector. In other words, the FHA's focus was on the *supply* side rather than on the demand side; and though the housing shortage of the last twenty-five years has masked the fact, the FHA still favors those who produce housing rather than those who ultimately use it.

One evidence of this is the multiplicity and complexity of federal programs. A whole professional subclass—"facilitating beneficiaries"—has come into existence for the purpose of manipulating the many federal programs. The individual citizen is nearly helpless and dependent upon middlemen and housing suppliers who naturally place their own interests first. The nonprofit CPT and BRL organizations were both shaped in response to existing legislation. The FHA assists both as housing producers; whether they actually help the dweller or not is almost incidental.

A sponsor such as CPT is a perfect foil for this supplier-centered system. As a philanthropic organization, CPT gives the appearance of concern for the poor; yet because of its limited and unsophisticated housing experience, CPT inevitably inflates costs through inefficiency and the purchase of unnecessary professional services. Furthermore, it appears that the more architects, lawyers, materials suppliers, and builders are involved in subsidized housing programs—and their involvement is very great—the less such considerations as user needs, quality, maintainability, and social consequences can be taken into account.

The need for ever more subsidies seems built into our federal housing legislation. Sponsors are encouraged to depend on facilitating beneficiaries—planners, architects, contractors, and so on—and must inevitably assume the cost of their services. Soon the well-meaning sponsor finds himself backed into the need for still *more* federal help and is constantly *more* reliant on federal programs.

This is not to say that all, or even the majority of, facilitating beneficiaries deliberately set out to provide poor housing at inflated costs for people whose wishes have been ignored. It is simply a question of who controls the process and where the incentives lie. As a client advocate, concerned more with long-term individual and community goals than with pork-barreling professionals and contractors, BRL has essentially been in conflict with the FHA. Though it has had some success in adapting FHA programs to its needs, particularly when it can work with the local office, BRL has been limited by a number of constraints which are irrational in terms of long-term community goals. These constraints are many. In this study we will touch on only a few: FHA program definition, turnover time and coordination of events, and FHA packaging.

Program Definition

Section 221(h) limits assistance to families with a set income ceiling and requires "substantial rehabilitation," which is defined as a percentage of total costs spent on labor and materials in rehabilitation to FHA specifications. BRL's efforts have thus been restricted to a narrow range of severely deteriorated houses and to lower-income families willing to do a substantial amount of rehabilitation themselves. A family must either do a great deal of work or—as the FHA expects—a contractor will do it. Relaxing the need for substantial rehabilitation while monitoring the quality of work performed would open the opportunity for organizations such as BRL to serve a much wider spectrum of potential homeowners. Such people could then acquire hand-me-down (though not badly deteriorated) houses and earn their closing costs through supervised but less demanding repair work.

The 221(h) and 235(j) programs are too narrowly defined to reach other housing types, such as Boston's triple deckers; and now that the program has been revised into 235(j), the incentive for home ownership is diminished as well. Under 221(h), dweller-families carried a monthly amortization payment which stayed fixed regardless of income changes. Under 235(j), an income increase means higher mortgage payments by the dwellers, making the advantages of ownership over rental less evident to them at the outset.

Turnover Time and Coordination of Events

Under the BRL program, families admittedly require spare time to accomplish in months what professionals could do in weeks. Even though interim costs are borne by the families, though they acquire valuable skills in the process, and though more durable housing results, the FHA is impatient with a median fourteen-month time lapse between commitment and final closing, as measured by the simple yardstick of new production in suburbia. Ironically, much of this period is consumed in title search (inner-city properties frequently have tangled titles), FHA inspections, and red tape.

Figure 3 suggests a part of the reason for the FHA's impatience. Three relatively simple operations must be coordinated with four FHA events—through a field office miles away.

Fig. 3. *Turnover Time and Coordination of Events*

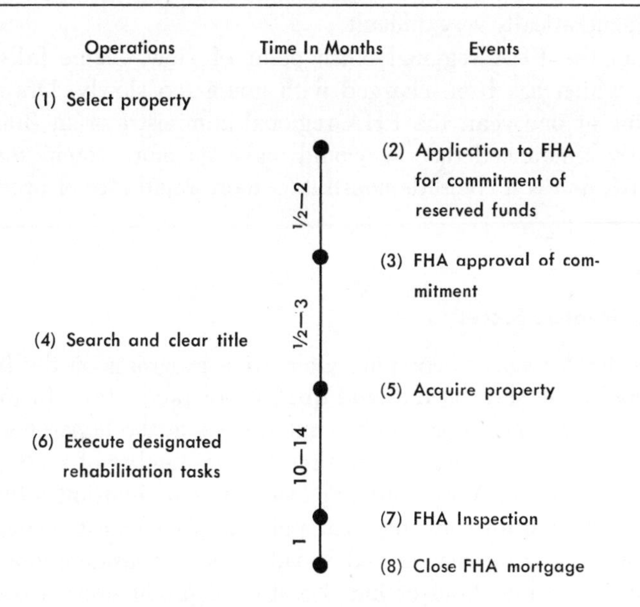

FHA Packaging

BRL must coordinate its packaging as well as its sequence of steps to conform with FHA practice. The FHA requests that units be grouped into sets of eight for processing. This introduces minor benefits and major drawbacks.

An advantage is that blanket commitments are obtained in the name of the sponsor, which allows for acquisition before the participating families have their financial affairs in hand, although in the BRL experience this does not represent a risk factor. Thus, through blanket commitments, the rehabilitation process can begin sooner than it otherwise would.

On the other hand, acquisition and the rehabilitation of properties can hit snags. As a result, when one unit is held up for some reason, the whole eight-unit package will be delayed. Even though completed units could theoretically be "spun off" from the blanket commitment, BRL has found it almost impossible to do this, since making changes in the "contents" of a package is bureaucratically very difficult.

From the FHA regional office point of view, blame falls on BRL, which has been charged with going too slowly. Drawing the line at one year, the FHA regional administrator in Buffalo recently announced that he would make no more commitments for BRL unless it could demonstrate a more rapid rate of production.

How to Measure Success

The FHA seems to compare alternative programs on the basis of initial costs and the rate and quantity of production. In many cases, it is willing to pay higher initial costs in the hope of some dramatic statistical success measured by the number of units produced over time. Yet a rational evaluation of housing alternatives, judged from a twenty-year point of view, must recognize that ongoing maintenance and broader social considerations far outweigh considerations of initial cost or of production measured solely in terms of numbers of units.

To be fair, the FHA merely reflects criteria of success accepted too often by our society at large. We place a premium on quick, visible, statistically impressive results; and since the FHA is politically sensitive to the demand for "action," it is drawn to crash programs which are understandably popular with the professional and industrial interests who are bound to benefit, whatever the final results.

Short-term criteria of success artificially separate the production of housing from the consumption of housing. Yet the BRL experiment demonstrates that production and consumption are closely interrelated and have subtle trade-offs between them. Dweller participation in the rehabilitation process may take longer, but it can reduce the initial cost of rehabilitation. And even more significantly, whether or not it lowers initial costs, dweller participation pays great dividends during the occupancy phase when the new homeowner looks after most of his own housing maintenance, and in the process becomes a more responsible member of the community. As we noted earlier, the durability of the BRL units is conspicuous in comparison with those rehabilitated by CPT, and in a large measure, this can be traced to the education BRL participants received in the course of financial counselling and actual reconstruction.

Attempts to deliver finished housing units in quantity and at a high rate of production make it impossible to educate the consumer to play a role in providing his own housing services and may be a key factor in subsequent deterioration. Leased-housing tenants, for example, are often not aware of the cost consequences of their actions or inactions. Why should they be? They have been given no incentive to count the cost.

We can say, then, that by concentrating on the rapid production of demonstration units and excluding dweller participation from almost all subsidized housing, present policy is doing much less than it could to change abusive living patterns which shorten the useful life of the dwellings after occupancy.

This is not an argument for forcing home ownership or dweller participation upon those who do not desire it. It is an argument, instead, for offering home ownership as an option in circumstances where that option is presently quite rare or does not exist at all.

The closing note must be a pessimistic one. BRL is in trouble. Its vigorous nonbureaucratic director has not "won over" the staid FHA personnel, and further, BRL's intangible and long-term criteria of success have put it at odds with the FHA. While the program can survive with a neutral bureaucracy, it cannot survive active discouragement. The HUD regional office in Buffalo is no longer willing to support the BRL approach. Its director remarked, "We're a housing, not a social action agency. We can't afford the time to undertake social action." Yet ironically, if HUD broadened its evaluation criteria and diverted more funds toward approaches similar to BRL's, it might produce substantially more housing units *in the long run.*

4

HANS H. HARMS

The Housing Problem for Low-Income People

THE PROBLEM OF HOUSING appears quite different when seen from the national and aggregate level by a public policy maker or a large commercial developer than it does from the perspective of a low-income dweller. At the national level, massive housing deficits are most apparent, and solutions which combine speed, economies of scale and industrialization seem perfectly appropriate. From the user's point of view, on the other hand, primary considerations are *availability* (low rent or price level), *quality*, *location* in relation to jobs, good schools, transportation, and sufficient *control* over one's living space to make a personalized home.

This chapter will concentrate on those people whose housing situation is the worst, whose hopes for betterment under present circumstances are the least, and who therefore have the greatest need for decent housing.

As Anthony Downs wrote in *Agenda for the Nation:*

> Most Americans have no conception of the filth, degradation, squalor, overcrowding and personal danger and insecurity which mil-

> lions of inadequate housing units are causing. Thousands of infants are attacked by rats each year, hundreds die or become mentally retarded from eating lead paint that falls off cracked walls, thousands more are ill because of unsanitary conditions resulting from jamming large families into a single room, continuing failure of landlords to repair plumbing or provide proper heat, and pitifully inadequate storage space. Until you have actually stumbled through the ill-lit and decaying rooms of a slum dwelling, smelled the stench of sewage and garbage and dead rats behind the walls, seen the roaches and crumbling plaster, and recoiled from exposed wiring and rotting floorboards and staircases, you have no real idea of what bad housing is like.[1]

To this catalogue of miseries must be added lack of outside play areas, inadequate schools, shopping places, and public services, and decreasing job opportunities.

In a market economy, needs are fulfilled according to financial ability, not according to urgency. Or in traditional economists' terms, supply is provided according to "effective demand." As a rule, those people with the least income have to be satisfied with the lowest quality of housing and living environments as provided by the commercial market. This creates a sharp discrepancy between official or governmental housing standards and actual living conditions among neglected sectors of the population.

Clear distinctions should be made between "effective demand" in the market sense, "needs" in terms of adequate housing and living conditions as experienced by the users of housing, and the concept of official and legal standards of housing, which separate "decent" from "substandard" housing as defined by local or federal governmental agencies.

The housing industry and its set of actors (manufacturers, suppliers, developers, contractors, realtors, lending institutions, insurance companies, etc.) are primarily concerned with the effective demand for housing as a product, or with those households, out of the total population, which are able and willing to

[1] Anthony Downs, "Moving Toward Realistic Housing Goals," in *Agenda for the Nation*, Kermit Gordon, ed. (Washington, D.C.: Brookings Institution, 1968), p. 142.

pay the price for a housing product the industry and the market can supply profitably to them.

Official housing standards set the minimum quality theoretically acceptable to government agencies and their inspectors. Minimum standards, like all standards, are based on the values and professional judgments of those who set them. These standards are supposed to act as quality monitors and safeguards for the owner or tenant, lending and insurance institutions, and society at large.

Effective demand is a market concept, legal *minimum standards* is a concept developed by public officials, whereas *user needs* exist independently of the market and the government. They are based on human urgencies as felt by the users themselves.[2] The supply side of the market is of course interested in user needs, but only insofar as they can be turned into effective demand. Under the present practices and processes of financing, management, technology, and marketing are controlled by the housing industry and, to some extent, by government regulations. Private enterprise supplies the market only with those housing goods which guarantee a profit at a limited risk.

The Quantitative Housing Problem

We have to ascertain *how many* badly housed low-income people there are, *who* they are, and *where* they live. We will discuss the traditional mechanisms for meeting the housing needs of the poor, and the underlying assumptions, ideologies, and results of these approaches.

In 1950 15 to 17 million American families (37 percent) lived in substandard housing. In 1960 the figure was 11 to 12 million (20 percent). In 1968 Lyndon Johnson talked about more than 20 million Americans, approximately 9 million families (13 percent) who lived in poor housing. The decrease in the aggregated numbers of substandard housing gives the impression of a trend

[2] John Turner defines "demand" as dependent on the felt needs of users, their available means and *willingness to invest* (Chapter 6, p. 161).

toward improvement. Yet, as the Douglas Commission pointed out, the extent of the "achievements" depends on how one reads the available figures and the criteria on which they are based. In fact the achievements have been highly selective, largely bypassing two overlapping groups, the poor and racial minorities, mainly blacks (who constitute 92 percent of the nonwhite population). Kristof's housing need study for the Douglas Commission points to the widespread gap in rent-income ratios by income class:[3]

> —Of renters with incomes under $2,000, 90% paid 25% or more of income for rent, and of these, 13% paid 25 to 35% of income for rent; 77% paid 35% or more of income for rent.
> —Of renters with incomes between $2,000 and $3,000, 63% paid 25% or more, and of these, 32% paid 35% or more of income for rent.
> —Of renters with incomes between $6,000 and $7,000, 6% pay 25% or more, 1% pay 35% or more for rent.

The lower the income, the higher the housing tax the poor pay by way of a disproportionate outlay for shelter. An additional tax is paid by minority groups, the other population segment bypassed by "housing progress." The National Advisory Commission on Civil Disorders documented the financial burden of being nonwhite, and found that racial minorities were paying a definite "color tax" of well over 10 percent on housing.[4] This condition prevails in most racial ghettos and has not changed since Jacob Riis' documents at the turn of the century.[5]

In Massachusetts 260,000 (17 percent of all households, black and white) live in substandard housing. Half of them earn less than $4,000 per year (average four persons per family), two-thirds of them earn less than $5,000, one-quarter paid more than 35 percent of their income for shelter, half of them live in over-

[3] Donald Canty, ed., *The Ill-Housed* (Washington, D.C.: Urban America, Inc., 1969), p. 8. Figures apply to 1960.
[4] *Ibid.*, p. 10.
[5] Jacob A. Riis, *How the Other Half Lives, Studies among the Tenements of New York* (New York: Dover Publications, 1971). First published, 1890.

crowded dwellings, and three-quarters of them are tenants. The largest group consists of families with small children.[6]

Although only 20 percent of all U.S. households live in substandard housing, 50 percent of all nonwhites do.[7]

The geographic distribution in the U.S. shows a larger percentage of substandard housing in rural areas, but with an increasing proportion in urban areas. In Massachusetts 84 percent of the families living in substandard housing are located in the ten metropolitan areas.[8] And in this context, the official designation "substandard"—for all its many faults as a measure of value—does give a fairly reliable idea of the dimensions of the problem.

Between 1950 and 1960 the suburban black population of all metropolitan areas grew a total of only 60,000 per year, whereas the white suburban population grew 1.72 million a year. This means that 96.6 percent of all suburban growth consisted of whites. Between 1960 and 1966 the suburban black population growth declined sharply to 33,000 per year. There was actually an emigration of blacks from the suburbs into the center city. Meanwhile the white suburban population growth increased to 1.75 million per year. In 1966 there were 12.5 million nonwhites living in all U.S. central cities, of whom 12.1 million were blacks.[9]

The National Advisory Commission on Civil Disorders noted that:

> Since 1960 the growth of non-white population in central cities has continued unabated. White population growth in all those cities has, however, ceased entirely. . . . The absolute rate of growth of ghettos per year has gone up to its highest level in history. In contrast the white population of central cities in 1965 was 46.4 million, or 1.3 million less than 1960. So for all 224 central cities considered as a whole, all population growth now consists of gains in Negro population.

[6] Bernard Frieden, "Housing Creating the Supply," in *The State and the Poor,* Samuel Beer and Richard E. Barringer, eds. (Englewood Cliffs, N.J.: Prentice-Hall, 1970), pp. 107–33.

[7] *The Ill-Housed,* pp. 8–10.

[8] Bernard Frieden, *op. cit.,* p. 113.

[9] Anthony Downs, "Alternative Futures for the American Ghetto," in *Daedalus,* Fall 1968, p. 1331.

From 1960 to 1966, 89% of all non-white population growth was in central cities and 11% was in suburbs. Non-metropolitan areas (including the rural South) actually lost non-white population. This indicates that heavy out-migration from rural areas to cities is still continuing to take place.[10]

The Commercial Market and the Filtering Process

The traditional mechanism which presumably alleviates the housing plight of the poor is the so-called filtering process in the housing market. The filtering process links various submarkets of an area. One consists of new housing priced for middle- and upper-income people. Other submarkets consist of older housing stock of varying qualities and locations, some priced within the means of low-income people.

Filtering actually includes two distinct processes: a) the "filtering up" of households or users, which results in a substitution of dwelling units at certain points in the life cycle of households, either according to change in the need for size, quality, and location, or according to changes in income, taste, and status, or because fears of major racial, ethnic, or economic shifts in the neighborhood; b) the "filtering down" of dwelling units to lower-market value and price, which can result in changes of occupancy from higher- to lower-income households.[11]

The assumptions of the filtering process are that there is a constant upward mobility of households in society and that if enough new middle- and upper-income housing units are built in response to an effective demand, the now less desirable houses vacated will be filled by moderate-income people, who in turn will vacate buildings of still lower quality.

The poor, of course, are at the end of the line. They have to wait until everybody else moves. In times of great shortage of new housing or at a time when the increase in households is

[10] Report of the National Advisory Commission on Civil Disorders (Washington, D.C., March 1968), p. 121.

[11] See also William G. Grigsby, *Housing Markets and Public Policy* (Philadelphia: University of Pennsylvania Press, 1963).

greater than the increase in new housing starts, the filtering mechanism begins to fail. If the middle classes don't move from older housing to new or otherwise superior dwellings, then the housing opportunities for the poor are diminished. When the economic upward mobility of the population stops or declines and the production of new middle- and upper-class housing falls off, many people are forced to move or pay higher rents in proportion to their income. Only those who can pay the increasing rents or household costs can get or keep the housing they want.

Because of a limited supply of secondhand older housing, and therefore high prices, the poor seeking alternative housing are "forced out of the market" and have the following choices:

1. Double up with other families;
2. Move into very dilapidated housing of lower rent;
3. Pay more than 20 to 25 percent of their income (FHA regulation for rents in low-rent public housing); or
4. Combine any of the three possibilities.

It is not only in times of recession or tight money that the filtering process falters. Filtering depends, first, on a supply of new housing for the middle- and upper-middle classes, and second, on a supply of used vacant housing in fairly good condition at relatively low prices for the lower- and lower-middle classes. As soon as a substantial vacancy rate in new and higher-priced housing develops, however, the situation can turn into a buyer's market, so that at times when filtering begins to function freely, private developers begin to limit the supply of new buildings. They are interested in a seller's market, and the poor are again caught short.

The traditional building industry, with its large number of very small-scale developers and contractors, reacts very sensitively to fluctuations both in the market and the economy, and reduces the amount of building to minimize its financial risks. Furthermore, because of seasonal work and the danger of layoffs, the building trade unions have developed a policy of high hourly wages and strict limitations on the number of union members and apprentices. These practices, together with restrictive building codes, conservative bankers' attitudes, and soaring speculative land prices, not only keep the costs of new housing out of reach of the poor, but also limit the stock of good used housing available to poorer families.

Another reason for the failure of the filtering process is the shortage of existing low- and moderate income housing. This shortage is aggravated by the demolition of older housing stock in urban renewal areas in favor of middle income and luxury housing, or nonresidential land uses such as public buildings and highways, or new office buildings to "increase the tax base" of the central city.[12] At the same time, migration of the poor from rural areas into the cities increases the demand for low-income housing, while zoning restrictions ("snob-zoning") and racial discrimination in the suburbs prevent out-migration of lower-income people, particularly blacks, into white middle-class suburbia.

The Kerner Commission notes that,

> During the . . . 1950's, only 4 million of the 16.8 million new housing units constructed . . . were built in the central cities. These were counterbalanced by a loss of 1.5 million central city units through demolition or other means. The result was that the number of non-whites living in sub-standard housing increased from 1.4 million to 1.8 million . . .[13]

And the trend is continuing.

Filtering would work if enough old housing at low prices were available. The often-cited analogy with the used car market is erroneous. There is a big difference between the used car and the used housing market. Used cars depreciate (in exchange value) quicker than they deteriorate (in use value). The prices of second or thirdhand cars are far below those of the original

[12] Under Urban Renewal approximately 400,000 housing units have been demolished. By definition, low-income people lived in most of these units. The number of units planned or built is 200,000, or half the number demolished. But only one-tenth—20,000—are low-rent units (see *The Ill-Housed*, p. 49).

[13] Report of the National Advisory Commission on Civil Disorders, p. 467.

new cars. In used housing the situation is often the reverse. More often than not, an appreciation of exchange value has occurred, whereas the deterioration and need for repairs on the house may be high.

The total price of a house includes the market value of the structure *and* the land. In areas where land prices go up, as in most urban areas, the combined price for a house normally goes up too. In times of inflation this process increases, which makes home ownership through the filtering process hard for middle- and lower middle-income people, and impossible for low-income and poor people.

The common belief that the filtering process serves as a supply source for low-income housing is based on the assumption that the present market mechanism can provide decent housing for all. Supporting assumptions about the free-market economy in housing are:

1. Perfect knowledge and mobility among users
2. Equal opportunity of choice for buyers and sellers
3. Free entry and departure of producers and users at any time
4. The incentive of maximization of profit on the supply side

Imperfections are seen as "frictions" in the market rather than as inherent inequalities between the positions of the housing producers on the supply side and the users (especially low-income users) on the demand side. The traditional middle-class belief in equality among "a plurality of partners" and in the rules of fair play in the market is not shared by low- and lower-middle income users of housing.

As we have noted, their mobility and opportunity for choice is highly restricted through locational segregation by income and race. This segregation, and with it the perpetuation of slums, is reinforced through such practices as "red lining" by lenders and insurance companies who refuse to take risks in many black and/or low-income areas. The concept of a "free market" implies that there is a symmetry of freedoms on the supply side and the demand side. Yet what the poor do experience is that producers are far "freer" in the market than low-income users.

On the supply side, *producers* have freedom of choice as to location, entry, or departure in the production process. They also have a thorough knowledge of the market and its risks and opportunities for profit maximization, aggregated business associations, sharing of information, and political lobbying efforts.

On the demand side, *users* have very limited freedom of choice, mobility, knowledge of the market, little or no knowledge of tenants' rights, of building codes, of housing and health standards and their enforcement agencies or procedures, and very limited access to information about alternatives. Furthermore, they are highly individualized and isolated. (Militant tenant aggregations are a very recent phenomenon.)

Besides these inequalities in the market process, filtering often has functional deficiencies for the poor, due to differences in user needs between the former upper- or middle-class owners and the new low-income tenants. To mention only a few, there are often great differences in the geography of employment patterns and opportunities and need for public transportation and other services such as schools, play and recreation areas, health services, and shopping opportunities. Overcrowding, deterioration of services, and shifts in labor demand aggravate the deficiencies.

It is obvious that the market mechanism does not and cannot provide adequate and sufficient housing for low-income black and white people through the filtering process. The inadequacies are inherent in the system. Since the poor can pay the least, they are liable to get the worst housing—often substandard housing—even without the added factors of race and class discrimination.

The demolition of substandard housing as an isolated measure does not help the poor. In fact, it worsens their situation because it reduces the available number of dwelling units. As a result, overcrowding occurs in other units in still larger numbers, which increases deterioration if maintenance expenditures stay low. At the same time, rental costs in the diminished supply of older units go up. Thus, although slum areas may be shifted, they are actually perpetuated. Wherever block layout and housing stock make it possible, rehabilitation of dwelling units seems to be a better solution, especially at a time when very little or no additional units are available to low-income users.

Public Policies and Housing Programs

This raises questions of the government's social responsibilities and of public attitudes toward the poor and minority groups. What are the public policy approaches that deal with the housing problem?

Historically speaking, governments in many countries have intervened in the processes related to housing only in crisis situations, such as large-scale migrations, rapid urbanization, economic depressions, political unrest, natural disaster, or postwar periods.[14]

Depending on the values and prevailing ideologies of governments in power and on the traditional administrative cultures, the accepted responsibilities can range:

—from a few interventions in housing distribution and in financing mechanisms either to help the market or for social policy reasons;
—to the actual building of dwelling units for the especially disadvantaged or other groups;
—to more comprehensive policies, including reorganization of the housing industry through government intervention in the context of the so-called housing production and delivery system (building materials industries, labor relations, codes and standards, housing financing mechanisms, tax structure, local government activities, and macro-economic policies related to prime rates, etc.);
—to assisting the users of housing directly by aiding individual, cooperative, and community-initated efforts, and by setting up a network of services available without red tape to individual users or to community groups and, by so doing, changing the housing production system and the socioeconomic context to make it not merely responsive to the various housing needs of people but directly accountable to those who need housing. At present this last option does not exist. Yet it is the one alternative which guarantees users the greatest autonomy.

In this country the first steps toward a federal housing policy were taken during the economic crisis of the Depression. In 1934 the Federal Housing Authority (FHA) was created. Its initial

[14] For details see D. V. Donnison, *The Government of Housing* (Baltimore: Penguin Books, 1967), especially Chapter 3.

programs were low-rent public housing and federal insurance of home mortgages at market interest rates.

The intent of the programs was not so much to provide housing for the needy as to stimulate the economy, "to prime the pump," to get lenders to lend and the builders to build again. It was thought that the housing problem would take care of itself once the economy started functioning again. These government strategies did not constitute a housing policy. They were economic measures to help producers, rather than social measures to help users.

Since 1934 the range of federal programs related to housing and residential environments has increased considerably. The frequent changes of programs and the administrative complications have contributed to great confusion. Yet one can still make out two broad categories:

1. Programs of direct or indirect assistance in the production of housing units, e.g., public housing, 221(d)(3), FHA mortgage insurance
2. Programs that have to do with the development of areas or the development of communities, e.g., aid for the improvement of suburban water and sewage systems; federal funds for highways connecting the suburbs to downtown; urban renewal; Model Cities; and open space programs.

We shall concentrate on the first type of programs which contribute more or less directly to the production of dwelling units.

HUD-FHA housing programs can be ranked according to the income levels served.

1. Low-Rent Public Housing
2. Rent Supplement
3. Below-Market Interest Subsidy
4. Market Rate Mortgage Insurance

1. *Low-Rent Public Housing* (established 1937) is the oldest and the main program for channeling federal subsidies to municipalities so that they can house the poor. After almost thirty-five years the program has produced a total of approximately 700,000

units, most of which are located in inner-city areas where employment opportunities are now declining.[15] Local housing authorities have to be established to serve as the applicants for federal subsidies (loan commitments) to build public housing. The local authorities then sell income-tax-free bonds to private investors in order to finance development costs.

The rental income of public housing projects must be sufficient to meet operating expenses, overhead, and payments in lieu of taxes (10 percent of shelter rents). Individual rents are related to tenants' income. Income limits are set by the local authority.

Public housing projects are always subject to local political pressures and objections by real estate interests. Middle- and upper-income families don't want public housing projects near them for fear that both their social status and their property values will decline. In fact, many suburban communities and small towns have never set up housing authorities. In cities and larger towns, public housing projects are frequently located in the heart of ghetto areas or on sites so isolated (e.g., Columbia Point, Boston) that no influential people will bother to complain. As a result, the location of public housing has perpetuated class and race segregation.

In recent years some additional methods have been used to increase the supply of low-rent public housing and to overcome some of the political obstacles. Among the new approaches are:[16]

–"Turnkey" public housing. Private developers acquire sites and build new or rehabilitate existing structures on the understanding that local housing authorities (backed by federal commitments) will purchase the units on completion.

–"Leased housing." Local housing authorities contract for space in private buildings and subsidize the rent of low-income tenants. Landlords are protected: the tenants pay their portion of the rent (25 percent of their income) to the local housing authority, which pays the full subsidized rent to the private owner, who is required to manage the building according to housing authority standards.

[15] This figure has to be seen in the context of the estimated *annual* need of 600,000 units for low and moderate income families (Kaiser Commission).

[16] *The Ill-Housed,* p. 29.

2. *Rent Supplement* (established 1965). This program was initiated to subsidize monthly rents in subsidized or unsubsidized housing. The rent supplement program differs from "leased housing" in that the government pays the supplement directly to the renter. The amount of the supplement will be the difference between the regular rental cost of the unit and 25 percent of the renter's income. The maximum allowable subsidy under this program is 70 percent of the market rent.

As the tenant's income rises, his share of the rent rises accordingly while the "rent sup" decreases. He will not be displaced from the unit as he can be from public housing, if his income rises above an allowed maximum. Beneficiaries of this program usually have higher incomes than those eligible for public housing. The program also facilitates a certain mix of families with different incomes in the same building. This program is nearest to a "housing allowance" or a direct allocation of funds to needy families.

3. *Below-Market Interest Subsidy* (established under the Housing Act of 1961). The essence of the various interest subsidy programs (221(d)(3), nonprofit cooperative and limited dividend sponsor; 236, profit sponsor; 235, home owner; 202, elderly; 220h, 220k, rehabilitation) is that the federal government subsidizes the interest rate on the mortgage to the developer of moderate income housing. The developer submits plans and a feasibility study for a housing project to FHA and, upon approval, receives a commitment from FHA to subsidize the mortgage down to 3 or 1 percent. Under 236, for example, the developer obtains a mortgage from a commercial bank and pays the bank 1 percent interest. FHA pays the bank directly the difference between 1 percent and the market interest rate. Thus, the bank receives the going market rate of return at public expense and with no risk.

4. *Market Rate Mortgage Insurance* (established 1934). This program guarantees commercial lending institutions that the mortgages of moderate- to middle-income families will be repaid. The FHA charges the mortgagee an insurance fee of one half of one percent. In case the mortgagee cannot meet his monthly payments to the bank, the FHA takes over the mortgage. Again the bank receives the market interest at no risk. The program

permits lower than commercial market down payments and allows middle-income groups, who otherwise might not be able to receive credit from private banks, to become homeowners. This program has been responsible for much of the suburban expansion since World War II. Figures published by HUD show that this program served mainly middle-income people.[17]

All federally subsidized programs together provided in the mid-1960s 50,000 to 60,000 units a year. The number increased in 1967 to 100,000 units, in 1968 to 120,000 units, in 1969 to 165,000 units, and in 1971 for the first time the numbers of new and rehabilitated units exceeded 400,000. This is still far below the Kaiser Commission's estimated need of 600,000 units per year up to 1978. The total number of rehabilitated dwelling units in all urban renewal and enforcement areas under section 312 loans and section 115 grants was 61,568 up to November 1971.[18]

The discrepancies between the needs proclaimed by the government, the financial commitments made, and the units built reflect a general tendency of Congress to authorize programs for low-income people, but then consistently to allocate funds for very low levels of operation. The HUD Act of 1968 called for $1.5 billion for the following three years, but Congress funded only one-third of that amount.

One has to compare these figures with other funding allocations in order to see clearly the priorities set and interests represented in Congress and the administration.

The total subsidies to farmers for not growing crops is far higher than the total budget for HUD, and a large percentage of agricultural subsidies goes to farming corporations linked to industrial interests. Meanwhile the tax losses or indirect subsidies to the oil industry through oil depletion allowances amount to more than $3 billion per year—not to speak of the vast sums allocated for defense ($76 billion in 1970) and the space program which, like the farm subsidies and the oil depletion allowances, benefit large corporations and their stockholders, rather than the urban and rural poor.

[17] *HUD Newsletter,* vol. 2 no. 41 (November 8, 1971), p. 3.
[18] *Ibid.,* p. 1.

Table 4 Comparative Funding Allocations, 1962–67

$356.3	billion	national defense
32.2	"	farm subsidies
24.2	"	space program
22.2	"	federal highway construction
8.1	"	housing and urban renewal
1.25	"	federal housing subsidies

Compare: HUD's own estimate of the cost of 6 million subsidized units needed by 1978 was $2.8 billion; the Kaiser Commission's estimate was $3.4 billion.[19]

The dogma that government intervention in the market is an unhealthy sign of socialism and against the American creed is strongly supported when benefits go to the "undeserving" poor, yet there are no ideological scruples if the benefits go to big business or the "deserving" rich.

Who benefits most from present government housing policies? So far we have looked at the four major types of official housing programs. Although they are supposed to aid low- and moderate-income families, they provide a rather "indirect" assistance to housing users, since most of the funds go at first "directly" to the supply side of the market, namely the banks, the commercial developers, builders, and land speculators in the form of guaranteed profits at no risk. The housing produced this way is then made available to low-income people. The only "direct" financial aid to the users comes through the trickle of the Rent Supplement Program.

As an example of how government help to low-income people actually works, we may look at the rehabilitation of housing in Boston's South End. From June 1966 (the start of Urban Renewal in the South End) to January 31, 1970, the number of dwelling

[19] *The Ill-Housed*, p. 13.

units rehabilitated or in process was 1,365. Within the next few years, all remaining 19,130 units not planned for demolition are scheduled for rehabilitation.[20]

In October 1969 the Boston Redevelopment Authority (BRA) set operational priorities for rehabilitation in the South End (1) to low- and moderate-income owner-occupants (section 312, now section 235); (2) to nonprofit sponsors (221(d)(3), later changed to 236, which favors profit sponsors); (3) to landlords who accept leased housing; and (4) to all others. But BRA priorities have had little effect on who receives housing aid, because the financing and funding arrangements go through the FHA without coordination with the city or the BRA. The prime beneficiaries of the program have been middle- and upper-income families, "urbanites" who come from other areas back into the center city. The average income of Section 312, now 235, beneficiaries ("low and moderate-income" owner-occupants) was $16,000 per year![21]

To give an adequate picture of government housing policies, two "hidden" programs have to be mentioned in addition to the HUD-FHA programs described above. Both are administered by the Internal Revenue Service.

The first consists of the deduction from taxable income of property taxes and mortgage interest payments. This amounts to a subsidy of enormous proportions to middle- and upper-class homeowners. As Anthony Downs writes:

> All homeowners who pay federal income tax benefit from three hidden housing subsidies:
>
> 1. They can deduct their interest payments
> 2. and their property taxes from the federally taxable income.
> 3. The real benefits they get from occupying their homes are not counted as income [e.g. total monthly costs of homeowners for mortgage payments, maintenance and utilities are far lower than rents for the same size and quality of homes. Sales prices of homes after several years of use are mostly higher than original buying prices.]

[20] Nate Betnum: "An Economic Analysis of the Rehabilitation of housing in the South End of Boston." MIT graduate student paper, May 1970.

[21] *Ibid.*

It has been estimated in 1962 that these subsidies amounted to about $2 billion per year for just the 20% of U.S. households with the highest income. Since the subsidy to wealthier families *rises* as their incomes increase and tax deductions become more valuable, their total annual subsidy may well equal $4.8 billion by 1980. Thus, extending these subsidies to lower-income households would rectify to some degree the present favoritism toward wealthier people.[22]

These estimates are also corroborated by Alvin L. Schorr, Director of the Income Maintenance Project in the Department of Health, Education, and Welfare, who wrote in 1968 in his report to the Douglas Commission:

We are already investing heavily in housing as a nation, but the lion's share of the subsidy, through income tax deductions, is going to the well-off. . . . The government spent 3½ times as much on those who were not poor as for those who were. Closer examination shows that the subsidy is heaviest for the largest incomes. . . . A family in the upper fifth received about twice as much on the average as a poor family.[23]

The degree of inequality has changed, if anything, for the worse, since the rules of the subsidy game have shifted even more to the benefit of the upper-income levels since the 1969 Tax Revision Law.

To quote Downs once again:

The total subsidy cost of a gradual build-up to the target of six million subsidized units by 1980 would be about $26 billion for the entire decade. This is about 4.5 times all the federal cost of Urban Renewal in 18 years (1949–1966). In reality these subsidies to relatively low-income households would not be much larger than the housing subsidies which will be received by middle-income and upper-income households during the same period.[24]

The second "hidden program" is also administered by the IRS

[22] Downs, *op. cit.*, pp. 161–162.
[23] *The Ill-Housed*, p. 14.
[24] Downs, *op cit.*, p. 161.

with the help of the National Housing Partnership. It stimulates increased capital participation in the development of low- and moderate-income housing by large corporations and individuals in high income tax brackets through the sale of tax shelters and provisions for accelerated depreciation schedules. So far, this stimulant to the production of low- and moderate-income housing through incentives to investors has shown itself to be of far more benefit to the investors than to the ultimate users of shelter so produced.

The present system of market incentives, which gives favors to middle- and upper-income users and investors on one side and neglects the poor and racial minorities on the other, works as long as the poor and the minorities are quiescent, cooperative, and "know their place."

Only after ghetto explosions, tenant strikes, and other rebellions against the inequality of treatment did the system respond in some token way with renewed talk about the "urban crisis," palliative measures, and increased police budgets.

As long as the users of housing, especially low-income people, are kept uninformed and individualized, the supply side of the market will overwhelmingly continue to determine the rules of the game—with the help of a government that creates a climate in which risks are diminished and profits to producers are guaranteed and publicly paid for.

Summary and Conclusions

We have seen that the way the problem of housing is defined depends on the interests of the actors involved. We have seen that, in our present system, the effective definition of housing needs is made by politicians, bureaucrats, financiers, and suppliers—all of whom profit while the needs of low-income dwellers are last to be considered.

The analysis of the traditionally proposed solutions to the housing problem of low-income people through the market and filtering process, plus the existing housing programs, has pointed to some basic contradictions:

1. The concept of the market is based on the assumption of equality of partners on the demand and supply side, whereas the filtering process which is closely linked to the market presupposes inequality as its basic operating principle.
2. Public policies in housing supposedly try to mitigate the inadequacies in the market and to resolve the contradictions noted above through programs which present another set of contradictions and inequalities: funding allocations through HUD-FHA and the bureaucratic paperwork that goes with it, keep poor people dependent on agencies and professional "facilitating beneficiaries,"[25] whereas tax reductions and tax shelter allow rich investors to receive two to three times more, through tax shelters and other such benefits, than the poor who are ostensibly the beneficiaries of housing aid.

To understand the problems, to reach the roots of the contradictions, and to arrive at new directions for solutions, we have to consider several approaches.

First, we need a much better analytical and conceptual understanding of the political and economic processes, the various roles and actors in the system, and their linkages. Second, we have to deal with the problem of institutional change and change-agents. The initiative for change is not going to come from those powerful groups who benefit under the present system. But where can it come from? What alliances are needed? Third, we have to explore alternatives to the present housing process which will give users and community groups greater autonomy and self-determination.

So far most concepts and relationships are unclear. The key cost factors and their multiplying effects in terms of monthly user expenses have to be identified. How do land costs, financing costs, various construction costs, maintenance costs, and tax rates proportionally influence the monthly payments of the dweller? What role do tax shelter and depreciation play in the cost to users?

Since the mid-fifties the costs of housing have risen sharply,

[25] To obtain funds under 221(d)3 required the filing of more than 40 forms.

and today many low-income people pay from 30 percent to over 40 percent of their income on housing. A major cost increase is due to financing charges. Land costs are growing faster than building costs. The land and site cost averages for an FHA-insured house was $2,477 in 1960 and $4,982 in 1970.[26] Costs of building structure increased 31.1 percent over the same period. Cost-reducing industrialized technology has had little effect. The Kaiser Commission estimated that through technological innovations in an effective national effort (including modernizing codes and labor practices) monthly housing costs might be reduced by perhaps 10 percent.

The underlying reasons for the rising costs of new housing, as well as of existing and rehabilitated dwelling units, have to be understood.

Why is it that, as a housing survey by the Metropolitan Area Planning Council in Boston notes, a house costing $19,000 in 1960 costs $28,000 in 1970 and will cost $36,000 in 1980?

What incomes will be necessary to buy or rent at these soaring prices? Who benefits? Who is outpriced and what can be done about the problem if the cost distribution of a traditional $22,000 house is as follows: $12,000 for construction with one-third equally for raw construction, utilities, and interior finishes, and the rest of $10,000 for land, packaging, and financing?

The second problem area of institutional change has to be seen in the political context of power relations and potential new alliances. Aggregations on the demand side through local and national tenant organizations, housing and Community Development Corporations, and an increasing call for user control of the housing processes—including financing, more job opportunities, and community management of housing—are on the horizon.

Different types of technologies must be explored that allow initially lower standards, which can be upgraded in time by the users, rather than the continued production of completely finished houses which then depreciate quickly to the benefit of investors. New types of technologies are needed which will be easy

[26] *HUD Newsletter*, November 8, 1971, p. 3.

for unskilled people to handle and which will provide more job opportunities for the presently underemployed.

Finally, alliances between community groups and socially concerned professionals must be formed in order to counter alliances between industry, financing institutions, and government agencies and to increase the expertise and political power of low-income people. This could open opportunities for greater control over their individual and community lives. If such an alliance is to come about, however, there will have to be a commitment on the part of professionals to enter into a new kind of relationship with low-income people. This issue is treated at length in Chapter 8.

5

PETER GRENELL

Planning for Invisible People: Some Consequences of Bureaucratic Values and Practices[1]

RECENT EVENTS in countries as different as India and the United States suggest that some basic planning values and development practices are beginning to be seriously questioned. In India drastic rescheduling and reordering of the Fourth Five-Year Plan priorities, growing recognition of the permanence of and need for improving urban *bustees*,[2] and a gradual disenchantment with Western-style development have focused attention on some major shortcomings of current development philosophy and techniques. In the United States national priorities and governmental and corporate structures have been criticized for creating more problems than they solve in their pursuit of unlimited and uncontrolled economic growth.

[1] I am indebted to Cora Du Bois, Zemurray Professor of Anthropology at Harvard University (retired), for introducing me to the term "invisible people." Any differences or distortions of the original usage are mine. Most of the research upon which this paper is based was supported by a grant from the American Association for Indian Studies during 1965–66.

[2] *Bustee* literally means "settlement," but has become almost synonymous with "slum" for many government officials and the Westernized upper classes.

For example, both countries have severe housing problems, in spite of the United States' great wealth and India's surfeit of manpower. Leaders of both nations believe these problems can be solved through modern technology and organization if sufficient resources are available. A fundamental consequence of this optimistic view is an underestimation of the variability and complexity of human needs, and also of the great resource represented by the people themselves. On the one hand, limits on what large development-oriented institutions, public or private, can accomplish are usually explained away by referring to "shortages of funds." On the other, official lip service to "planning from below" and "equal opportunity" obscures a deep-rooted conviction that individual understanding and initiative are of little value in achieving overall development goals—goals which ordinary people have played little part in shaping.

The result of these attitudes and their underlying values is to make people seem "invisible" to those persons—chiefly members of large bureaucratic[3] organizations—whose professed task is to serve them. It is only when invisible people have made their presence felt, through political agitation or sheer force of numbers, that governments have been compelled to recognize their existence and to institute new or revised goals and programs. This is as true in India with its islands of affluence amidst a sea of poverty, as it is in the United States with its pockets of poverty in almost universal plenty. The similarity of the two governments' approaches to their respective housing dilemmas is not surprising, given India's adoption of a Western-style bureaucratic form of government administration, whose many implicit values have reinforced traditional hierarchical values.

The confrontation of individual initiative and social complexity

[3] Bureaucracy here refers to all three of the usages distinguished by Crozier: (1) government by appointed staff organized hierarchically and dependent on sovereign authority; (2) rationalization of collective activities with attendant concentration of production according to impersonal rules; and (3) the common usage evoking slowness, routine, complexity, and frustration. All have direct relevance for a discussion of organizational blindness to "client needs." See Michel Crozier, *The Bureaucratic Phenomenon* (Chicago: University of Chicago Press, 1964), p. 3.

with the standardization, paternalism, and preoccupation with technique common to large bureaucratic institutions has implications crucial to a transitional economy like that of India, and to a highly industrialized economy like that of the United States.

India is an especially instructive context to study because the elements of bureaucratic blindness are often more clearly apparent than in the United States, where the extent of the problem is masked by comparative affluence, extremely high standards, and mass consumption patterns. The case study of Indian new town planning and construction presented below attempts to clarify the nature of invisibility, its influence on actual development, and its importance as an underlying cause of much misdirected and ineffective social change.

The Phenomenon of Invisibility

Before describing the plight of invisible people in one of India's new towns, some general remarks are needed about the phenomenon of invisibility. People become invisible in the housing process to the extent that officialdom either does not see them at all or sees them only in terms of quantities of stereotyped human beings. This blindness is the result of a genuine desire to improve the living conditions of as many people as possible; a fixed idea of what constitutes "good" housing; a recognition of severe limits on public and private commercial sector resources to attain these goals; an emphasis on standardization of design and production efficiency; and a consequent discounting of the role of the dweller in the provision of housing. The latter is based on assumptions that public participation is inefficient and time consuming, that people "don't know what they want," or simply that trained technicians "know better" about laymen's needs than they do.

In an effort to achieve targets and to increase production, the nature of housing needs is assumed a priori by government policies and programs. People in general, and poor people in particular, become invisible to officialdom; their needs are reduced to the barren and abstract specifications of codes and standards, however well-intentioned. They are either prevented from exercising real control over one of the basic elements of existence, or are continually harrassed by governments bent on preventing haphazard or substandard development. To be sure, some people are more invisible than others. In India low-level government servants are more "visible" to their superiors than manual laborers or rickshaw pullers. The relationship of invisibility to hierarchical structure is a critical one; it suggests that many conventional bureaucratic approaches are inappropriate for achieving real redistribution of wealth and social change.

Planning a New Capital City: Some Background

As World War II ended and India drew close to independence, the provisional government of the Province (now State) of Orissa on India's east coast made plans to build a new capital city in order to provide a more efficient base for administering post-independence development. The site eventually chosen was a large, practically uninhabited tract of government-owned land located 20 miles southwest of the existing capital of Cuttack, a town of approximately 100,000 people on the main railway line connecting Calcutta and Madras. The new capital site was across the railway from the ancient temple town of Bhubaneswar. The new Bhubaneswar was to become India's first planned city, preceding Le Corbusier's Chandigarh by a few years.

Soon after the initial commitment had been made, the government of Orissa invited Dr. Otto Koenigsberger to prepare a plan for the new capital city. Koenigsberger, a European who had adopted Indian citizenship, was at that time working for the maharaja of Mysore. Hardly had Koenigsberger begun to prepare a preliminary sketch plan when it was announced that Prime Minister Nehru would lay the capital's foundation stone on April 13, 1948, at Bhubaneswar. So great was the pressure to provide adequate accommodation for the provincial administration that construction began in June, barely four months after Koenigsberger had agreed to do the new capital plan. Thus, although Koenigsberger saw Bhubaneswar as a grand opportunity to blend modern physical design with indigenous spatial patterns, to infuse new life and vitality into the old temple town, and to build an efficient urban community which embodied India's newly won democratic freedoms, the government of Orissa was almost totally concerned with the rapid construction of an official colony to provide sorely needed working space.

The main results of the government's narrow conception of the new capital—in part brought about by objections from the residents of Cuttack who feared economic and political decline with the shift of the capital—were that (1) Bhubaneswar grew slowly, was not expected to expand beyond a small administrative enclave, and presumably would not reach Koenigsberger's projected first-stage population of 50,000 for many years; (2) private development was not encouraged by the government, and practically no provisions were made for the new city's service population of shopkeepers, tradesmen, rickshaw pullers, and other private service people; (3) little attention was paid to Old Bhubaneswar beyond an initial cleanup and improvement of utilities, which only occurred through the prodigious efforts of the administrator of the new capital area in persuading the Orissa Government of the old town's needs; and (4) the principal features of Koenigsberger's plan were not implemented beyond the overall linear street pattern which formed neighborhood units roughly one-half-mile square (see map).

However, the Orissa Government finally made it clear that the shift to Bhubaneswar was permanent by enlarging the capital construction program in 1957, and by leasing out public land for private residential construction. Whereas five years earlier no one had wanted land in Bhubaneswar, now the demand was high. Since the government could not provide sufficient housing for all its employees and needed office space as well, many government servants took out government loans, leased plots (for 99 years), and built houses, which they then leased to office or residential tenants.

By 1965 the new capital had grown to around 45,000 persons, a little less than Koenigsberger had projected for that point in time. The city had an attractive visual aspect to the Western eye, especially where trees had grown up. Its overall physical and health standards were higher than most other Indian cities. Both authorized and unauthorized private housing construction con-

MAP OF BHUBANESWAR, ORISSA

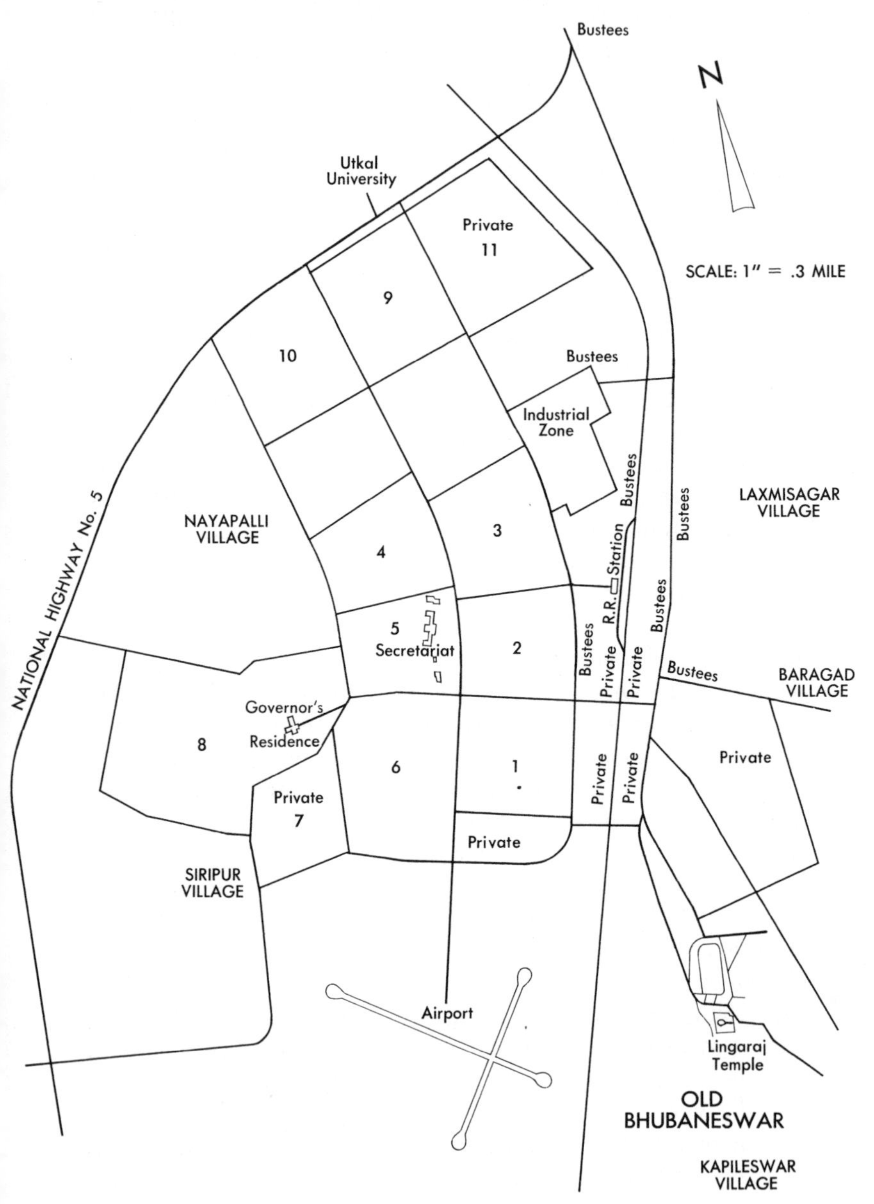

tinued at a brisk rate, yet the housing shortage created by the government's expansion remained acute. This was particularly true for the lowest levels of the governmental hierarchy and private service people, who lived mostly in shanty towns called *bustees.* These *bustees* were located on the fringes of the capital or along the railway track, and contained the worst living conditions in the city. Higher-ranking civil servants, meanwhile, got most of the scarce government units and, because of their higher salaries, had more opportunity to rent or build private living space.

Thus, fifteen years after the start of construction, Bhubaneswar had become a twin city: the railway separated the new capital, with its orderly and well-spaced rows and blocks of government quarters, from the densely settled old temple town, while the *bustees* were interspersed between and around these major settlements. Finally, five small villages, Nayapalli, Siripur, Kapileswar, Baragada, and Laxmisagar, which were adjacent to the capital site and originally surrounded by scrub jungle, were now in the path of the capital's expansion.

Land Development for the Government

Dr. Koenigsberger's original master plan called for mixed government and private development within the string of neighborhood units stretching along a main traffic artery. The linear design allowed for continuous expansion along this artery, avoiding unnecessary encroachment on the old temple town and surrounding villages. The linear design also anticipated a simple and efficient transportation system for the capital and (for capital residents) easy access to the countryside. As Bhubaneswar matured, however, it became quite different from the city Koenigsberger had envisaged.

First, developed residential densities in the new capital were much lower than planned figures. Each neighborhood unit provided for 3,000 people instead of the 5,000 people originally envisioned. Lower densities were mainly the result of the government's modest estimate of future growth potential, combined with an initially plentiful supply of government-owned land. Furthermore, the model for the new capital was New Delhi, with its broad streets of bungalows and open spaces in the British cantonment style. Since Bhubaneswar was to be Orissa's symbol of modernization and change, the cantonmentlike spaciousness was considered to be a desirable part of the sought-for higher standard of living. The fact that the dispersed settlement pattern made informal social gathering—especially for women who usually stayed close to home—very difficult; that the open spaces were impractical in a hot climate and hard to maintain; and that people had to go further to work or to market was of less concern to the government than building a clean, modern-looking administrative center.

Second, the Koenigsberger plan proposed a mixture of housing types for each unit to encourage social interaction between different social and bureaucratic strata, and to strengthen ties necessary for effective democratic local government. The State Government thought otherwise, however. It limited residency in new capital units exclusively to government servants and maintained control over the capital's administration, while a local self-government structure was neglected. These policy steps were taken to minimize contact between government officials and private persons who might attempt to illegally influence the former in their duty, and to reduce the potential for disruptive political agitation in the seat of government. The authorities did build a mix of government housing types in the units, yet, at least in the early stages, the mix showed a certain insensitivity since the most modest one- and two-bedroom quarters were placed next to six-room bungalows for senior officials. This caused mutual antagonisms and jealousies, and hardly fostered neighborhood solidarity. Planners and administrators thus failed to take into account a major aspect of change generated by the new capital: the rising importance of new physical symbols of social status. How close one's house was to the secretariat, how many rooms, windows, or water taps it had, and whether one had a flower or vegetable garden became critical indicators of one's social standing in new Bhubaneswar. The new capital thus became a physical analogue to the bureaucratic hierarchy: One's rank in the governmental hierarchy determined one's salary (and one's status), which in turn determined what type of quarter a government servant was eligible for. The bungalows of the senior officials were placed prestigiously close to the office complex and the Governor's Residence to facilitate accessibility to work, in spite of the fact that top administrators had cars. A man's place in the hierarchical structure of the government colony was clearly defined economically, locationally, and socially.

Third, a variation from the proposed development pattern involved the government's relative indifference to the capital's impact on the surrounding settlements. The villages became crowded with low-level civil servants who could not find accommodation elsewhere. No real attempt was made to deal with economic and social problems which arose in the wake of the dislocations caused by the capital construction. On the contrary, at least one invisible village which stood in the path of the new city's expansion was threatened with total relocation. Much of this disruption could have been avoided had the government kept to the linear development plan and higher densities.

Problems in Old Bhubaneswar were similarly given low priority by the administration. By the 1960s, however, younger temple town residents had begun agitating for municipal status and elections. They felt justifiably that development funds allocated for Bhubaneswar were going mostly to the new capital, and that the government was not concerned with the old town at all. The State Government wanted to forestall political activity in Bhubaneswar, and although it agreed to eventual municipal status, postponed elections indefinitely. This was not surprising, for the administration had long ago decided to forbid major industrial development in the new city in order to avoid labor troubles at the capital, just as it put the new state university campus on the far outskirts of the capital in order to limit the possibility of student demonstrations in town.

Standards and Economics of Government Housing Design

The Orissa Government had only a small budget with which to make good its commitment to provide a high standard of housing for its employees at Bhubaneswar and to create a model for future development. The generally accepted minimum housing standard, as voiced by Prime Minister Nehru in the late 1950s, called for a permanent (*pucca*) structure containing two rooms, kitchen, bath, attached latrine, and veranda per family. This was considerably "higher" in Western terms than the earthen (*kutcha*) houses typical of Indian villages and many towns, including much of Old Bhubaneswar. Economically the new standard was and still is impossible to achieve for every household in Bhubaneswar, let alone India as a whole. Nevertheless, the Orissa Government attempted to house as many of its employees in Bhubaneswar as possible, and by 1965 had actually managed to build quarters for more than half of them. This was made possible by a gradual transfer of offices from Cuttack to the new capital, by cutting costs during construction and later design revisions, and eventually by a transition from single-story bungalows and row houses to multistory blocks of flats.

While the new capital was considered to be a model of modern development, many of its inhabitants found their new surroundings left something to be desired. A few examples will highlight the confrontation between basic human needs and traditional life styles on the one hand, and modern design, economic constraints, and bureaucratic attitudes on the other.

Living Space: Bureaucratic Status vs. Family Needs

Eight types of housing units were initially designed for the new capital, ranging from one-room row quarters (Type I) to six-room, free-standing bungalows (Type VIII). Distribution of quarters was made according to a civil servant's rank and salary in the government hierarchy. Rents were scaled to match. Peons and messengers earning Rs. 100 per month or less were assigned to the smaller units while departmental secretaries and other senior officials received the largest quarters. After only a few Type I units were built, they were discontinued when a two-room minimum standard came into force. Type III units were barracks for single men, and were also discontinued after they were found unsuitable.

TYPICAL PRIVATE RESIDENCE IN OLD BHUBANESWAR
(Ground floor)

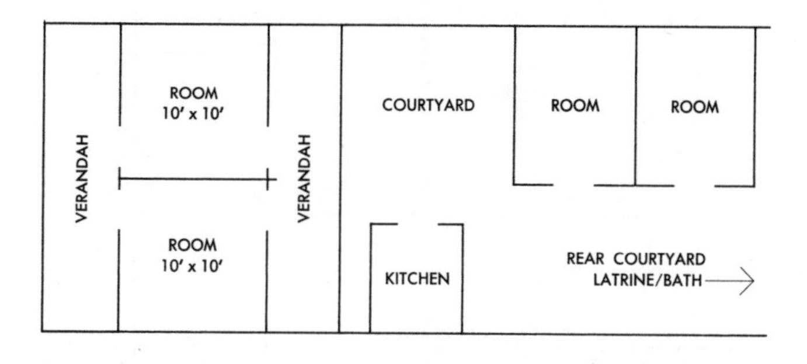

TYPE V QUARTER

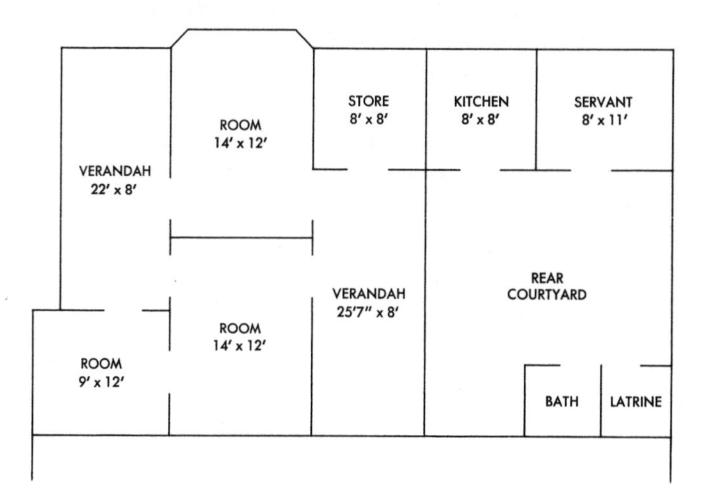

TYPE II QUARTER

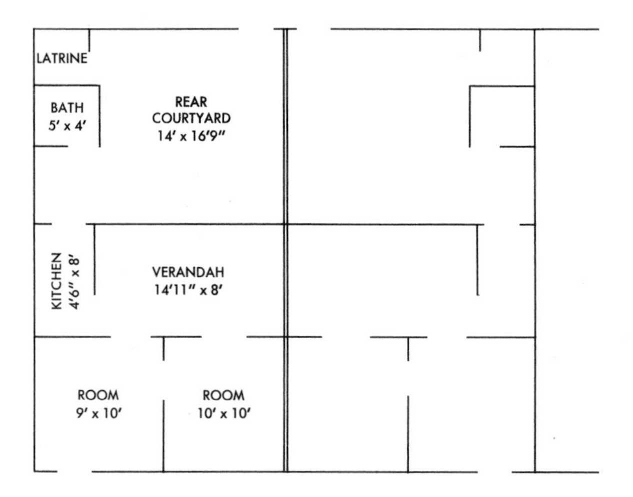

While the system of housing distribution according to government rank seemed equitable and public (everyone's salary was known from his rank, which implied a certain level of seniority and merit and hence knowledge of the quarter to which he was entitled), it created certain problems. The most critical problem was the shortage of living space for families of low-level civil servants, who, in addition to having wives and children, often had other relatives living with them. Overcrowding of two- and three-room quarters was not uncommon, and created considerable hardships on those forced to endure these conditions. Furthermore, although the government maintained that the hierarchical allocation of quarters was reasonable, in practice its inability to provide accommodations for all its employees led to frequent departures from the system. This gave rise to frustration and heightened dissatisfaction on the part of many people who considered themselves entitled to, or badly in need of, larger accommodations.

TYPE VIII(C) QUARTER

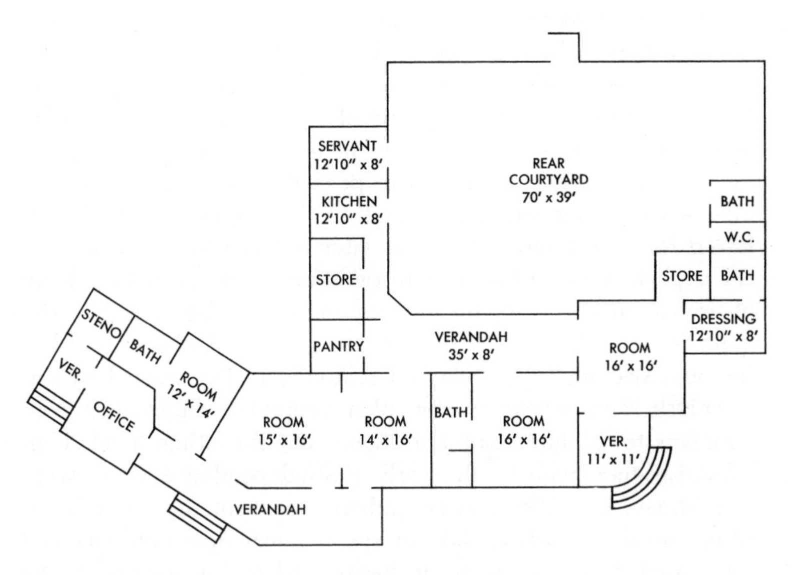

TYPE 2RA FLAT
(Upper floor)

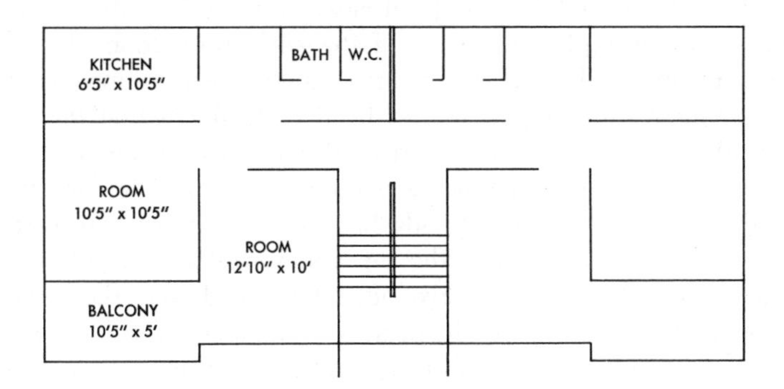

Differences in Life Styles and Spatial Needs

Both high-ranking administrators and elected representatives and ministers made a distinction between the needs of the Westernized upper echelon bureaucrats and the rest of the population. This was stated explicitly by one of the capital architects, who noted that "rear courtyard treatment to every house is essential for the Indian ways of living, except in the higher grade officers' qtrs. where a regular plot of land of about 5 acres is to be allowed for each house." This was later reduced to about an acre each. There was thus a clear recognition of the need for plenty of private outside space for cooking and eating, keeping domestic animals (especially cows), vegetable gardens, bathing, laundering, and sleeping during the hot season, a feeling shared by Dr. Koenigsberger, whose master plan proposed single-story construction to facilitate outdoor living. On the other hand, high administrators, who in the early postindependence years were Englishmen and Westernized Indians, many of the latter being from outside of Orissa, did not spend much time outdoors and often used their yards only for flower gardens (as opposed to the more utilitarian vegetable plots). Moreover, although these officials did not sleep outside during the hot months, the planners assumed that many Orissans did, as people do in other parts of India, ignorant of the fact that the high humidity of the Orissan coastal region precluded outdoor sleeping for most people.

More serious miscalculations occurred in spite of the government's obvious but limited awareness of some life style differences. For example, occupants of the early three-room Type V units complained that the front verandas were unnecessarily large (some said they were not needed at all), while the rear verandas were too small. A related complaint concerned the front and rear courtyard arrangements. These and similar grievances indicated that local family life was much more introverted and privacy-conscious than the top administrators and architects had suspected. One defensive official claimed that the people "thought they were living in palaces" compared to village housing, and so did not complain to the government, even though the new quarters were found inappropriate to traditional life styles.

This same official observed of his enterprising neighbor who kept a cow in his parlor that "my neighbor's cow enters from the front and his women enter from the back" of the quarter. The government produced a revised Type V design, but only after considerable dissatisfaction was finally registered by the residents.

In another case, some people objected to the arrangement of windows in the truncated corners of one of the early Type IV two-room designs, because this enabled neighbors in adjacent quarters of the same row to look inside. The arrangement also made it easy for young men to have visual tete-à-tetes with the daughters of these conservative households. Subsequent Type IVs were altered after the designers realized how unpopular the original layout had been. Some extremely useful semiprivate spaces were accidentally created for the capital's row housing. Initial conceptions had eliminated the service lanes between back-to-back rows of quarters, which traditionally provided sweepers with access to house latrines for manual cleaning. Lanes were included in the final plans because it was not known when funds for modern sewerage would be available. (Note that sewerage was provided in all government quarters, however.) These lanes quickly became routes for door-to-door tradesmen, play areas for small children where they were safe from traffic on front streets, and informal sheltered social spaces for the womenfolk to gather in, away from the eyes of passers-by.

Bachelors and other low-level civil servants who had left their families in their villages did not fare even as well as families in the search for adequate housing. The Type III barracks built for these men were far from comfortable, afforded little individual privacy, and were immediately unpopular. Single men either moved in with relatives or friends, or eventually grouped together to rent privately built houses. The barracks were soon converted to offices and, although they were also unsatisfactory for this purpose, continued to be used as offices because of the critical shortage of working space.

Residential designs were modified several times, to some extent as a result of occupants' criticisms. Besides the problems already mentioned, residents complained of insufficient storage space, poor ventilation, leakage during the monsoon, lack of electric fans, and no accommodation for cows. The main reason for design revision, however, was financial. While the new capital project was always short of funds, construction costs rose steadily, leading to reductions in plinth areas, ceiling heights, wall thicknesses, and other alterations for the sake of economy. Thus, as the years went by, the older quarters, in spite of their shortcomings, became sought after by new capital residents for their more generous floor space and higher-quality construction.

The Shift to Flats

By 1960 it was clear that the earlier policy favoring dispersed single-story development needed revision, for the housing shortage continued, the supply of land dwindled, and land prices soared. The decision was made to switch to multistoried construction, and blocks of three- and four-story flats corresponding to the older type designs by number of rooms began to appear in the new outlying sectors of the capital.

The flats were predictably unpopular, not only because of smaller floor areas and lack of outside space (hardly compensated for by tiny balconies). Conservative families were distressed by the lack of privacy, which was even more pronounced due to common entries and higher densities. Less space was available for storage of fuel and other household necessities, and none for cows. The common entries, being public space, were cared for by no one and became cluttered and dirty. Older people found the stairs difficult to surmount. Ventilation was also more of a problem because of interior design as well as site planning, both of which often did not make good use of Bhubaneswar's prevailing breezes.

Economic imperatives precluded major modifications of the designs of the flats. Alternatives to flats involving government single-story development were considered uneconomic by the government. Furthermore, the planners had begun to consider flat tenancy an inevitable part of urban living; people would simply have to get used to it, one architect declared—and he felt that they would, as they had in Bombay and Calcutta.

Encouraging Private Development

Almost five years before the construction of flats began in earnest, however, the Orissa Government decided it had to lease out portions of the capital for private residential development. The Chief Minister, who had been the major influence in getting the Bhubaneswar project started during his earlier term in office, returned in 1957 to the task of completing the new capital. Commencement of private construction thus coincided with a spurt of government building, both in response to an increased need for office and residential accommodations.

Although token private development had occurred before 1957, the official policy of keeping the capital as an administrative settlement had acted as a damper until the need for space became acute. The government then established several private cooperative building societies through which different branches and levels of the administrative service could acquire plots and build houses. Quotas of plots with 99-year leases were allotted to the societies, which in turn distributed them to their members. The latter then took out building loans through their cooperatives, hired contractors, and erected their houses. Cooperative society members were mainly but not entirely middle-level government servants—people who would have been eligible for Type IV, V, and VI government quarters. Their houses were usually rather modest because the size of their loans was based on their equally modest salaries. Senior officials also had a cooperative, and many built costly houses which they rented back to the government for offices.

The spatial distribution of income levels in private units strongly followed the pattern established in the older government-built units. The biggest houses on the largest plots tended to be closest to the main office complex; the smaller, less costly houses at higher densities were located farther away. However, residential densities in private areas were in all instances much higher than in the official units. This allowed more people to build, in spite of the fact that they built single-family units, and also gave the government more income on lease premiums and rents. It also maintained the clear spatial differentiation of income and social classes laid down by the government's own construction.

The government made much less effort to control the visual character of the new private development, except in the prestige area near the airport. The resulting concentration of structures and variation of heights and façades contrasted sharply with the more uniform government neighborhoods. Officials expressed dissatisfaction with this "inharmonious" visual image, but wrote it off to economic necessity.

Squatters and Slum Clearance

When pressed sufficiently hard to find a solution to its staff housing problem, the Orissa Government created opportunities for middle- and upper-echelon officials to provide their own accommodations. The administration made little effort, however, to supply dwelling space for the service population of the new capital, consisting of rickshaw pullers, mechanics, barbers, tailors, launderers, food sellers, milkmen, manual laborers, and other traders and small businessmen. More than any other group, these were the most invisible people. Bhubaneswar was consequently subject to uncontrolled *kutcha* construction along the railway line, in Old Bhubaneswar, and on the outskirts of the new capital.

The squatters were generally tolerated by the capital administrators and the State Government, who were well aware of the services they performed. But since government policy called for removal and prevention of temporary and haphazard development, the squatters were eventually faced with eviction. Slum clearance began in the new capital during 1957–58, when construction started on the first private cooperative residential area opposite Neighborhood Unit I. The shacks in this area belonged mostly to rickshaw pullers, who provided the only form of public transport in the capital until regular bus service was at last inaugurated.

Having no legal claim to their plots, the rickshaw pullers were forced to move to some vacant land opposite Unit 2, from which they were evicted again when a cooperative society began clearing land for construction a year or so later. Moving up the railway line to a spot opposite Unit 3, the rickshaw pullers obtained leases from the State Government and established their own colony of huts. Around 1964 the government tried to move them a third time, so that their land could be developed for more lucrative purposes. By this time, however, the rickshaw pullers had acquired some political influence and were able to forestall eviction. Eventually the government built some very modest quarters for the rickshaw pullers next to their shacks. The rickshaw pullers quickly sublet these new quarters for extra income and stayed in their shacks, indicating clearly what their priorities were.

A similar official attempt was made in 1963 to evict many of the small traders and marginal businessmen. A number of *kutcha* shop-cum-residences were removed on orders of the Chief Minister as part of the government's big clean-up campaign prior to the 1964 All-India Congress Convention in Bhubaneswar. The merchants had organized into an association, however, and demanded payment or compensation. The government ultimately arranged to allot new plots, and loans were granted to finance construction of new structures after much negotiation. This group was clearly more visible than the rickshaw pullers by virtue of their greater monetary resources and political connections.

In addition to these major slum-clearance attempts, the state-appointed Notified Area Council, which administered the capital zone, maintained a continuous program of demolition of unauthorized constructions scattered around Bhubaneswar. Demolition occurred after two warnings were issued to the violator. Although there was considerable discretion exercised in the carrying out of this policy, many individuals, including old Bhubaneswar residents who had made extensions to their houses, were harassed by the NAC in its effort to keep the capital area free of uncontrolled *kutcha* development in spite of the housing shortage.

Invisible People in Bhubaneswar

The capital construction transformed Bhubaneswar from a small settlement, whose livelihood, social organization, and ritual focus were dominated by a major temple and the needs of its service, to a company town, whose principal activity was administration and whose patron was the government. After initial working space was provided, the new capital project became a low-priority item for the government, because its attention was turned to more pressing matters of economic development elsewhere in the state. The impact of the capital on the old temple town, provision for the new city's service population, and construction of housing for its civil servants, especially for those in low-level and low-paying posts, were issues of minor importance to the administration, except in occasional periods of crisis, e.g., the first stage of construction from 1948 to 1951; the commencement of large-scale private development in 1957; the switch to flats around 1960; and the major slum clearance efforts in 1957–58, 1960, and 1962–64.

The government was committed to build accommodations for as many of its employees as it could; and its wish to keep the new capital clear of sizable nongovernmental development for political, economic, and social reasons reinforced the original official view that the capital should be a model of modern development. These factors, coupled with a chronic shortage of funds, led to a consistent neglect of the needs of Old Bhubaneswar, the service population, the surrounding villages, and the lowest-level civil servants. At best, minor improvements in utilities were provided for the old town, monetary compensation paid to villagers for land taken for capital expansion, and some quarters or plots were provided for the other groups. At worst, private individuals were prohibited from building except according to the government's high and Westernized standards, unless they squatted without authorization and at the risk of official harassment; surrounding village lands were taken without thought of integrating these settlements into the master plan; and low-level civil servants fortunate enough to be allotted a government quarter tolerated cramped and often alien living conditions.

The most critical problems, however, were encountered by the most invisible people of all, the service population. The new capital was not built for them; they were an embarrassment, albeit a necessary one, to the main settlement, and their *bustees* were considered temporary, thus making them subject to removal at any time. Although the government tolerated their presence, no land was set aside for them for many years, in spite of the fact that Dr. Koenigsberger's master plan had strongly recommended mixed public and private development.

The emerging physical pattern of development at Bhubaneswar thus reflected the prevailing traditional and Western values of the senior administrative and elected officials. Most obvious were a distinct spatial separation of government and private sectors, and spatial differentiation of income groups and levels of government service according to the official hierarchy, with the top bureaucratic levels in the choicest locations closest to the office complex, the Governor's residence, and the airport. There was also a rather rough physical separation of castes according to the hierarchy. This was inadvertently linked to the government's policy of quarter allocation by salary and service level, as the top official echelons were composed mainly of the high caste people who traditionally had most direct access to education and employment. This system also led to rigid allocation of the largest quarters to the highest official levels, and a tendency in housing design toward Western concepts of space utilization in spite of a vague awareness of indigenous life styles and space needs.

A principal consequence of the government's approach was the constraint placed on the number, location, and type of construction possible by private individuals. The government saw no virtue in the erection of temporary housing for or by people who were either transients in the new capital or who might eventually became permanent residents, even though such people could not afford anything else at the outset, and in spite of their obvious value to the city in providing essential functions and services. As a result, Bhubaneswar was relatively free of the very dense, visually disorderly *bustees* which are a common feature of most Indian cities. But it suffered severely from a lack of commercial and recreational facilities, and a monotonous lack of vitality characteristic of other Indian new towns built on the single-industry principle. More serious, however, was the fact that such *bustee* dwellers as there were in Bhubaneswar tolerated substandard conditions even in Indian terms, such as grossly inadequate supplies of fresh water. These conditions could have been avoided with a relatively small measure of government planning and provision for land and utilities, as was done for the cooperative societies. Unfortunately, this step was never seriously considered by the government for the service population.

If private development at Bhubaneswar had been unrestricted from the beginning of the capital project, the settlement pattern typical of new growth around other unplanned Indian cities probably would have evolved. Considerably more *bustee* development would have occurred, and much of this would have been gradually transformed through various stages, from *kutcha* lean-tos and shacks to one or more stories of *pucca* construction, as individual resources permitted. Other bustees would have remained *kutcha* according to the longevity and needs of their inhabitants. More private *pucca* buildings would have been erected as well, in response to the need for more middle-income housing. Indications of all these trends were evident in private areas on the Old Bhubaneswar side of the railway, on the outskirts of the new capital, and within the capital itself during periods of official tolerance of temporary settlements. Had the government instituted a program of providing sites and utilities to all kinds of private persons from the outset—and not just government servants through cooperatives—the worst excesses of totally unassisted growth could have been avoided while enabling the provision of sufficient essential services to the community.

Bhubaneswar and Other Indian New Towns

In these respects, Bhubaneswar was no different from other Indian new towns; fear of re-creating the worst physical features of Calcutta and Bombay, the regulatory and control-oriented influences of postwar British and American planning education to which Indian planners were exposed, and the bureaucratic practice of allocating funds through several independent channels, each for specific and narrow purposes, all contributed to the planning and growth of new towns as single-purpose settlements in government capitals like Bhubaneswar and Chandigarh, or in industrial centers like Durgapur and Rourkela.

These new towns were conceived and developed as small communities—only Chandigarh had a projected population of over 100,000—whose population would be composed mainly of employees of a single major employer, be it government or a steel plant. Rather than focus scarce public resources and energies only on the few key public locational and investment decisions, which would influence the course of all further development, inordinate attention was given to preparing master land-use plans, zoning ordinances, and slum clearance. For example, master plans were drawn up showing circumferential roads around the planned towns with areas within the roads delineated in some detail; land beyond the roads was often simply marked "Future Development." No recognition was given in the plans to the fact that development would take place on both sides of the circumferential roads. "Outside" development clearly was considered to be beyond the scope of the current plans, and, in any case, temporary, and to be removed subsequently. Such was the official attitude in Bhubaneswar in more than one instance toward the peripheral villages around the capital.

Furthermore, the prevailing government approach in allocating funds to a multiplicity of different programs tended to obscure the character of the problems supposedly being addressed. In housing, for example, Orissa (like the government of India) had programs for different levels of government servants, middle-income private housing, low-income housing, industrial-workers housing, slum-clearance (relocation) housing, and so on. In addition, various public sector corporations like steel plants or port authorities built their own housing without reference to other governmental priorities and programs. This structure, which has its counterparts in the United States and other countries, resulted in programing overlaps and gaps, and decreased the efficiency sought by officials who looked askance at public participation in development because of its presumed inefficiency.

In Bhubaneswar, as in other Indian new towns in later years, official programs could not keep up with housing demands; the government eventually recognized the necessity for relaxing restrictions on private construction and provided leased plots and loans for the purpose—but only for its own employees, and according to its own regulations and standards. The government apparently had not recognized the legitimacy of the variety of needs represented by the heterogenous population of the new town; nor had it accepted the impossibility of providing housing to its accepted standard for all these people. Finally, it had not accepted the usefulness of transferring the dwellers' role in housing from the village to the city. In the former context, people built their own houses, individually and together. In the latter, the government considered that people either did not know what they wanted or did not care. In this assumed situation, as one senior official phrased it, "guided democracy" was required until people were educated enough to determine and articulate their needs to government. This, too, has its United States counterparts in the Model Cities program, many so-called home ownership training programs for low-income families who are considered ignorant of modern housekeeping methods, and the standards and certain administrative practices of agencies like FHA and Farmers Home Administration with respect to low-income housing.

Dr. Koenigsberger made other assumptions which were, in retrospect, also somewhat unrealistic. His expectations that creating heterogeneous neighborhoods would lead to cooperative community action; that the government would seriously consider establishing elective local self-government in the new capital; and that no preparations need be made for the nongovernmental population beyond the mixed neighborhoods were all doomed to disappointment because of the conflicting official policy. Had the latter not been so, it is likely that the usual course of urban growth would have resulted in the same outcome.

Some Generalizations

While cross-cultural analogies must always be tentative, the case of Bhubaneswar does seem to have a telling significance for the United States and other industrialized nations. It is not possible, nor is it necessary, for any government to know all the needs of its constituents sufficiently to bear the burden of serving those needs according to a single set of standards and goals. As Harold Orlans concluded about the planning of the English new town of Stevenage, "there are no universally acceptable architectural or sociological principles for engineering the happiness and success of a neighbourhood or community, but only different principles catering to the needs of different social groups and planners."[4] Those groups whose needs are ignored or are assumed by other groups (including planners) become invisible, except insofar as their efforts to maintain themselves are designated as "haphazard" or "uncontrolled."

Low-income families in urban slums, migrant farm workers and other low-income rural families, blacks and other ethnic minorities in any location, and American Indians are all invisible to government planners and administrators in the United States. The major difference between the latter context and India is that our invisible people are tucked away in pockets of poverty instead of in shacks encroaching on major thoroughfares by the thousands. The fact that there are degrees of invisibility—that, for example, migrant workers are more invisible than urban ghetto dwellers—is of less concern (except to the migrant workers) than the fact that existing bureaucratic institutions inherently discriminate against those who do not have access to the upper levels of the hierarchy.

In Bhubaneswar, the businessmen managed to gain a fairly satisfactory settlement by virtue of their position as contributors to political campaigns; the rickshaw pullers got harassed until they, too, acquired some influence. In one Florida county in the United States, some migrant workers were able to obtain Farmers Home Administration loans to finance their self-help home construction until the local VISTA volunteer departed; now the FmHA insists that the families have contractor-built homes, even though they cannot afford them. And in California, other self-helpers were not permitted to install sliding doors in their homes, even at their own

[4] Harold Orlans, *Utopia, Ltd.* (New Haven, Conn.: Yale University Press, 1953), p. 101.

extra cost, because the local authorities considered that sliding doors were not appropriate fixtures in low-income housing.

Should it appear that a straw man is being erected, the following anecdote will indicate that certain underlying values of bureaucratic institutions are quite widespread. A dedicated Indian construction official of the U.S. Bureau of Indian Affairs could not accept the idea of building adequate, though spartan, housing for his people in the absence of funds for up-to-standard accommodations, even though to build nothing would mean that many Indians would remain in tents and hovels through cold winters. The concept of building substandard housing was too abhorrent. This view was prevalent among government officials in Bhubaneswar and elsewhere in India. Only necessity has forced a reconsideration of the validity of high physical standards as operational indicators rather than as long-range targets.

In Calcutta, for example, the West Bengal Government developed plans for an extensive *bustee* improvement scheme after deciding that it was impossible to clear all the *bustees* and provide enough new housing for their inhabitants. And in the new steel city of Durgapur (also in West Bengal), planning was initiated on a new housing policy, which would provide for a variety of housing needs for single men and families, permanent residents and transients, owners and renters, rich and poor, and those desiring accommodation and those desiring to build their own residences. The latter occurred some time after it was noticed that many men earning sizable amounts in the steel mills were content with minimal communal shelter or with shacks of their own construction, because they either sent most of their earnings back to their villages or were saving to build permanent accommodation later on.

This lesson—that operational standards cannot grossly overreach the ability to attain them—is yet to be learned in the United States, where over half of the entire population currently cannot afford the new single-family suburban homes now being produced. The fallacy of the "purified" government city envisioned by the Orissa Government has its rough analogue at a much larger scale in some suburban United States communities. Both seek a level of physical and social homogeneity which in itself is acceptable, except that it becomes the standard by which all other development is judged. It is not surprising that postwar United States and English planning concepts of high standard construction, master planning, zoning, and slum clearance found ready acceptance in India, with its age-old caste hierarchies and rural orientation. It is also not surprising that these concepts failed in practice because they oversimplified people's needs and did not account for the dynamics of Indian urban growth.

Even more important, however, is the fact that housing and urban development are being attempted mainly through bureaucratic institutions, which find it expedient to function through hierarchical structures according to set procedures. These structures and procedures are inevitably biased toward those operating them; and the larger they get, the more difficult it is to deal with them. The proliferation of nonprofit housing sponsors in the United States attests to the strongly felt need for a middleman between the government and building industry, and the growing number of disenfranchised invisible people.

The latter are disenfranchised to the extent that their freedom to build—their ability to determine and satisfy their own needs—is increasingly limited by legal, administrative, and economic restrictions devised and implemented by institutions which have a vested interest in maintaining those constraints. Yet at the same time, these very institutions exhort the poor to accept institutionalized housing products on the ground that they are entitled to them, even though, in a variety of ways, they cannot afford them.

This gap between dweller needs and resources on one hand and institutional standards and values on the other is the root of the problem faced by invisible people. And development policies which widen this gap instead of seeking to close it threaten everyone's freedom to build.

6

JOHN F.C. TURNER

The Reeducation of a Professional

FOR SOME MINOR MISDEMEANOR at the English public school I attended, a prefect made me read and precis a chapter of Lewis Mumford's *The Culture of Cities.* Mumford quoted his own teacher, Patrick Geddes, whose name stuck in my mind. Later, Geddes' work caused me to doubt the value of my professional schooling and, when I eventually escaped into the real world, his work also guided my deschooling and reeducation. Through his writings and notes, Geddes taught me to think in terms of the relationships between man and his environment—a habit of mind that is essentially incompatible with professional compartmentalization. He was a student under Sir Thomas Huxley, and though he continued his botanical studies after an illness which affected his eyesight and ended his work with microscopes, Geddes turned more and more to the study of cities.

Geddes' background and training in the natural sciences led him to a systematic interpretation of man and his environment, which I have used and tried to develop ever since I accidentally recovered some of his manuscript notes in a garden studio. These notes, mainly describing his "thinking machines" to his friend

Henry Wilson, a former neighbor of my own family, fascinated me. They were evidently an attempt to establish the linkages between the sciences, a problem which I was especially preoccupied with as a young student of architecture in the optimistic years immediately after the end of the Second World War.

With Bruce Martin's help, Paffard Keating Clay and I unravelled Geddes' methodology, which, I later realized, anticipated modern general systems theory by over half a century.[1]

These interests, which seriously interfered with my studies at the Architectural Association School in London, supply the background for the following account of my subsequent experiences in Peru, which were both the direct and indirect consequences of Geddes' theoretical work and of his practice in India.

I was invited to work in Peru by Eduardo Neira, a Peruvian architect who had studied urban and regional planning at the University of Liverpool,[2] and for whom Geddes was (and is) a prophet —one especially relevant to the contemporary Third World because of his profound understanding of the relationships between contexts, cultures, and urban form.

Geddes seemed much more relevant that Le Corbusier and the Congrès Internationaux d'Architecture Moderne (CIAM), the organization established to propagate the causes of modern architecture; but it was only after living and working in Peru that I began to articulate the dissatisfaction shared with so many contemporaries. We felt and knew that architecture cannot be practiced as if it were an independent variable—as though the architect had

[1] See Appendix 1 part 2, The Geddes diagrams: their contribution toward a synthetic form of thought by the author with W. P. Keating Clay in Patrick Geddes, *Cities in Evolution,* second edition edited by Jaqueline Tyrwhitt, Williams and Norgate, London, 1949.

[2] Geographer John P. Cole, social anthropologist José Matos Mar and architect-planner Eduardo Neira were all members of a small group of professionals who first drew attention to the real and potentially positive nature of the *barriadas* or urban squatter settlements of Peru. By 1955 Neira had set up a pilot technical assistance service to the squatters of Arequipa (the second city of Peru) in his capacity as an official of the Ministry of Public Works. My first job in Peru was obtained through Neira and was with the Oficina de Asistencia Técnica a las Urbanizaciones Populares de Arequipa (OATA).

no social or political responsibilities—yet neither could we accept the Marxist antithesis. It seemed as absurd to believe that social structure could be changed through architecture as it was to believe that architecture should be entirely subjected to the official interpretation of popular taste. Geddes' own work, in Scotland, in India, and elsewhere, led another way, even though we could not see the goal.

Geddes' method, clearly enough, was to involve himself as closely as he could with all the people concerned, especially with those who were suffering most from the consequences of urban dysfunctions and blight. The possibilities for a young and inexperienced professional to get as involved in such a thoroughly institutionalized country as the United Kingdom seemed remote.

Therefore, when Eduardo Neira offered me the chance of working in Peru, some years after our first meeting in Venice, I jumped at it. I felt that if I could get out from among the underbrush of technological innovations and intellectual formulations and into the much simpler situation described by Neira, I might be able to see my way. And this is what did happen. For me, as for many anthropologists who have had analogous motives for undertaking the study of primitive tribes, the connotations of words describing simpler and often harsher situations and conditions of life have changed. "Primitive," "backward," "underdeveloped," and the more recent euphemism "developing" do not change the essence of life or the nature of people, as the views we were brought up with imply. It is just that it is easier to see and understand ourselves when we are not surrounded and burdened by so many things.

Although houses and construction technologies are immensely different from place to place and time to time, the basic activity of housing is not. In the next chapter I present an interpretation of the structure of this basic activity as a universal invariable or constant. It is a necessarily abstract argument, however, and it is easier to follow if introduced with illustrations of the situations which gave rise to it and which the theory attempts to interpret.

Three episodes from my life in Peru are described here: the disastrous school project of Tiabaya; the absurd but, within its own terms, largely successful aided self-help housing project in the squatter settlements of Arequipa; and a project that came close to applying the lessons learned from those first two experiences: the supervised housing credit experiment carried out in a squatter settlement extension of Lima called Huascarán.

In 1957 Tiabaya was a very beautiful village of small farmers and commuting factory workers set among intensively cultivated terraced fields—the *campiña* of Arequipa, an oasis surrounding the small Spanish colonial city just below the western *cordillera* of the Southern Andes some 700 miles south of Lima and Callao.

The council of the district of Tiabaya had received an authorization from the Ministry of Education in Lima for a new school building, together with a plan and some funds. A representative of the council then brought a formal petition for technical assistance to the Office of Technical Assistance to the Popular Urbanizations of Arequipa (OATA), where a young Peruvian architect, Luis Felipe Calle, and I were then employed. We had found little demand for OATA's services in the *urbanizaciones populares*, the appropriately named squatter settlements surrounding the city. We were therefore glad to respond to the council's request, and offered to do more than we were asked.

Luis Felipe and I were both appalled by the wretched sketch sent by the Ministry (which, in fairness, soon afterward greatly improved its architectural services).[3] We persuaded the council that they could get far more for their money if we redesigned the school.

I was responsible for the design. It was economically and technically rational and I think it would have been aesthetically approved by both conservative and modern schools of design. Very

[3] When historian and educator Jorge Basadre became Minister of Education in 1958 he assigned architect Carlos de Martis Bazo the task of reorganizing the design and construction of rural schools. One major achievement was their highly successful self-help school construction program designed and carried out by architect Patrick W. Crooke in the year 1960 (during which over 20 village schools were built, by the villagers, in widely scattered locations in the southern Andes between Cuzco and Arequipa—and at less than half the usual cost). This program is described in "Communal Building and the Architect," *The Architect's Yearbook*, No. 10 (London: Paul Elek, 1962).

properly concerned that the village should get the most for its money and that the school should provide the best possible environment for teaching and learning, I discarded the expensive and uncomfortable brick and concrete construction, along with the very poor plan, specified by the Ministry. In its place, I substituted an improved version employing local materials and construction techniques; thick and therefore thermal walls of stabilized earth with narrow windows and wide reveals to soften and diffuse the extremely strong daylight; a light trussed and acoustic roof of bamboo, treated against termites, which could economically span much wider, squarer, and consequently more flexible classrooms. Most of these materials and all of the labor could be provided at little cost by the village itself, which meant that the whole school could be built with the budget allocation intended to cover the costs of the first stage of the construction.

No village council could withstand this onslaught of economic and design logic; our plans were in the course of time accepted and authorized. But our own enthusiasm was not audibly echoed or even noticeably shared by the council members; we were subjected to an intensive cross-examination on all points, especially over the proposed soil cement walls, for which we promised a demonstration prior to its employment.

We recommended as general foreman the builder of one of the most beautiful homes I have ever seen, which was built of traditional local materials and construction.[4] Jorge Vizcarra, whom I already knew through Eduardo Neira, was duly instructed and proceeded to carry out the soil cement block tests. They were not satisfactory: the volcanic soil had chemical peculiarities that interfered with curing and hardening. We agreed that brick should be substituted and that one classroom less be built at this stage, but, otherwise, no major changes were to be made in the design or construction.

On an unsolicited inspection shortly after work began, I found that foundation trenches had been excavated according to the

[4] See "Village Artisan's Self-Built House," an illustrated article by the author in *Architectural Design*, London, Volume XXXIII, No. 8, August 1963, pp. 361–62.

layout I had prepared, but with a disconcerting change. Footings for the conventional modern concrete columns were being prepared. The embarrassed Vizcarra admitted that he had been ordered by the council to build an orthodox modern structure with concrete columns, brick panels, and a reinforced concrete slab roof. The plans had not been modified accordingly, however, so that the village, in all innocence, was committing itself to an enormously expensive structure. As the villagers had set about building the school, I made a quick calculation of the reinforced concrete beams needed to span the classroom width, made economically possible by the light roof I specified. This calculation showed that it would be impossible to finish even *one* classroom.

Some days after our chagrin at this discovery there was a disastrous earthquake which demolished the unfortunate village, literally burying our plans in the rubble, and with them a classic misunderstanding between professionals and their clients.

Before discussing the meaning and implications of this episode, I will describe a second.

The same earthquake of January 15, 1958, which destroyed or badly damaged about 10,000 homes in the Department of Arequipa, precipitated new funds for housing. OATA's budget had been just enough for our exiguous salaries and the office overhead. Except for surveying the settlements and drawing up our own improvement plans, which, at best, evoked a mild and polite interest overlaying the suspicions and distrust of the local leadership, there was little we could do. Without funds our technical assistance services were not in demand, and we had not learned how to stimulate that demand. Shortly after the earthquake, however, the situation changed.

In comparison with the damage, the earthquake relief funds allocated for housing were pitifully small. This obvious fact encouraged the young mayor of the city to accept OATA's suggestion of using the aided self-help method (as developed in Puerto Rico) in order to stretch the funds. We claimed that commercial contract unit costs could be reduced by 30 to 50 percent. We promised to build as many as 150 houses for the contract price of 100. In fact 140 were built for the contractor-built cost of 100. In a strict account, including the *real* if unpaid administrative overhead, the theoretical difference would have been greatly reduced —a point I return to below.

Aided and mutual self-help housing methods have been and are being successfully used in the U.S. and elsewhere. It is not my intention to criticize the practice in this paper, and I refer the interested reader to Chapter 2. However, it is an inevitably complex administrative procedure, and, in this particular case, its use was unnecessary and paternalistic.

With the exception of an initial blunder (mentioned below), which was soon corrected, the OATA team faithfully followed the Puerto Rico aided and self-help housing manual. The manual demanded that groups of would-be participants be organized. In our case these were families who had previously rented inner-city tenements which had collapsed in the earthquake, and who also owned, or rather laid claim to, lots in the squatter settlements in the district of Miraflores. This is an area on the north side of the city in which there were, at that time, seven settlements, each with its own representative organization.

In collaboration with the local Patriotic Association of Fathers of Families Pro-Home Ownership, Alto de Selva Alegre, and others similarly named, we organized seven groups, one in each settlement, with an average membership of twenty families. All families had to have at least one able-bodied member willing to work one full day a week until all the houses of the group were finished. The houses were to be structurally identical, but many individual variations were possible, thanks to the well-thought-out design system developed by Federico Mevius, an architect who stayed with the project until it was completed some two years later. The participants were to be charged only the cost of the materials, and the repayments were scheduled so as to maintain a rotating fund.

In this particular case, administration was further complicated by the geographic dispersal of the individual lots, the variety of lot shapes, sizes, and slopes, and the fact that the properties were already owned, or rather effectively possessed. Conventionally aided and mutual self-help builders usually work on one block of identical lots which, even if assigned to individual participants before the houses are built, are not usually their inalienable property, at least not until the project is finished. In the Arequipa project, however, there was no way of recovering material and human contributions made to a subsequently delinquent participant. If one dropped out after his own home had been built, that was everybody else's loss.

In addition to the lack of control over participation and the logistical problems of delivering materials and getting the participants to work on many sites scattered over a 4-to-5-square-mile area, an unusually large number of interest groups were involved. OATA itself had become, by that time, the local branch of a special division of the Ministry of Public Health and Welfare, the Fondo Nacional de Salud y Bienestar Social (FNSBS), which paid overheads and salaries of the permanent staff. The foreman and assistants' salaries, contracted specialist labor, materials, and the maintenance of one of the two half-ton pick-up trucks were all paid for out of the Earthquake Relief Fund administered by the City Council. Then, of course, there were the seven local associations with defacto jurisdiction over the settlements we were working in. These did not always identify with the seven participant group committees, and some open clashes occurred. The participant groups themselves had many internal problems—though less than a pessimist would have anticipated—as a result of the many intense and, as it turned out, unnecessary sacrifices required by the system.

In addition to these sixteen organized interest groups—seventeen if the local OATA and central FNSBS offices are counted separately (they did have quite different sets of motives)—a further political complication cropped up. While the project was getting underway, a new semiautonomous regional organization came into existence in order to centralize all reconstruction and development efforts in the region. This contributed to internal political changes in the FNSBS and the loss of the support we had had from the original directors. Fortunately for our project, the City Council greatly resented the regional agency and resisted its efforts both to cancel the self-help project and to disband the OATA. Having unwisely attempted to obtain President Prado's intervention, through the good offices of Ernest Weissmann (Director of the United Nations Center for Housing, Building, and Planning), I was among those dismissed.

It is rather embarrassing for me to contemplate the committee and group meeting man-hours dedicated to the project. To begin with, there were weekly evening meetings with each of the seven participant groups which went on for several months. These didn't leave much time for the OATA staff's family and social life. Then there were many meetings with the Mayor's special committee, created to supervise the disbursement of the earthquake relief funds for the project. Meetings with this committee became rather frequent as the likelihood of OATA's demise and the problem of staff funding increased. Considerable investments of administrative time were also made at the national level.

Many of these meetings were the result of the special circumstances of the project, including the fact that it was the first of its kind in Peru. Yet even under the ideal conditions assumed by the aided and mutual self-help manuals, many administrative operations were specified or recommended. (A manual based on considerable experience acquired in Colombia, for instance, calls for some 25 discrete and complex operations.)

The basic principle of aided and mutual self-help is the employment of the free labor of the participating families who thus earn "sweat equity." By working in groups, it is possible to divide, train, and specialize labor and maintain continuously working teams under expert supervision. This, of course, involves a very wide variety of tasks for the organizers and supervisors, ranging from technical design, to the social organization of groups, costing and supervision, time accounting, and the solution of the many personal and intragroup problems that inevitably arise during the construction period, which is ideally not more than six months, but generally more, and often much more, than a year.

The plausibility of this concept fades somewhat in the light of people's own unaided self-help efforts—the same low-income families for whom aided self-help projects are so well intended by the authorities and agencies concerned.

The OATA project was carried out in the middle of a sea of unaided self-help or owner-built houses. The great majority of the houses in the *urbanizaciones populares* of Arequipa, as in the peripheral *barriadas* of Lima, are substantial, if mostly incomplete, structures of brick (or the white volcanic rock *sillar* in Arequipa) reinforced with concrete piers. Contrary to the generalizations made by the mass media and an uninformed middle-class, these squatter settlements are no more slums than any building or development under construction. Most dwellings start as temporary shacks; therefore most new settlements are, temporarily, shanty towns. But, in Miraflores and other squatter suburbs where the settlers are fortunate enough to obtain de facto ownership, they quickly convert the initial encampment into a thriving construction site. However, it takes most "progressive development" settlements of this kind fifteen years or so before they take on the character of a more or less fully developed residential neighborhood.[5]

The physical types and quality of the houses built under the auspices of the OATA project were indistinguishable from those of their unaided neighbors. The only significant difference, and apparent advantage, in the OATA project was the difference in the length of construction time. A self-financing owner-builder of the same income level needed from seven to ten years to complete a unit similar to those built by the mutual-aid groups in eighteen months or two years. This, of course, represents an enormous advantage. The OATA project participants' patience in suffering inferior living conditions—eight and a half years in a high-rental tenement of very low standard or in a shack or incomplete build-

[5] The "progressive development" of low-income settlements that occurs naturally and traditionally when the settlers have secure tenure (de facto if not de jure) is illustrated in Plates 15–17. Case histories of squatter settlement development are given in the author's article *Barriers and Channels for Housing Development in Modernizing Countries,* in the Journal of the American Institute of Planners, Vol. XXXIII no. 3, May, 1967, reprinted in William Mangin, ed., *Peasants in Cities,* Houghton Mifflin, 1970, and in David Lewis, ed., *The Growth of Cities,* Paul Elek, London, 1971. Also, see William Mangin with the author, *The Barriada Movement* in *Progressive Architecture,* New York, May 1968, reprinted in Paul Oliver, ed., as *Benavides & The Barriada Movement in Shelter & Society,* Barrie & Rockliff: The Cresset Press, London, and Praeger, New York, 1969.

ing is a cost that explains the OATA project participants' patience with the many conditions they were obliged to accept in order to receive the credit for the materials and specialized labor—the same items they would have had to pay for but over a longer period when going it alone.

Whether the aided and mutual self-help method, in the Miraflores or any other situation, is really economic or viable as a large-scale alternative is a question hotly debated by the protagonists and antagonists of such programs.

Antagonists claim that the administrative overheads are uneconomically high, and it has often been admitted that they run to 25 percent or even higher, about twice as much as in the relatively top-heavy direct construction of publicly sponsored housing projects. It is also argued that it could be extremely difficult or even impossible to recruit and train the dedicated and self-sacrificing professionals and para-professionals needed for extending programs of this kind. And it is also very commonly and persuasively argued that the cost of participation to the self-helper is as great or even greater than the subsidized sweat equity he earns.

Protagonists counter with arguments justified more by social desirability than administrative feasibility. The aided self-help advocate claims that the most important products are of literally incalculable value: that, in Nehru's words, "We are building families as well as homes." Supported by much recent research on the correlations between well-being and improved housing, the protagonists argue that merely physical improvements are of no value unless supported by social development of the kind built into the self-help programs. Yet before stating my own position in this debate, I must step back and review the lessons I learned, primarily from the Tiabaya school and Miraflores self-help housing projects.

The principal effect of these and other experiences in Peru was to change my attitude toward the people I set out to work for. I stopped trying to work *for* and started trying to work *with* people.

I realized that I knew far less than I originally assumed, and that the people I was supposedly qualified to order about knew far more. As Harms points out in Chapter 8, the same assumptions are not made by professionals or administrators when their clients are from their own or "superior" levels of society. Harms discusses the vital but commonly ignored difference between the user-client and the sponsor-client. When the specialist is paid by his user-client, and as long as the latter is not cowed by a professional mystique, there is dialogue and a learning situation. On the other hand, when the paying client is not the user but an institution supplying him with goods or services, the professional's opportunities for learning are drastically reduced—generally to the limited existential sphere of his peers which, of course, tends to reinforce his own views, which are often profoundly unrealistic.

As I came to realize the perverse nature of the premises on which professionalism and the institutionalization of services (and values) are based, I began to understand how and why the established system is so often counterproductive and so rarely enjoyable. In fact, to associate delightful feelings with institutionalized services or mass production seems foolish and almost indecent. Yet a common and heartening scene in villages and squatter settlements throughout Peru is the celebration of roofing a house, a ritual occasion that brings family and friends together. When the house becomes a commodity supplied through paternalistic agencies, there is no room for the enjoyment of the process itself. To the professional trapped by institutional frameworks, or isolated by his own secretiveness, all measures of value are invested in the material end product. To the extent that I and my colleagues were associated with institutionalized housing, we contributed to the human and material costs imposed on those least able to afford them.

The disaster which would have overtaken the well-intentioned Tiabaya school project—had it not been for the even greater earthquake disaster—would have been the direct result of power to *impose* decisions from above which must come from below if good use is to be made of local resources. The same can be said of the astonishing waste involved in the Miraflores project.

Each illustrates a different side of the issue, however, and these should be separately recognized. We, the authorities, overpowered the Tiabaya School Committee with words, and though more respectful of our Miraflores clients' felt architectural needs, we overwhelmed them with our political power.

As I state in the opening paragraph of my theoretical paper, "Housing As a Verb," Chapter 7, these are two sides of the same basic existential issue of autonomy versus autocracy. Looking back on the Tiabaya school experience, I see it as a lesson in communication and the power of language. We architects were deaf and even blind to the now obvious differences between our own language and that of our clients. It was not so obvious then because we were meeting people already confused by the transition from a traditional, rural, semi-subsistence culture to a modern, urban, semi-industrial situation.

Neither Luis Felipe Calle nor I were more than superficially attuned to the historical context of our activities. Confronted with automatically respected professionals who recommended traditional rather than modern ways, the mayor, the teacher, and the other council members were doubly confused. Even worse, one of the professionals was a foreigner, an Englishman like those who had built the railway and introduced the first modern industries.

To the members of the council, the objective beauty and harmony of the architectural shell of the village symbolized their assumed backwardness and their relative poverty. Our enthusiasm for the superb Vizcarra houses must have been incomprehensible. To them, the respected Don Jorge was a quaint survivor of an older era of even greater hardship.

The school, on the other hand, was to be a symbol of progress. A modern institution for the emerging generation would have to have, of course, according to their logic, a modern dress. This much was clear enough to us, if only half understood. We did our best to convince the villagers that our design was supermodern, far more sophisticated than the contemporary conventions they really wanted. As already stated, our unanswerable economic arguments, together with our prestige as professionals, forced them to accept what, in effect, were our own decisions on the design and construction of their school.

That we were perhaps entirely right, technically, economically, and even culturally speaking, is an academic matter. The reality of the village was quite different from what we saw and the language of the villagers different from our own. For them the school meant a way out of an old and hopeless situation into a new and visibly hopeful one. The probable fact that that hope was unfounded—speaking here with a pessimism neither I nor my colleague shared at that time—does not alter the conflict, even though it may profoundly change the interpretation of the root problem.

The reality we found ourselves up against was the will of the people on whom the execution of the project depended. Since the money to build with lay, quite properly, in their hands, we could not impose our specifications. The decisions we made were illusory, and their apparent acceptance of them was a lie. Quite consciously, I am sure, and after discussion among themselves, the council decided to use our plans and nothing more. They liked the plans, and fully appreciated the far better use made of the site; they certainly understood the material economies of a proposed construction system essentially similar to those employed in the village since its foundation 400 years before. But, whether they were convinced or not that the technical improvements were genuine, they knew for a certainty that they would get little support from the rest of the village for such a building. And of course our project depended on voluntary village labor.

The school committee members did not admit this—not to us anyway. Perhaps they were ashamed to do so, or more likely, they decided that it was less trouble to humor us and wait for us to go away, leaving them with the plans they wanted. They assumed, erroneously, that they could build the way they wanted according to the floor plans we provided. Unfortunately, they did not understand the dependency of those plans on the lightweight roof construction I had specified. If they wanted a heavy concrete roof, then they had to accept the narrow, corridorlike classrooms, such as those in the plan sent by the Ministry in the first place. In other words, they really were dependent on informed technical advice to an even greater extent than they realized.

This natural dependency of the layman on the specialist and the entirely reasonable division of labor it implies is entirely different from the artificial and imposed dependency on the secretive professional. In this case, illustrated by our relationship with the Tiabaya school committee, the mutually assumed inaccessibility of our knowledge deprived our clients of their freedom to hire and fire us as it suited them. Once in our hands, they were left to guess the risks they had to take by dropping our services—the very uncomfortable situation we all find ourselves in, for instance, as we become more dependent on the increasingly institutionalized medical profession.

When we started on the OATA aided and mutual self-help housing project, we were more sensitive to the "felt needs" factor. In fact, we were so sensitive to it that we started off on the wrong foot by insisting that the participants build only provisional dwellings from materials they could later use in their own ways and without any interference from our side. Rosa Bustamante and Blanca Galvez, our social workers and group organizers, quite rightly and wisely warned us against this unjustified lack of confidence in their building skills. Shortly after starting, we had to change over to the construction of permanent dwellings. After another false but fortunately tentative start with an attractive and economic brick vault roofing system (which conflicted with the demand for building second stories), Federico Mevius developed a highly successful and adaptable plan allowing for a wide variety of conditions and internal layouts without changing the quantity of materials or labor or, therefore, the costs and accounting system.

Even to sympathetic neighbors and certainly to the participants themselves, the project must have seemed rather silly, but I think most of them appreciated our effort to come to terms with their own situation. The fact that the staff worked so hard to overcome the problems they created for themselves through the administrative superstructure, and that they worked so closely with the participants, certainly won respect. In comparison with the conventional contract-built housing projects, which were invariably too expensive for families able to participate in our project, we scored a success which deserved its national renown.

The predominant issue raised by the Miraflores project is the political rather than the conceptual one. The participants and the project staff understood one another well enough; in fact, we had a good personal understanding with most of them most of the time; yet the relationship was still one-sided, though in a different sense from that experienced in Tiabaya. Unlike the Tiabaya committee our Miraflores clients were not in control, even though they participated more directly and fully. OATA made all the key decisions about what houses should be built and how they should be built. It had the money, and so we called the tune.

The great and, retrospectively, the somewhat absurd mistake of the Miraflores project was the assumption that the professional staff knew *how* to get houses built better than the people themselves. Today this seems an even greater mistake than the assumption that the professional knows best *what* should be built.

It is still hard for me to understand why we thought that it was necessary to do so much for the people of Miraflores. As mentioned above, the seven *urbanizaciones populares,* with a total population of about 5,000 households at the time, consisted mainly of solidly built though mostly incomplete dwellings. To be sure, there were many cases of poor design and wasteful construction, but few structures were unsound or would have been unlivable when finished or semicomplete. The settlements were all planned by the squatter associations, with or without the assistance of the district municipality. Most of the twenty associations in the urban area of Arequipa had also built their own meeting halls and at least one school. Several had already installed electric light services and a few had started to install water supply systems. The associations, all active, were quite strongly supported for the most part by their local resident populations, as well as by many members and plot owners who were still living in the city. All or nearly all of the associations belonged to the aggressive *Asociación de Urbanizadores Populares de Arequipa* (AUPA), an organization which was generally opposed to OATA's existence and activities, but with whom Luis Felipe and I had made an uneasy peace shortly before the earthquake occurred. In other words, we were dealing with vigorous, capable, and organized working-class people.

Why, then, did we feel it was necessary to organize such people into groups to do what they were so obviously capable of doing individually? If they were going to be provided with credit for materials which they normally buy themselves and for skilled labor which they normally hire themselves, then why did we think we should do all this for them? Did we really think that the work would go faster or that they would save money by the addition of so many tasks and administrative complexities?

If we had been at all conscious of our assumption that we would be saving everyone time and effort by organizing the groups, by keeping elaborate time sheets, by buying and distributing materials, and by keeping an account of the dozens of different materials that go into each job as well as of the tools and the skilled labor supplied, then, I am sure, we would have spent at least a few hours analyzing this assumption. We would have taken the trouble to find out how the typical family actually builds, and we would have compared overhead costs. We didn't because it never occurred to us that our own organization could be more wasteful than theirs. We never anticipated the towering administrative superstructure we were setting up and could not imagine that it would be largely superfluous.

I and my colleagues still shared the liberal establishment notion that the great resource of the people is their labor, and that properly organized by the government—or, even better, by government and private institutions in concert—sweat equity could make great contributions to national development. Of course we were aware of the people's own organizations, but we were much more conscious of their negative motives. For us, AUPA at that time seemed no more than a clique of illegal speculators, who were far less interested in the welfare of the people they claimed to represent than in their own profit. This half-truth we subconsciously extended to all manifestations of autonomous organization.

In fact, the staff of OATA, including myself, held the liberal authoritarian view that all local autonomous organizations tended to be subversive—as, indeed, they are to systems concentrating power in an elite, however benevolent and successful they may be at redistributing wealth in the form of institutionalized services. Fortunately for the genuine liberals, this view is untenable in situations where the institutionalization of basic services such as housing is materially impossible. Once confronted through professional contact with local realities and the people who live them, the creative specialist or open-minded professional is bound to change his or her attitude.

If we had fully realized this at that time, however, we would never have been able to make a politically acceptable proposal. If OATA had approached the mayor with a supervised credit scheme such as that squeezed under the administrative wire a few years later in Lima, it would not have been considered for one moment. Consequently, the OATA staff, and the staffs of several other local and national institutions which followed their lead, would never have experienced the confrontations with local realities or have been affected with the subversive knowledge that any sensitive person must soon acquire from the common but uncommonly capable people of the *barriadas*. A few years after the Arequipa experiment, enough of this new understanding had filtered up to the higher levels of public administration—mostly with the promotion of the infected professionals themselves—where genuinely radical alternatives could be tried.

By mid-1962, a very large low-income housing program, financed with a loan that I had in part helped to negotiate from the Interamerican Development Bank, was floundering. Luis Marcial, a brilliant young architect who was later tragically killed in an airplane crash, was the chief architect for the government institution administering the program. I had the job of assisting him with the development of self-help techniques on which the entire program was supposed to be based. By that time Luis and I had come to the conclusion—evident from the Miraflores experience several years before—that the only way to effectively simplify and generalize self-help was to transfer the bulk of the administrative load onto the program participants themselves. Although we had a few well-administered and effective self-help programs underway—notably the large program in the northern city of Piura directed by another extremely capable and then very young Peruvian architect, Victor Wyskowski—only a small proportion of the 30,000 unit national program was, in fact, being built through self-help. Only rarely was it possible to recruit teams of field personnel willing to work exceptionally long hours for exceptionally low pay and, at the same time, find suitably located land for which the demand did not immediately generate local social and political conflicts that made the organization of self-help groups virtually impossible.

The *barriada* of Huascarán contained an area that was large enough for some twenty single-family dwellings, which the settlement association had acquired and wished to distribute to member families who for lack of their own plots had been living doubled up with relatives in the settlement. When the association approached our agency for funds and technical assistance, Marcial and I suggested to the chief executive (Luis de los Heros, with whom we had negotiated the IDB loan) that the agency simply lend the plot recipients the cash and let them get on with it under a minimum of supervision. Although many of our colleagues and contemporaries were opposed to the idea, our elderly and very conservative friend agreed that we should go ahead.

The procedure was extremely simple. The local association allocated the plots to bona fide families who had no other urban properties and who contracted to build the minimum units specified within six months of receiving the first of five staged payments. The local recipients also undertook to repay the debt within a fifteen-year period on very easy, subsidized interest rate terms. If the property were to be transferred, the debt would also be transferred—we were not concerned who the eventual owners or users were. A new dwelling or dwellings would, in any case, be built at far less cost to the public than those built by commercial contractors in the direct construction projects. The total loans were small, just enough for the materials and skilled labor (bricklayer, roofer, electrician, and plumber), and less than half the amount given for similar units built by contract.

The first cost to the public agency, the construction cost, was substantially less than half. Not only were there no general contractor's profits and overheads to finance, but the agency's own overheads were substantially reduced to about 4 percent from the usual 7 or 8 percent on direct construction projects and from the 15 to 25 percent on direct labor or aided self-help projects.

Longer-term savings in such cases, including financing and related administrative costs, are even greater for the borrower, the lender, and the promoter. Since the total construction cost is reduced by about two-thirds to the public and by half to the borrower, it follows that the long-term savings and the reduction of risks and losses are very large indeed, especially when inflation progressively increases the cost of subsidies paid for out of hard foreign currencies.

Our doubting colleagues and opponents within the agency had the same attitudes and assumptions that I had had a few years earlier while working in Arequipa. Perhaps unfairly, we forced our friends to admit that they had no confidence in the morality of the ordinary working-class people whom we were proposing to trust with cash payments, even though these would be made in four or five stages and only after the certified completion of the previous stage. We were strenuously warned that even the very best people succumb to temptation when the going gets hard. In a crisis, we were told, a family would blow its check for medicines or a journey to the relatives back home, or on gambling or on other even more depraved activities. Our colleagues were by no means opposed to the principle of loans for home building or improvement in squatter areas, however. On the contrary, they were going ahead with their own variant, in which building materials and specialized labor were to be provided by the agency instead of cash. In this way, it was confidently claimed, the people would be protected against themselves. Moreover, the agency was supposed to be able to provide better and cheaper materials through bulk buying negotiated by experts who, unlike the inexperienced borrowers themselves, would not be cheated by unscrupulous merchants.

It did not work out that way. The first bulk purchase made by the materials loan method was a very great quantity of brick which had been obtained at a 10 percent discount. Large purchases by public agencies are, of course, tied up in a certain amount of red tape. In this case, along with other safeguards, three competitive bids had to be obtained through advertising. Three months passed before the first bricks were delivered to a self-helper. He and most of the other borrowers refused to accept the deliveries, claiming that the bricks were of too poor quality. And when the recipients refused to sign, the agency was stuck with its bargain.

Meanwhile, the Huascarán project participants had gotten their bricks with little or no delay. Another participant, a truck driver, took care of deliveries. One of them had a brother in a brick factory who negotiated such a good bargain with his employer that the project participants managed to get themselves a 5 percent better discount than the materials loan program.

If there were any complaints about the quality of the bricks, they were not directed at the agency. All the agency had to do was to get the money to the borrowers and see that the work they did with it met acceptable standards. If it did not, then the agency withheld the next payment until the builders brought previous work up to standard. The problem of collecting payments due was, of course, the same in either case. In Huascarán the accounting system was elementary and the accountants loved it. The materials loan system, on the other hand, was extremely cumbersome. Even with the rather simple construction techniques employed, between fifty and sixty different materials and components were used. The individual accounts were thus multiplied accordingly, and, on top of that, there were all the operations involved in buying, storing, and distributing the very considerable capital that had to be held by the agency from the time the purchases were made until they were received by the borrowers.

In other words, while the cash borrowers proceeded immediately to use their own network of suppliers and distributors, the materials borrowers were dependent on a hierarchic system set up by the agency. While the former were free to make any advantageous entry they could find in the local network system, the latter were stuck at the receiving end of an inflexible supply system—free merely to sign or refuse to sign the receipts.

It was only to be expected, therefore, that the materials borrower, frustrated by long waits for materials he could have bought for himself around the corner, often refused a delivery on one pretext or another. Paradoxically, it was the only *positive* action he could take.

No systematic evaluation has yet been made of these and other forms of self-help projects in Lima, or in Peru, or, as far as I know, in any one area where various methods have been tried. However, the rather unsystematic and superficial surveys that were made of the results of these and other projects carried out during this period in Peru showed that both methods were considerably more productive than conventional direct construction projects, or even orthodox aided mutual self-help projects. Both in Huascarán and in San Martín de Porres, where the materials loan method was first tried out, many borrowers invested far more than the amount demanded by the value of the loans. Very few invested less. Not one of the twenty Huascarán cash borrowers failed to invest more than the minimum one-story house required, and two years later, most of the houses had second floors. In a few cases the materials borrowers sold the materials delivered, and one used the cash to equip his wife's beauty parlor business. But who can say that this was not the best use that the borrowers could have made with the loan? If successful, the business would increase their income and enable them to spend much more on their house in the longer run.

This last question raises the quantitative and most obvious aspect of the basic issue that my colleagues and I were confronted with in the course of these experiences. The presumed authority with which we acted as officials and professionals seemed more and more absurd to those of us who became aware of the simple and overwhelming demographic and economic facts of the situation. The enormous population increase, largely concentrated in the cities through migration, and the tiny budgets of the government public works agencies proved to us how impossible it would be for a public authority to assume direct responsibility for housing the mass of the people.

Even in metropolitan Lima, with a per capita income and budget of about three times the national average, there was less than U.S. $100 per household per annum for all public services, including health services, education, sanitation, transportation, and policing. With the cities doubling every decade, at least 10 percent of the urban populations have to be finding or building themselves a home at any one time. Even if 10 percent of the public monies available were invested in housing projects (of the conventional varieties) not more than 4 percent of the "unhoused excess" population could be accommodated by the public sector (assuming an average unit cost of U.S. $2,500).

The first impulse, of the architect and builder especially, is to reduce the costs by technological innovation. The 10 to 12 percent reductions in first costs that can be achieved by technical modifications of publicly sponsored housing projects is still far too little to make any significant change in the potential contribution of public agencies under these circumstances.[6] These conventional innovations do not answer the question Ernest Weissmann put to me, which continued to bother me until the Huascarán experiment provided an answer. Though very encouraging and supportive when he visited our project in 1958, the then Director of the United Nations Center for Housing, Building, and Planning mentioned, with apparent casualness, that what we really need is not just to help people to build their own homes but to do it in ways that we can administer on a very large scale. The very high and humanly exacting administrative cost of the aided self-help method eliminates it as a general or large-scale solution. Even when the money is made available by a foreign agency, it has not been possible to find and train the army of dedicated field workers and local program administrators demanded.

[6] See Part II, Industrialization: Myths & Realities, in *Industrialized Housing, the opportunity and the problem in developing areas,* by Ian Donald Terner and the author, Office of International Affairs, US Department of Housing & Urban Development, Washington, D.C., 1972. In this analysis we observe that the savings that can be obtained *in theory* range from 10 to 25 percent. In the contexts discussed in this chapter, however, the maximum possible savings in the construction costs would be at the lower end of this range—far less, anyway, than the savings commonly obtained by self-helpers using conventional, labor-intensive techniques.

In addition to the issue of whether it is feasible for the public sector to assume more-or-less direct authority over housing, there is the question of its desirability. This aspect of the central issue of authority is not directly quantifiable nor is it so obvious, except to those who have experienced both authoritarian and autonomous housing systems. It is obvious enough, however, to those who have known the vast human difference between the two, even though the physical operations and the material products may be quite similar.

To put it simply, building carried out by a large and hierarchically organized agency, whether public or commercial, provides little room for dialogue between people. All decisions are vertical and all operations are carried out by more-or-less unchallengeable order. When people are building for themselves, on the other hand, or when the builders are building for the users, there is plenty of room for genuine relationships between the people brought together by the activity and, therefore, for creativity, pride, and satisfaction from the work itself. Of course, there are plenty of grounds for conflict and hate as well as love, but these are the matrix of life which is denied by the impersonality of authoritarianism.

This discussion of the feasibility and desirability of centralized administration in housing raises the basic issue of authority. It therefore directly involves any actions having or needing authority, including, of course, those of the professional architect. Hans Harms discusses the issue in depth in Chapter 8. In fact, we came up against the problem together while we were working for the same agency in Lima, in 1961 and 1962.

Hans was mainly involved with the monitoring of a large housing project while I spent most of my time trying to develop viable self-help programs. Sometimes we would discuss our various frustrations while visiting in the squatter settlements, an invariably stimulating and heartening experience. The initiative, ingenuity, perseverance, and hope so evident in the housing action of such a large part of the population and in the face of so many difficulties is, perhaps, the most important lesson an architect or urban planner can get. This is especially the case if the professional shares responsibility for the artificial barriers placed in the way of people and for projects that drain money away from them and waste it on unsuitable and expensive designs which the intended users do not want or cannot afford.

The students and young professionals, some of them foreign volunteers,[7] who managed to find situations in which they could work with people rather than for central agencies supposedly acting on the people's behalf, learned more than they ever could have in a formal school. Sometimes, the lessons were quite direct. An acquaintance and resident of a Lima barriada, Mrs. Romero of Tres Compuertas, once pointed out to me the logic of enclosing a plot with an expensive brick wall and even of finishing the street façade, before building a permanent room on the plot (which would cost much less). By doing that, she explained, the squatter protects his land, by far the most important part of his property; he creates a large private area, relatively secure from theft and with a greatly improved micro-climate; and, last but not least, he contributes to the creation of an urban street at an early stage of development—a great stimulus for all who live on it or use it.

Mr. and Mrs. Romero, whom I first met in 1960 when they were visiting and advising a barriada association in a small town about 150 miles to the north of Lima, were still living in a less than half-built house of their own when I last saw them shortly before I left Peru in 1965. They were two of the most dedicated professionals I have ever known.[8]

The certified professional makes a fool of himself, and often does a great deal of harm to other people, by assuming that he

[7] For accounts of work done by young volunteers in these contexts see: Margaret Grenfell and the author, *Barriada Integration & Development* in *Architectural Design,* London, Vol. XXXIII, No. 8, August, 1963, pp. 337–8 (illustrated). Also by the author: *British Volunteers in Comas Barriada, Lima* in *Peruvian Times,* Lima, Vol. XXIV, No. 1202, Jan. 3, 1964, pp. 6–10 (illustrated).

[8] At the time I knew them, Mr. Romero worked as a bricklayer and his wife as a part-time nurse. In their forties, they lived with Mrs. Romero's elderly mother in a partly-built house sited on a steep and rocky slope in one of the oldest barriadas of Lima. A great deal of the Romeros' time went into their consulting activities, as did, I suspect, much of the income they earned from it.

knows more than the "uneducated" by virtue of his schooling. All that second- and third-hand information and intellectual exercising does for him, however, is to reduce his ability to listen and learn about situations significantly different from his own social and economic experience—with consequences which can be tragic when he has the power to impose his solutions on those who are not strong enough to resist.

7

JOHN F.C. TURNER

Housing as a Verb

The Problem of Standards

THE MOST COMMON OBJECTION to changes in public policy which would increase the user's control in housing at the expense of central institutions is that standards would be lowered as a result. The standards the objectors have in mind, however, are not something which *can* be achieved with available resources but, rather, represent the objector's own notion of what housing *ought* to be.

The fact that the enforcement of unrealistic standards (unilaterally defined as the minimum acceptable) serves only to worsen the housing conditions of the poor raises the basic issue in housing—that of its meaning and value for people. The emotions which this universal aspect of housing problems stirs up prove its close association with deep human and cultural values.

The minimum standards for housing, building, and planning to which I refer are those which specify *what* should be built, and, very often, they go a long way to determining *how* the subdivision, dwelling, or ancillary equipment should be built as well. Almost all official codes, in the wealthiest and poorest countries alike, require that a building plot be fully equipped with modern utilities, and even with paved streets and sidewalks, before it may be sold to a would-be home builder. Even then the buyer cannot occupy his house until it is completed, at least to a minimum standard, which usually means separate bedrooms, an equipped bathroom, and a kitchen separated from the living area. An investment of this kind demands a mortgage loan, and if the property cannot be occupied until it is finished, or at least certified as habitable, it is extremely difficult for the owner to build it himself—he is virtually obliged to employ a general contractor or, more likely, to buy a ready-made unit in a speculative development or in a publicly sponsored project.

Subdivision codes of the kind and standard described above were instituted in Lima in 1915; these were followed in 1935 by conventional modern minimum standards for dwelling units. It is easy to anticipate the problems created by regulations like these in cities with large and rapidly growing low-income populations such as Lima (which is more typical of the contemporary world than the cities of Europe and North America). Insofar as such standards are enforceable, they price the great majority of would-be home builders out of the market, and even without the added discouragement of rent freezes, they inhibit legitimate, inspected, taxable private investments in low-income housing, whether for rent or for sale.

Hence it is not surprising to find that two-thirds of all new dwellings built in Lima since the early 1940s and over 90 percent in the poorer provincial city of Arequipa were put up by squatters or buyers of lots in clandestine subdivisions. Neither is it surprising to observe that since it became illegal to build tenements which the mass of the people can afford, those remaining have become grossly overcrowded while illegal shanty towns have proliferated. (I refer to conglomerations of rented shacks that must be distinguished from the *pueblos jóvenes* and the *urbanizaciones populares* consisting of owner-built dwellings of far superior standards.) In fact, housing conditions for the poorest fifth or quarter of Lima's population are far worse now than they were in the 1890s, and demand substantially higher proportions of personal income to boot.

Although building codes have made great contributions to human welfare in countries with high per capita incomes, their rigidity often contributes to a shortage of safe and sanitary housing. In many cities of the U.S., for example, owner-building is virtually prohibited, and in many more the administration of building codes is an important factor in the precipitate abandonment of older housing, so badly needed by the urban poor.

The disastrous abandonment rate of structurally sound but obsolescent housing—which each year in New York City alone currently amounts to the stock for a fair-sized town—is in part due to housing codes and their administration. A license has to be obtained in order to replace a defective roof, for example. But if the building is obsolescent, this may not be granted unless the entire building is brought up to standard and by licensed builders. Therefore, because the owner or a willing tenant is forbidden to do a job he would have been quite able to do, and very cheaply, an entire building is lost, thus accelerating the decay of the neighborhood.[1]

This begins to suggest that minimum specification standards are frequently, if not generally, counterproductive under at least two sets of conditions. First, when there is a significant gap between the levels of investment they require and the effective demand; and, second, when that gap cannot be closed with subsidies, whether through lack of financial resources or lack of will on the government's part.

If governments cannot, or will not, make up the difference between what housing laws require and what the effective demand can purchase, then why do they create these problems? Why is the common sense solution of allowing and encouraging people to make the best use of what they have treated as subversive nonsense by the technocratic and bureaucratic authorities? Why do these authorities and the institutions they control refuse to let people

[1] See, for example: the *National Urban League* and the *Center for Community Change,* The National Survey of Housing Abandonment, Washington, D.C., April, 1971, and George Sternlieb, *Abandonment and Rehabilitation: What Is to Be Done?* Sub-Committee on Housing Panels, Committee on Banking and Commerce, U.S. House of Representatives, 92nd Congress, First Session.

live and move between the extremes of neglected, dangerous slums and residences suitable for middle-class Joneses? Why, in other words, are the "problems" so universally defined in terms of what people *ought* to have (in the view of the problem-staters) instead of in realistic terms of what people *could* have?

The Issue of Housing

The questions that end the last section cannot be answered without first analyzing the alternative meanings attached to the word "housing," and identifying the different value systems underlying the problem of standards.

In English, the word "housing" can be used as a noun or as a verb. When used as a noun, housing describes a *commodity* or product. The verb "to house" describes the process or *activity* of housing. While the idea of housing as a collective noun is obviously associated with housing activities, the word itself does not generally indicate this fact. On the other hand, the activity of housing is difficult to conceive without including the houses promoted, built, or used.

It follows that the criteria for the measurement of housing will differ with the meaning of the word. The measures of housing products or commodities are, of course, the alternative physical standards commonly used (which may be the "specification" standards described above or the more sophisticated and open "performance" standards already adopted in some European countries and increasingly favored in the U.S.)[2] The measurement of housing activity, however, is another question altogether. Some components of housing action are clearly measurable—dwelling units, for instance. It is also possible and practical to measure financial costs, time invested, and even human effort. But the vital aspects of housing are not quantifiable at all. The

[2] See, for example: National Bureau of Standards Report Number 9850 *The Performance Concept: A study of its application to housing,* U.S. Department of Commerce, Washington, D.C. 1968, and the proceedings of the American Public Health Association Invitational Conference on *Health Research in Housing and its Environment,* Airlie House, Virginia, 1970.

most important "product" of any human activity is, of course, the satisfaction or frustration of needs.

If there were simple or invariable correspondences between material products and human satisfactions (and frustrations) there would be no issue and the problem of standards would be easily resolved. As the later sections in this paper spell out in detail, there is, however, a very wide margin of independent variability between material products and human feelings and behavior. This is a truism in everyday life, but evidently not in the minds of producers, distributors, technicians, and administrators concerned more with things than with the people for whom they supposedly exist.

Given this independent variability of things and their human uses, it is perverse to attach human values to things or the measures of things. Yet this is exactly what is done in common housing practice. Housing problems are defined by material standards and housing values are judged by the material quality of the houses produced, or by the material quantity of related products, such as profit or equity. From the viewpoint of a central planner or an official designer or administrator, these are self-evident truths. From such a viewpoint, more is better: more plumbing is better than less plumbing, more space per person is better than less space. Given all the local constraints, then, there will be an imperative for the establishment of standards that are minimally desirable or acceptable—in the view of those with the authority to make them, of course.

According to those for whom housing is an activity, these conclusions are absurd. They fail to distinguish between what things *are*, materially speaking, and what they *do* in people's lives. This blindness, which pervades all institutions of modern society,[3] explains the stupidity of tearing down "substandard" houses or slums when their occupants have no other place to go but the remaining slums, or are forced to create new slums from previously "standard" homes. This blindness also explains the monstrous low-cost projects (which almost always turn out to have very high costs

[3] An especially eloquent statement of this phenomenon is that by Ivan Illich in *Deschooling Society*, Harper & Row, New York, 1970.

for the public as well as for the unfortunate "beneficiaries") erected for the evicted slum dwellers or others with nowhere to go (and these are not always in the lowest income brackets).

Standards of course have their uses; it would be impossible to plan or carry out any complex operation without them. But it is entirely improper to use them as *measures* of human value. If enough is known about a process or an activity, such as housing, then the standards and measures of things produced and used can be more or less accurate *indicators* of their values to the people concerned. In the final analysis, though, it is only the people who experience the activity and its products who can evaluate them.

In this paper, I am primarily concerned with the impact of housing activity on the lives of the housed, since these issues and problems must be better understood before the wider, secondary effects on society can be properly evaluated. Such an analysis is especially justified for activities which are relevant to personal life; that is, those which can act as vehicles for personal fulfillment, assuming that fulfillment and maturity in turn depend on personal responsibility for making decisions that shape one's own life. Housing is one such activity, as are all those on which the immediate ends of life depend: the cultivation and preparation of food, the clothing of ourselves, the care of our bodies, the procreation and nurture of children, and the sheltering of these activities. Other activities, essential as they may be, are less amenable to personal direction or direct participation: the installation and operation of major communications systems, for example, or dealing with any mass-produced and mass-marketed item, whether one is a factory operative, a distributor, or a consumer.

If this distinction between existentially significant and insignificant activities is not recognized, then what I consider to be the basic issues will seem irrelevant or meaningless; that is, the linguistic difference between housing as a noun and housing as a verb, and the political difference between legislating standard rules and executing standardized games.

These alternatives, naturally, have profound implications in all spheres. On the one hand, we will have, as we commonly do have, supralocal agencies which plan *for* and provide *for* people's housing needs, with the result that the people so planned for and provided for turn into consumers or passive beneficiaries. On the other hand, if housing is treated as a verbal entity, as a means to human ends, as an activity rather than as a manufactured and packaged product, decision-making power must, of necessity, remain in the hands of the users themselves. I will go beyond that to suggest that the ideal we should strive for is a model which conceives housing as an activity in which the users—as a matter of economic, social, and psychological common sense—are the principal actors.

This is not to say that every family should build its own house, as the urban squatters do, but rather that households should be free to choose their own housing, to build or direct its construction if they wish, and to use and manage it in their own ways. In fact these are traditional characteristics of local housing systems and are still practiced by those with high incomes.

The vital difference between organizations which use people and organizations which are used by people raises crucial issues at the policy level. If local decisions are made by central bodies, those decisions are bound to implement more or less standardized programs and projects for particular social groups in particular places and at particular times. But if local decisions are made by local people, those decisions must be ordered and supported by institutionalized services which must be open to all, in all places and at all times, within the normative framework of those institutions.

Any housing system depends on a series of more-or-less-organized and institutionalized services, the number and complexity of which vary with the nature of the context. No house can be built and maintained without land, without tools and materials, without skilled labor (and management), and without an exchange system which allows the users to obtain the resources they do not possess themselves.

In housing based on open services, the builder, buyer, or householder is free to combine the discrete services in any way his own resources and the norms governing their use allow. In other words, local executive decisions (and generally supralocal normative decisions) are fully differentiated. For the local decision-maker or user, the open service system has a high degree of, or the capability for, providing many different ways of achieving the same end—in the present case, the construction of a house. If, for example, each of the four basic services can be used in four diffent ways (or provide four different types or sets of components) then there are 5^4-1 or 624 combinations for a user who requires at least one of these services to build or maintain his home (see Fig. 4).

Figure 4 represents such a network composed of four services or submarkets, each of which, for the sake of a simplified illustration, provides four alternatives (choices between four sites, four ways of financing, four systems of contracting, and four sets of construction tools and materials, as described in the captions to

Fig. 4. *The Open Services Network*

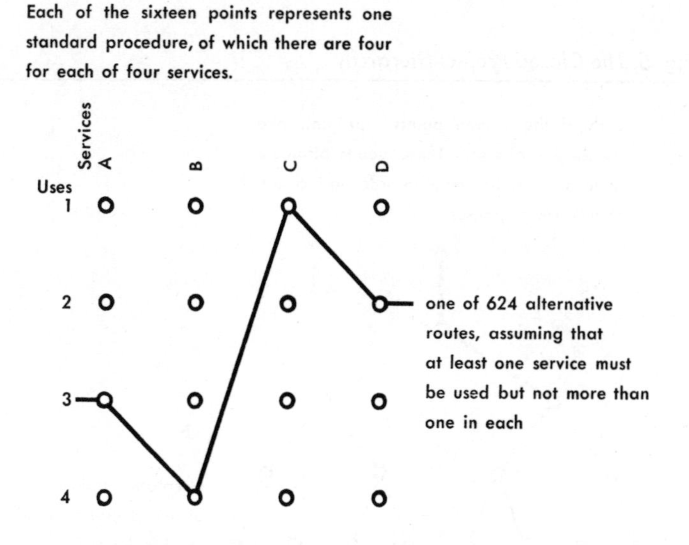

the figure). In reality, there would be many more alternatives in an agile and responsive market, at least for sites and alternative sets of tools and materials or individual building types. In the figure it is assumed that all the alternatives are compatible, although, in markets providing much wider ranges of choice, there would be many incompatible combinations—a single-family dwelling in a central city location, for example.

According to the definitions of this paper, a system is closed or limited to few uses and, very often, to few users when the local or supralocal decision-making powers are centralized. In the more extreme (and relatively common) cases of housing built or administered by public institutions or private corporations, all decisions are subsumed by a central directorate or administration (see Fig. 5).

Figure 5 represents the hierarchy which results when these rule-making and game-playing functions are concentrated in one person's or agency's hands. All decisions, in this authoritarian system, flow down from the peak to the base, at which level the prod-

Fig. 5. *The Closed Project Hierarchy*

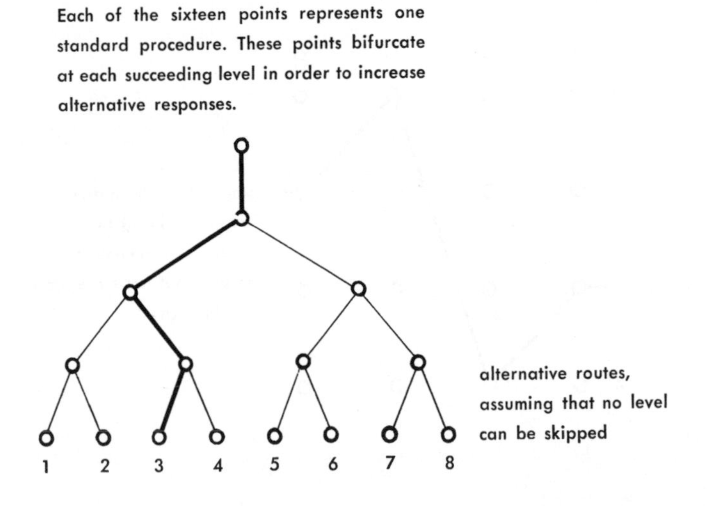

ucts are received by consumers whose decision-making role is limited to a possible choice between a very limited number of prepackaged alternatives.

The illustration suggests a typical publicly sponsored housing project of the kind administered by governments of countries with low per capita incomes. Generally, only one major project is carried out at one time in cities other than the very largest ones. Often only one financing contract is offered, although the illustration assumes two (subsidized and unsubsidized mortgage loans). A choice of two contracting systems is also offered: aided self-help and general contracting. And, finally, under each of these contracting systems, two alternative dwelling unit types are offered. This relatively wide range of choices provides eight alternative combinations, probably about as many as any director of a centrally administered project would tolerate.

It must be recognized that the two housing systems define a spectrum rather than a duality, since there are many combinations. Most contemporary housing systems are mixed and lie between these extremes.[4] The conventional real estate developer and the increasingly popular sites and service programs for lower-income households in low-income contexts,[5] for example, provide package deals for these components, but leave the buyer free to design and build his own house.

In practice, a policy-maker must know what system or mix is the most appropriate in a given situation if his decisions are to be productive. An entirely open service system is wholly inappropriate for the aged or infirm (if they are obliged to be the direct users), and a closed project system is extremely frustrating for a

[4] *Ibid.*, Chapter 4: The Institutional Spectrum.

[5] Site and service programs are publicly sponsored subdivisions providing building lots and (generally minimum) services or utilities for low-income owner-builders. At the time of writing there is a discernible trend away from publicly sponsored low-income housing projects in low-income countries. This is partly because they have proven to be so costly to the public (the loss of 60 percent or more of the funds invested through the beneficiaries' failure to repay loans is common) and partly because of the far greater effective demand for land without dwelling units (which most low-income people prefer to build themselves anyway).

young family which wants to save money by building its own home.

The practical policy issues of feasibility are raised by such considerations and apply to developers, builders, and realtors producing for buyers of finished housing, as well as to producers of component goods and services for users who demand their own particular housing type.

In principle, if not in practice, the greater the degree of centralization or the larger the scale of the housing operation, the *less* economic it becomes, except in times of crisis or when the hierarchic system is essential for the generation of basic resources—an argument that anticipates the steps which follow and which is further elaborated in Chapter 11.

Housing Action as an Open System

Obviously, the agility and flexibility of a housing market depends on the openness of the system at all levels of production in order that the number and variety of producers and compatible and interchangeable products are maximized. In both material and human terms, the more open the system, the greater the potential benefits. The best results are obtained by the user who is in full control of the design, construction, and management of his own home. It is of secondary importance whether or not he builds it with his own hands, unless he is very poor.

As Grindley reports in chapter 1, the middle-, moderate-, and relatively low-income owner-builder in the United States often achieves first cost savings of 50 percent or more, and these savings are proportionally matched by many very low-income squatter-builders in countries such as Peru. A squatter with a suitable building plot and secure tenure can and often does build a house which would cost twice as much if it were built by a government agency.

Savings in first construction costs are considerably greater, of course, if operating expenses are taken into account; interest, insurance, taxes, and utility costs over a twenty-to-thirty-year period are about three times as great as the initial construction cost.

Mortgage carrying charges constitute the largest part of operating costs, and these are greatly reduced when the principal is halved (or, as in the case of squatter "progressive development," mortgage financing is eliminated altogether).

The human side of the account is much more difficult to assess. Most, if not all, who have observed or experienced owner-building agree, however, that user-controlled housing (when it is also materially economic) is far superior as a vehicle of personal, family, and social growth or development than housing which is merely supplied.

Once again, the worth of the physical product cannot be assumed to lie in its physical qualities, but rather in the relationships between the object and the user. These relationships change as the conditions of the household vary; as the dwelling itself is altered through improvement or deterioration, modernization, or obsolescence; and through changes of use and market value as the urban context changes.

In other words, if housing is perceived as functions of what housing *does* in the lives of its users—of the roles which the process plays in their life history—and not in the material qualities of the physical products, then the material worth of the objects and the manner of their production are entirely dependent on their highly variable uses. These uses, in turn, vary along with the changing demands imposed by changes in the context, or in the location of the process in the same context.

This point is developed and clarified if stated in simple general systems terms. The equivalents (of the general systems terms) in our present discussion are shown in Figure 6. The simplest description of housing as action must include the actors, their actions, and their achievements. This process, which is really simultaneous and not linear as the left-to-right notation implies, takes place in a context. The context will be altered to some extent, however, by the actor's actions; that is to say, by their achievements which become part of the context.

A further element is equally essential for a realistic representation of the process as a whole: the feedback loop, in this case the expectations which motivate the actors in the first place. No con-

Fig. 6. *A Simple General Systems Definition of Housing*[6]

This assumes that the context, including the products of the process, is different from the context which instigated it.

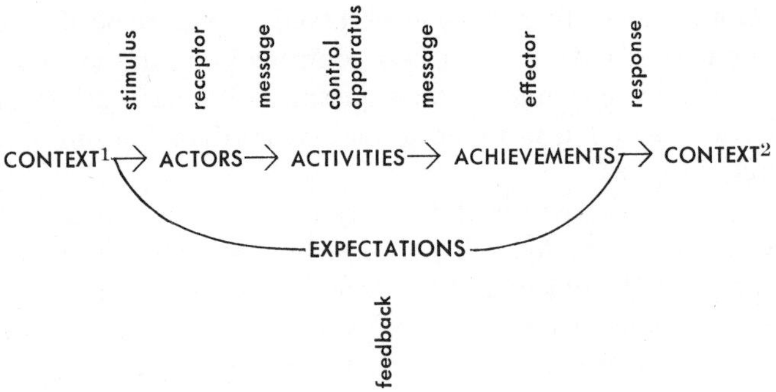

stimulus
receptor
message
control apparatus
message
effector
response

CONTEXT[1] → ACTORS → ACTIVITIES → ACHIEVEMENTS → CONTEXT[2]

EXPECTATIONS

feedback

scious or complex action is likely to be taken unless those on whose decisions it depends expect the benefits to outweigh the costs of inaction.

Of course, several and often many actors or decision-makers are involved in any one housing action, and their interests can vary a great deal—some may be against the enterprise. But the balance must be favorable if it is to be carried out. In general, it is both necessary and sufficient to recognize three classes of actors: the private (and generally commercial) sector, the public sector, and the "popular" sector—the users themselves. Clearly the nature of the housing process depends as much on the relative influences of actors motivated by commercial profit, political power, and personal use as it does on the nature of the context determining the specific needs and means of all the actors.

It follows that the program of operations or the actions required by the actors is dependent on the cast and roles of the decision-makers, just as these are determined by what they can imagine

[6] This figure is an adaptation from Ludwig von Bertalanffy's description of a simple feedback scheme in his *General Systems Theory*, George Braziller, New York, 1968.

and expect in the situation perceived. Expected housing achievements consist not only of houses and other material parts of a dwelling environment, but also of the ways and means by which they are sponsored, designed, built, used, and maintained.

Demand as a Function of Expected Supply

It is clear from this schematization that there are a number of major and more or less independent variables that must greatly affect the nature of the process and its products. The key variable for the present discussion is the demand. Demand is a dependent variable of the anticipated costs and benefits of the action and products required to meet the demand; that is, the felt needs of the actors and the means they possess *and are willing to invest.*

In authoritarian or hierarchic systems, the user has no significant control over the nature of the process or the form of its products, yet certain processes and the life of the product nevertheless depend on the users' willingness to support the maintenance costs of the original investment.

Where the housing supply does not match the home buyer's or renter's demands well enough to generate the will to pay or to care for the property, the seller or landlord depends on coercion. This can take two forms: direct police power or reification through propaganda, which tries to persuade the consumer that what he really wants is just what the producer is selling him and that value lies in the product rather than in its usefulness. Which of these two ways of enslaving man is the worst is a much-debated question. For the present purpose, however, we can wish the plague on both these authoritarian houses, and build some hope on the fact that excessive police power and excessive advertising are far too costly for most nations' economies.

Those who are poor in material fact but who are not socially degraded simply because they live in a poor society are relatively impervious to reification. The typical Peruvian urban squatter, for instance, must be highly pragmatic if he is to capitalize on his very small savings margin and his relatively limited skills. The many thousands of families with very low incomes who have built themselves homes that have potential or even actual market values amounting to five years' income or more—double the usual limit—are sufficient proof of this. The typical Peruvian squatter has also proved that he—and even more frequently, she—is also highly resistant to the exercise of police power. This has often taken the dramatically literal form of pitched battles between squatters and riot police. The existence of hundreds of squatter settlements surrounding cities such as Ankara, Manila, and Nairobi, as well as Lima, provide further evidence of squatter stamina.

People already hooked on totalitarian systems or forced to depend on them need little additional coercion to accept a standardized housing package—the mere lack of an alternative is generally sufficient. But as the margin between income and subsistence living costs shrinks, housing demands lose their elasticity, and individual priorities become increasingly rigid. The demand for residential location near work places, for example, can be so rigid in cities like Calcutta and Delhi that the very poor will sleep on the street rather than accept a subsidized house on the periphery.

Middle-income households, with incomes five or ten times the minimum needed for survival, can afford the diseconomies of unsuitable housing and can often compensate for them by means of alternative expenditures. If the only dwelling available to middle-class users is poorly located, for example, they can compensate through the use of automobiles or telephones, while these luxuries are far beyond the reach of the vast majority in countries with very low median incomes. The lower the income level, therefore, the better the match must be between the demand and the housing process, if both the household and the housing economies are to be maintained.

We need to provide an analysis of housing costs and benefits in order to explain why the human and material economy of the housing process depends on a precise matching of people and their dwelling environments, especially in the context of low or very low income populations. When the values of housing are sought in the material characteristics of the dwellings produced, it is hard or impossible to explain the apparently "irrational" behavior frequently complained of by administrators of low-income housing programs. Why do so many poor households resist paying what they are quite able to pay for physically improved housing? Or when minimal rents, or even when no rents, are charged, why do they so often let their environments deteriorate to virtually uninhabitable levels?

The wealthy have traditionally avoided the real issues of authority and autonomy by convincing themselves that the poor are congenitally ignorant, incompetent, and feckless—an absurd notion in any context and impossible to maintain in the face of the enormous housing achievements of the urban poor in cities such as Athens, Lima, or Seoul.[7]

The apparent paradox of the simultaneous existence of bankrupt or rapidly disintegrating low-income housing projects and flourishing and rapidly developing squatter settlements in the same city and occupied by people with similar characteristics is difficult to explain if *conventional premises are accepted.* The reluctance of families to pay for, or even to maintain, apartments in subsidized projects is baffling to the observer with conventional views when confronted with the fact that the same families make extraordinary sacrifices in the building of their own homes.

However, when the basic issues of the meaning of housing and the significance of autonomy are recognized, the paradox is easily

[7] In these three cities, which are typical of a wide range of countries with low per capita incomes and undergoing rapid urbanization, between a quarter and a third of the entire metropolitan populations live (at the time of writing) in squatter settlements or illegal subdivisions where they have built, or are in the process of building, their own homes. In countries with these characteristics—with at least one third of the world's present population—squatter settlements, or other forms of autonomous urban growth, generally increase at twice the already very fast growth rates of the cities as a whole. For a general review of these developments in the Third World, see the author's paper on *Uncontrolled urban settlements: problems and policies* in the International Social Development Review No. 1—Urbanization: development policies and planning, United Nations, New York, 1968; reprinted in Gerald Breese, ed., *The City in Newly Developing Countries*, Prentice-Hall, 1969. See also William Mangin, *Latin American Squatter Settlements: A Problem and A Solution* in the Latin American Research Review, Vol. II No.3, Summer 1967; and Aprodicio Laquian, *Rural urban migrants and metropolitan development*, Intermet, Toronto, 1971.

explained. Either the self-sacrificing squatter-builders have in fact achieved what they want or, failing that, are making the best of a situation for which they accept full responsibility.

Material and Existential Needs and Priorities

The quality of the *shelter* provided by housing is only one of the specific functions of housing. All the functions are dependent variables of human goals which particular households have at any particular place and time.

Location, in addition to the material standard of the dwelling unit, is now generally recognized as an equally important factor in housing. The significance of alternative forms of *tenure* and the significance of physical, emotional, and financial security, on the other hand, has yet to be understood by most authorities.

Even those authorities and housing analysts who do recognize the independent variability of priorities for high standards of shelter or comfort, for locational convenience, and for secure tenure—and who therefore reject dwelling unit standards as a measure of housing value—cannot easily explain or anticipate the wide variations of housing choices and action observed. Particularly wide variations in the housing priorities of the lower- and lower-middle income groups are evident in most, if not all, cities. Members of this generally large and rapidly growing sector of modernizing cities can be found living in almost all residential sectors and in a very wide variety of dwelling types and with all forms of tenure—from squatter tenancy to the ownership of mortgaged homes.

This elasticity of lower-middle income demand and the generally narrower ranges of common priorities of the lower- and higher-income levels (both of which tend to be more rigid for both social and economic reasons) can only be understood if the roles which housing plays in the lives of the households are known. In addition to the specific and material housing functions or needs mentioned above, it is essential to identify the human or existential and nonquantifiable functions or roles which the housing process can play. If, by way of illustration, these

Fig. 7. *Priorities for VITAL NEEDS x Income Level*

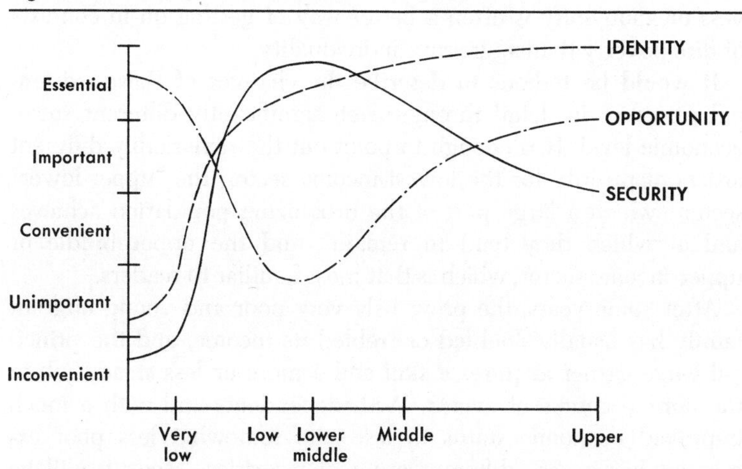

are taken to be *identity*, *security*, and *stimulus*, or more appropriately in the present context, *opportunity*,[8] then it is much easier to interpret or anticipate housing priorities and behavior in any given context.

This simple but important concept is illustrated in Figure 7, which shows how priorities of most active or upwardly mobile households change as income levels change; in this case, in the context of contemporary Lima. It hypothesizes that the lowest-income sector will have a very high priority for opportunities to get out of that situation. The upwardly mobile very poor are generally young adults recently arrived in the city and are, therefore, far more concerned about future than present security; indeed, present security will be the last thing they want if, as is likely, it entails socioeconomic stagnation. Nor will they be particularly

[8] These suggested or illustrative factors are borrowed from Robert Ardrey's book *The Territorial Imperative*, Atheneum, New York, 1966, pp. 334–35; Ardrey, in turn, borrowed them from Abraham Maslow, ed., *Motivation and Personality*, 2nd ed., Harper & Row, N.Y., 1970. As Michael E. Stone has pointed out to me, some distortions and inconsistencies have crept into the interpretations which make it doubly important to emphasize the illustrative and tentative nature of the set of terms used.

concerned with personal status or identity, for a certain facelessness or anonymity is often a better way of getting on in contexts of dire poverty than aggressive individuality.

It would be tedious to describe the changes of these existential priorities in detail through each significantly different socio-economic level. It is enough to point out the remarkably different orders of priority for the lowest-income sector, the "upper-lower" sector (which a large part of the urbanizing population achieves and at which they tend to remain) and the upper-middle or upper-income sector, which is that most familiar to readers.

After some years, the previously very poor and young migrant family has usually doubled or trebled its income, and the principal wage earner acquires a skill and a more or less steady job in the normal course of events. With dependents and with a much improved economic status to lose, the somewhat less poor ex-migrant has a very different order of priorities: security will be far the most important determinant of his longer-term plans; opportunity will be less important for the head of the household, although it may still be very important for the children; identity or social recognition will also be more important to him and

Fig. 8. *Priorities for HOUSING NEEDS x Income Level*

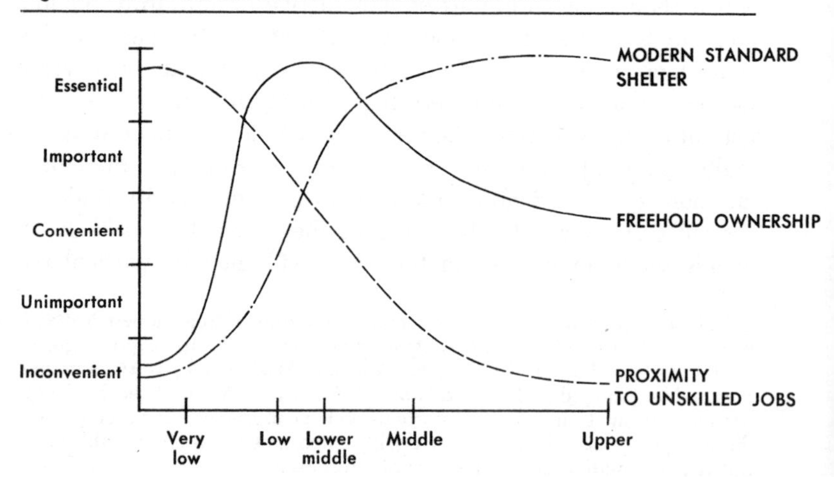

Fig. 9. *Matched Priorities*

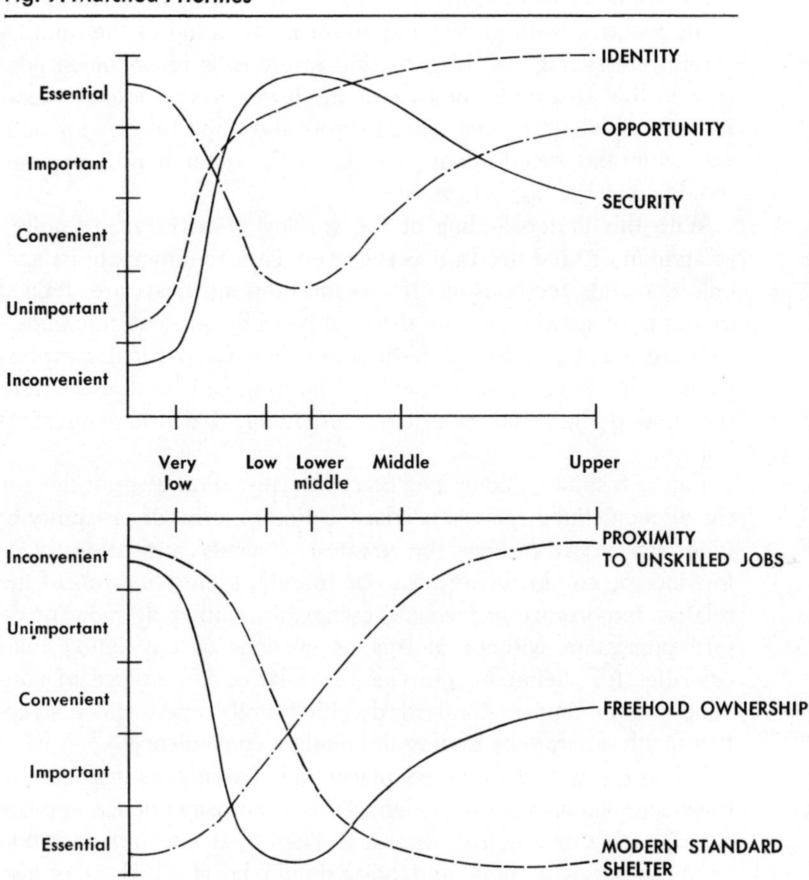

may increase if opportunities for higher incomes shrink as time passes.[9]

[9] For further elaboration of the relationships between environmental change, socio-economic mobility, and housing needs and priorities, see the sources quoted in footnote 5 to Chapter 6 (page 131) and the author's paper *A new view of the housing deficit*, in *Housing policy for a developing Latin American economy*, Charles Frankenhoff, ed., University of Puerto Rico, 1966. Reprinted in David Lewis, ed., *The Growth of Cities*, Paul Elek, London, 1971.

The common order of these basic priorities for an upper-income family of modern middle-class status will be different again; while security is often very important in the mind of the middle-class professional, say, his situation rarely calls for as much concern in this area as in the case of the lower-class worker, at least in contexts such as Lima. Social status and opportunities for both economic and social advancement, on the other hand, are commonly given the highest priority.

With this understanding of the varying priorities of a family's existential or vital needs, it is relatively easy to anticipate its specific demands for housing. If specific housing needs are defined in terms of another set of three universally present functions—location, tenure, and shelter—then priorities for particular expressions or forms of these elements of housing can be derived from the underlying vital priorities, providing that the context is known.

Figure 8 shows a complementary interpretation of priorities for the above-defined specific needs: location in terms of proximity to inner-city areas (where the greatest diversity and intensity of low-income employments are to be found); tenure in terms of the relative importance of freehold ownership (either de facto or de jure possession without mortgages or liens of any kind); and priorities for shelter in terms of the relative importance of conventional minimum standard dwelling units (permanent structures with separate bedrooms and modern conveniences).

When the two analyses are placed side by side, as in Figure 9, their complementarity is evident. If their correspondence appears unreasonable or illogical, then it is likely that one interpretation or the other is at fault and both should be checked. It is also clear from this approach that the observer can start his analysis either from the evidence provided by the housing action of the housed or from deeper studies of motivation and social behavior. Alternatively, and perhaps preferably, both approaches should be used in concert.

From this double-sided picture, anyone who knows the context well enough will be able to point out which alternative dwelling environments are in fact available to a given sector at a given time. If the basic and specific needs are well defined and accurately interpreted, and if the observer has information on the housing resources available from the private, commercial, and public sectors, as well as those possessed by the users themselves, then he can prepare a viable cost-benefit account and make a reasonably accurate prognosis of housing action.

The Impossibility of Authoritarian Solutions to Real Housing Problems

At this point it is helpful to return to the systemic definition of housing action. It is now clear that the "expectations" feedback loop should be split in two: one for materially measurable, specific housing needs and the other for the nonquantifiable, basic, vital, or existential needs which underlie them. Figure 10 shows

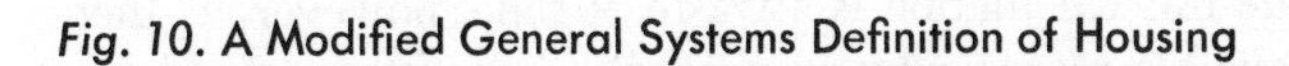

Fig. 10. A Modified General Systems Definition of Housing

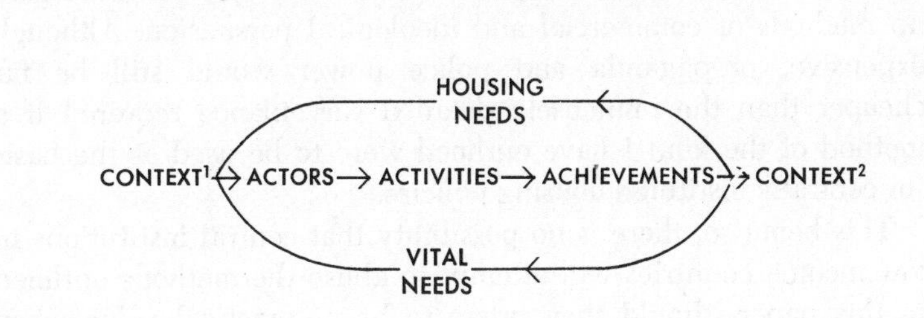

the complete expression, which helps us to avoid the fundamental error of confusing human ends and material means.

This rounded-out representation of any particular housing action or class of actions, when read in conjunction with the analyses which led up to the differentiation of vital and material needs, highlights another side of the issue of feasibility. Not only does the present analysis show that authoritarian housing systems are impractical in economies of scarcity, but it also suggests, very strongly, that a true match between housing demand and housing supplied by central institutions is politically, if not economically, impossible in economies of abundance and scarcity alike.

One only has to consider for a moment the number of more or less independent variables we have so far identified in order to boggle the mind with the immense number of possible permutations and combinations. Even if there are only half a dozen types of location in a given city, and the same small number of alternative forms of tenure and of house plans, we have 6^3 or 216 specific housing types. Even if this theoretical number is reduced by eliminating impractical combinations (such as single-family dwelling units in central city areas), the substantial residue must still be multiplied by the number of ways in which the dwelling can be sponsored, built, used, and maintained. And even then we have only dealt indirectly and partially with the other components of the dwelling environment. Unless types of location are to be specified in much greater detail to provide a much larger multiplier, another series of multiplying factors must be added.

To pursue this calculation is a waste of time, however, as there is no conceivable reason why an authoritarian system would give up methods of commercial and ideological persuasion. Although expensive, propaganda and police power would still be far cheaper than the immensely detailed surveillance required if a method of the kind I have outlined were to be used as the basis for centrally instituted housing policies.

This being so, there is no possibility that central institutions in low-income countries will attempt to abuse the methods outlined in this paper—should they prove to be of practical value when properly used. Before explaining this last and concluding part of the argument, the assertion that it is impossible to coopt local decision-making in economies of scarcity, through the analysis of individual demands or through the normal tools of authoritarian persuasion, must be more fully substantiated. If closed and authoritarian systems are as inflexible and therefore as inhibiting of personal and local initiative as I have suggested, then these methods are bound to be unproductive.

In an economy of scarcity, the mass of the common people, though poor, possess the bulk of the nation's human and material resources for housing. Their collective small savings capacity and their collective entrepreneurial and manual skills (and spare time) far surpass the financial and administrative capacity of even the most highly planned and centralized institutional system, whether dominated by the state or by private capitalist corporations.

The commercial market for new housing in low-income countries such as Peru is inevitably limited to the minority who can afford the costs of imposed standards and, of course, the profits demanded by capitalist enterprise in inflationary or high-risk economies. The publicly subsidized housing supply is also limited by the generally very small budgets available for housing and related facilities.

If neither the organized private sector nor the public sector of the economy can provide new housing for a huge and rapidly growing population (which cannot possibly crowd into the initially small and diminishing supply of old housing in zones of transition), then needs must be met by the people themselves, the popular sector.

This third sector is, in fact, the major producer of low-income housing in most low-income and rapidly growing cities. Norms practiced or legally required by organized public and private sectors, but impractical for the mass of the people, are simply ignored. For example, if building land is restricted by private commercial speculation, it will be taken out of the commercial market through organized invasion if no other land is available, or if poor people cannot pressure the political authorities into expropriation on their behalf.

A popular sector capable of organized action on a scale the formally institutionalized sectors cannot control and composed of households whose housing priorities are relatively inelastic is, therefore, the dominant actor in the processes governing the production and maintenance of new housing in economies of scarcity.

In general it is far better that people should act outside the law than not act at all. Housing conditions are worse and, by implication, social and economic progress is least where the constraints placed by the organized or elitist public and private sectors are strongest.

The analyses and evaluation of policy makers will be greatly influenced, however, by their political biases or assumptions. Those who assume that they know people's demands better than the users themselves, or those whose interests are best served by this assumption, will naturally favor authoritarian closed systems.

In contrast, those who assume that the user is the best judge of his own demands (as distinct from his rights) will try to limit their participation to the administering of services which guarantee the supply of land, materials, tools, and skills to the users, together with credit for the purchase of these elements. He will therefore support open systems in which the output is the product of a dialogue between rule makers and game players, without which there can be no existential freedom.

Standard Rules or Standardized Games?

The practical policy issue, which defines the problem of housing standards, lies in the choice between the elitist and authoritarian assumption that technicians and managers know what is good for people, and the humble acceptance of a pluralist and genuinely democratic system. In assuming that free people are the only real judges of what they need and of what they can do for themselves, I belong to the second of these two incompatible and necessarily warring groups.

My argument rests on the premise that there is no existential or real freedom without dialogue between the rule makers and the game players. As in chess, any one of the infinite number of games we can play is the product of an implied dialogue between those who set the rules ages ago and today's participants. To round out the analogy, an authoritarian housing system would amount to a pseudo-game in which the pieces are moved for the players. In this situation the intended players become pawns, and the real game is between the commercial and political powers that dominate instead of serve the people for whom they ostensibly exist.

Since hierarchic systems for such complex and personally important activities as housing are impotent in economies of scarcity, there is reason to hope that, at least in these economies, this fact will be generally recognized. In such situations, the rapid improvement of material housing conditions and the conversion of public investments in low-income housing from burdensome social overheads into vehicles for social and economic development can only come about through the extension of open housing service networks.

Governments of low-income countries have only two real choices, once they have lost or abdicated the power of suppression: they can ignore the process and abandon any serious pretense of planned urban development or they can support local action through public service institutions designed to help the mass of the people make the best use of their own resources in their own ways.

After an examination of the nature of housing as an activity involving particular people or actors, their organized activities and the costs and benefits of the process and its products, it is evident that the democratic alternative is the most desirable one in any context, and the only feasible one in an economy of scarcity.

If governments in countries with low per capita incomes wish to avoid the disorder and diseconomies of unplanned direct action by squatters and clandestine developers (who are the major suppliers of low-income urban housing in these contexts), then their housing strategies must change. The only way of reversing the present deterioration of housing and the collapse of viable urban development is for governments to redirect their relatively scarce resources away from the conventional, and now discredited, closed housing projects and into the development of open housing service systems.

Summary and Conclusion

To conclude the thoughts presented and to preface the work that must follow if the main points are accepted, we must return to the problem of standards stated at the beginning of this paper and reexamine it in the light of the issues raised.

Conventional minimum standards for housing were accused of

worsening rather than improving material housing conditions—dramatically so in economies of scarcity. It was hypothesized that this counterproductive behavior is a consequence of the conceptual error of understanding housing as a noun and of identifying values and objects instead of understanding housing as action and seeing values in the roles that procedures and products play in people's lives.

In the analysis of housing that followed, the reasons for the failure of conventional housing action—of programs and projects for the replacement of substandard dwellings—were shown to lie in the mismatches between people's needs and the housing supplied by institutions. The immense variability of individual household's needs and the inelasticity of low-income peoples' housing demands creates a difficult situation for any government; the satisfaction of housing needs by central institutions is an impossibility for governments with very small budgets and faced with rapidly growing masses of people with very low incomes.

As housing action depends on the actors' will and as the dominant actors in economies of scarcity are the people themselves, they must be free to make the decisions which most concern them. In order to make the best use of scarce housing resources, most of which are in any case possessed by the people themselves, each household must have an adequate choice of alternative locations, of alternative forms of tenure and, of course, of alternative structures and ways of building and using them. People who do not have these freedoms in housing are generally unable to use housing as a vehicle for their existential ends. If they cannot hope to get the combination they need, they will tend to minimize their housing action by doing and paying as little as possible.

While hierarchically organized or authoritarian corporations and bureaucracies cannot respond to the true heterogeneity of low-income housing demands, a network of discrete services can. This network needs and uses both institutions and standards, but in nonauthoritarian ways. By separating the legislative function of rule-making and the provision of social and economic services from the free use of those rules and services, or the executive function of game playing, it is entirely possible to ensure that things made, and the ways in which they are made, are of value to their users. Where social institutions guarantee the availability of the essential elements or pieces and order the ways in which each one may be used in relation to the others, then, like chess players, every game we play can be unique and will in any case be precisely adapted to our own capabilities.

I have used the game of chess as an analogy for the housing system. The game cannot be played without rules and without the authority that drew them up in the first place. In a game or activity as complex as housing, it is inconceivable that a set of rules as perfect as those of chess should ever be achieved. The authorized institutions must be constantly active, therefore, adjusting the rules to previously misunderstood conditions and to new conditions that arise with ever-changing circumstances.

Housing standards are no more the measures of housing values than the standard moves of chess pieces are the measure of a game. Both are indicators or descriptors of what takes place, and the informed observer can read them and know the quality of performance just as the engineer who reads the dials on the control panel of his machine. One measure or indicating needle may tell us nothing on its own. Similarly, we must know how much money the inhabitant of a slum has, what his expectations are, and what his alternatives are, before we can be sure that the slum, alleged or actual, is doing him more harm than good.

The problem which drew our attention to the issues and questions discussed in this paper is that standards have not worked at all well for most people in the contemporary world, whose average incomes or levels of material consumption are about one-twentieth that of most who will read this paper. It is obvious that we do not understand the games we are trying to regulate with the rules we institute.

In my own view there are two things we must do now: we must give up the futile or destructive attempt to impose our own will and we must support those who are fighting to regain the authority our executive institutions and corporations have usurped.

8

HANS H. HARMS

User and Community Involvement in Housing and Its Effect on Professionalism

THE VERY COMPLICATED PROBLEM of satisfactorily housing people on a national scale has not been solved in most countries of the world. And in the case of the United States today, it is clear that the solution requires a national commitment far beyond the one now being made, along with a change in our producer-oriented and supply-dominated housing systems.

As shown in "The Housing Problem for Low-Income People" (Chapter 4), the present housing production and delivery system, with all its various government supports, does not provide the housing services needed by low- and lower-middle income people. Their choices in urban areas are increasingly confined to deteriotated older stock or to subsidized new construction, which is often unsatisfactory in terms of design, location, and construction.

Problems of insufficiency and inadequacy are immanent in the present housing supply structure, which is oriented toward the supply side and the construction of units according to procedures set by industry and government, and which subsidizes industry, professional "facilitating beneficiaries,"[1] and the rich in order to

[1] See Chapter 3, p. 67.

provide housing for the poor. Direct subsidies go to commercial financing institutions, land developers, and construction companies, while subsidized fees go to legal, architectural, and management firms. Direct benefits go through tax shelter to rich investors in the over-50 percent tax bracket. (For example, a person in a $50,000-a-year income range can invest in a project under Section 236 and regain his investment three to four times over in five years.)

Larry M. Lefkowitz, Director of Public Affairs for the Nonprofit Housing Center in Washington, claims that this process pushes the cost of the subsidized units to nine times what it would be if the federal funds were going directly to low-income people. Officials at HUD dispute that figure, but concede that the cost is probably double.

An alternative to the present product- and producer-oriented subsidy system would be a system oriented toward people, toward the development of human resources rather than capital and corporate resources, and toward the development of service procedures that can be controlled by the people who need to be housed.

Direct subsidies to users in combination with a network of decentralized services could increase the autonomy of low-income families without setting up complicated mechanisms to regulate the lives of the poor or the process by which housing for the poor is created.

We need service and training programs to set up developmental learning situations, to increase existing capacities in people, and to stimulate capacities that are dormant or suppressed. For interest groups on the supply side, housing is an investment channel and a consumption product. For most people on the demand side, housing constitutes a basic human need for shelter, for privacy, and for a personalized place to raise a family and meet with friends. The present housing system in the context of bureaucratically regulated federal programs treats low-income dwellers as depersonalized and manipulated objects rather than as self-actualizing subjects.

As class and racial lines have been more sharply drawn, and as poverty and dependency seem more and more the permanent lot of certain portions of our population, those population groups, especially blacks and other minorities, have begun to develop a group self-consciousness and to react against degrading slum conditions, or equally degrading and unsatisfactory public housing conditions. As the Kerner Commission Report pointed out, the housing situation was a major contributing factor to the urban riots of a few years ago, and it continues to be the cause for rent strikes and other protest activities.

Practically speaking, how can low-income users win greater influence and control—particularly in the area of housing?

A necessary *first* step is through greater self-awareness and an awareness of how the social and economic system works to the disadvantage of those who are on the wrong side of the racial or income tracks. This first step is already being taken. Out of the ranks of poor blacks and other underprivileged groups have begun to emerge leaders who have developed a sense of how the producer-oriented process works, and who can articulate their experience and understanding to their fellow poor.

This is true for the lower-middle class as well as for the lower class. Blue-collar communities, which would have fatalistically allowed their neighborhoods to be dismembered by highways a few years ago, have become vehement opponents of such programs. And while poor blacks and lower-middle class whites are still anything but allies, their mutually growing consciousness of victimization offers some hope that they will, in time, begin to perceive a common interest in housing as well as in education and job opportunities.

Another way that people, particularly low-income people, can put pressure on the system is through organization, both at the local and national level. The National Tenant Organization and the National Welfare Rights Organization are examples of a move to gain power through this traditional and potentially very effective strategy. Both groups, though still quite new on the scene, have become visible in a political sense, and their influence will be significantly enhanced if a merger presently under discussion goes through.

Their common objective is to create a powerful housing movement in this country. As Jesse Gray, Director of the National Tenant Organization, has said, "Tenants are not only concerned about rents, but also with the whole range of housing services, and with the election of a pro-tenant government."[2]

A third way, supplementary to the others, would be the cooperation of professionals, committed to social change, with low-income people.

As an example of this type of cooperation, I will discuss a project being carried out with the help of the Community Projects Laboratory (CPL), an organization of the School of Architecture and Planning at M.I.T.

A group of architecture and planning students was introduced in the fall of 1968 to some of the concerned tenants of the Newcastle Court and Saranac buildings in the South End of Boston.[3] The two apartment buildings, both of which were threatened with demolition, housed more than one hundred low-income families in small and medium-sized apartments. The two buildings were structurally sound and had a significant potential for the development of good quality low-income housing. The rent levels were adequately low ($50–$75 per month), and represented about one-quarter or less of the tenants' incomes.

The South End is a mixed community, as is the population of these buildings, though the residents are predominantly black. The tenants, who form a stable community, definitely want to stay in the buildings and for good reasons: the rents are modest, the location is near public transportation and services, and some of the residents have lived in the buildings for over thirty years. There are also cases of two or three generations of the same family living in several apartments in the same buildings.

Despite the need for low-income housing in the Boston area,

[2] *The New York Times,* November 7, 1971, p. 33.

[3] David Judelson, et al., "Tenant Cooperative Housing Rehabilitation" (Cambridge, Mass.: M.I.T. Community Projects Lab, May 1970). David Judelson, then an architecture student, was the driving force behind this project. He worked with the tenant group from the beginning in 1968 and he is still working with them, now as a research associate in the Urban Systems laboratory.

the Boston Redevelopment Authority (BRA) intended to raze these and all other buildings in a four-block area, including many other apartment buildings.

A squatter demonstration organized by a coalition of community groups set the stage for action at Saranac-Newcastle Court. It occurred in April of 1968 and marked the first coalition protest against the decision-making process of the Boston Redevelopment Authority. The group, known as CAUSE, occupied a large empty site which had been converted into a parking lot after the typical four-story row houses had been torn down.

Low-income local people—blacks, Puerto Ricans, and whites—along with some people from MIT—built a tent city on the lot to protest the continued demolition of homes in the area. The police tried to evict the protesters on the first morning of the occupation on the ground that they were preventing cars from using the lot. Yet more than a hundred people came back with more tents, beds, and scrap materials to build provisional shelter. Bandstands were improvised, there was music and food, and people erected their own "city hall."

Tent City lasted for less than a week; but it was well covered by the media, and many outsiders came to look at it. In a very public way, therefore, the BRA found itself confronted with demands to stop the destruction of housing in the South End and immediately to start housing low-income people.

The result of this direct action and the coverage it received was that the BRA conceded a right of veto over its plans to the people of the South End and promised to hold elections to choose a committee which could represent the residents of the area.

Nevertheless, the BRA and the city administration stalled, so that when elections had still not been held after a year, a number of community groups called their own election and chose the "People's Elected Urban Renewal Committee" (PEURC). Although the BRA refused to sanction the election, it found itself once again on the defensive and soon after called the election it had promised two years before.

The results of this election, conducted under City Council and BRA control, produced the "South End Project Area Committee"

(SEPAC). And in fact, SEPAC was largely made up of home-owners and immigrant suburbanites bent on restoring old town houses, while PEURC consisted mainly of poor black, Puerto Rican, and white renters.

The veto and advisory power the BRA had promised went, of course, to SEPAC, but PEURC had shown a sufficient following and had generated sufficient political power so that no plans could be made against their determined opposition.

The Tent City episode had provided an opportunity for students and others from several universities to work together with low-income people. It led to further cooperation between the two groups. One major instance has been the Saranac-Newcastle Court project described below.

The South End Urban Renewal Plan of 1962 (approved 1965) showed an elementary school and a junior high school scheduled in the area; however, no planning of these facilities had been started by the fall of 1968.

Most community groups, including those particularly interested in education, were in favor of preserving the apartment buildings. In order to save Newcastle Court and the Saranac buildings from demolition, the South End Urban Renewal Plan had to be amended. According to the Plan, there were approximately 200 families living on the four-block site who would have to be relocated.

Meanwhile, diagonally across from the site lay vacant land surrounded by a sea of asphalt and a few empty brick row houses. For this nearly clear site, 225 new housing units were planned. Although there was a rationale for locating the school adjacent to an existing playground, tearing down 200 low-income housing units on one site for a school and then "replacing" those units across the street with moderate-income units could hardly have been considered rational in light of the existing housing shortage, but this has been unfortunately typical of the whole South End Project.

Major decisions were made by the following government agencies: the BRA, the Boston School Department, the Public Facilities Department, and the State Board of Education. Low-income community organizations were neither consulted nor involved in any way.

When the students and the CPL took on the project of working with the tenants, a conflict with the 1962 Urban Renewal Plan complicated the situation very much. However, the process which was developed to resolve this conflict, as well as the still not implemented solution for a low-income housing problem which it produced, might well have broad applicability. If it is successful, the project will have demonstrated a means whereby a residential community, on its own initiative, can overcome physical and institutional roadblocks in order to satisfy its housing needs. Furthermore, the process will test the degree to which a resident community is capable of developing its potential to deal with problems of this nature, and the form and amount of technical assistance needed.

In close cooperation with the tenants and their leaders, a generalized approach to rehabilitation and tenant control was developed which may provide a feasible alternative to the present, inadequate approaches.

The involvement of the Saranac and Newcastle Court residents began with a series of informal meetings which included the technical advisory group, a few tenants, and two VISTA community organizers. At that time the strategy for initiating a tenants' association was developed. The initial issue was the immediate maintenance problems in the buildings. After some results were achieved the emphasis of the group shifted to the problem of saving the buildings from demolition.

Early in May 1969 the tenants formalized their organization under the title of the Columbus Avenue Tenants' Association (CATA), elected officers, and adopted a set of bylaws. The bylaws contained the agreed-upon objectives of CATA, along with strategies for their implementation. These were:

1. *To prevent the demolition* (scheduled for 1970) of the Newcastle Court and Saranac buildings; in other words, to change the BRA Urban Renewal Plan. This goal was essential to the realization of the other two objectives. The strategy used was intended to demonstrate to the appropriate city and state officials and to the

community that the planned school could be satisfactorily accommodated on the site or built on an adjacent site, without requiring the demolition of Newcastle Court and Saranac. Five alternative plans were developed by the technical assistance group.

2. *To rehabilitate the buildings at a cost the present tenants could afford,* without a major program of temporary relocation. Rehabilitation is necessary from two points of view: (a) the BRA requires rehabilitation if the buildings are to remain, and (b) the present condition and layout of the apartments is inadequate from the tenants' standpoint; e.g., the apartments in Saranac have the equivalent of only one-and-a-half bedrooms where it is easily possible to convert them to three-bedroom units; many of the apartments in Newcastle Court have no real kitchens, etc. The rehabilitation strategy involves working in close cooperation with the tenants, planning new layouts for the apartments and their surroundings, and putting together a development "package."

3. *To gain some significant measures of control through ownership of the buildings by the present tenants.* This is seen as a relevant mechanism for a continuing process of community development, which will allow leadership to emerge and assume new responsibilities, enabling people, previously politically weak, to make meaningful decisions concerning their own lives, and to give them new opportunities for choice through the accumulation of capital.

The object of the process of tenant organization and community development is twofold. The first goal is to stimulate a discussion of common problems that will lead to a commitment to common purposes. The second goal is to actively involve the tenants in the technical processes necessary to achieve their objectives. In this way both competence and confidence will be developed in organizational operation, fiscal management, and political action, as well as in skills of housing development.[4]

[4] Attempts at an organization built around the future benefits of participating in a rehabilitation *cooperative* have been impeded by the lack of a working example of such a cooperative. The existence of a model would have greatly simplified the work of the combined technical assistance and tenant group.

Rehabilitation plans and specifications were developed through the joint efforts of the technical assistants and the tenants, specifically the executive committee of CATA, to try primarily to meet the needs of the present tenants in terms of size, layout, and quality of accommodations. Major additional considerations were to satisfy the needs of future tenants, to meet FHA standards and Boston building codes, and to work economically within the constraints of the buildings themselves.

Many families are too numerous for the apartments they now occupy and desire larger accommodations, while many of the smaller families living in large apartments wish to remain there. Some residents prefer one design solution over another—a plan with a better view or orientation instead of one with a more efficient layout, for instance.

The only way to resolve these sometimes conflicting demands is to work closely with the residents, exploring the available options through discussions. We also use a particularly flexible tool—a fairly realistic, large-scale (¾″ = 1′-0″) three-dimensional model, which can be manipulated both by tenants and professionals. Room sizes, room and furniture layouts, the relationships among apartments, cost considerations (such as backing kitchens and bathrooms to utilize the same plumbing stack) are easily visualized. In the model the structural walls are fixed, and all partitions are movable. The floor is gridded with a scale 1 foot square grid so that room area can be quickly determined. A plan of the existing layout is superimposed on the floor so that existing features can be located and orientations retained. The nonstructural walls between apartments can be moved, but the size and arrangement of both apartments must be considered together since the model is of one piece, i.e., the layout of one apartment cannot be optimized at the expense of the adjacent one.

In accordance with the needs of the tenants, the process of rehabilitation must be done at low cost and without long periods of temporary relocation. Rehabilitation will be phased in such a way that a majority of the tenants will always be living in the buildings. This will minimize the monetary and social costs of relocation and will assure that the tenants will be able to remain.

The initial plan was to begin rehabilitation on a group of between nine and sixteen apartments. The work would have taken about three or four months. About a month and a half after the first section, a second section would have been started on a similar sized group, and so on. Thus, there would have been seven or eight groups, each taking about three or four months to complete and each overlapping another group, and so on. In this fashion the rehabilitation would have taken about a year to complete, and at no time would more than 30 percent of the units have been under construction and unoccupied.

The tenants expressed a desire to go through this process, even with the nuisance of construction proceeding close by. Yet from the point of view of construction, this elaborate process would have been too costly; therefore, the presently planned process shows only two phases.

There are several approaches to creating a housing cooperative with mortgage insurance, yet none of them proved to be adequate for a situation in which low-income tenants want to join together without capital of their own. However, one of the alternatives was considered very carefully in light of the then new Federal Income Tax Law of 1969 as it relates to low-income rehabilitated housing. Under the law, the entire investment in rehabilitation can be depreciated on a straight-line basis over a period of five years. The very great benefits of this tax shelter provision to high-income investors makes them willing to pay the initial costs and more. Thus it was that the technical assistance group found a way to share the benefits of the tax shelter provision, which normally go to high-income investors, with the tenant group.

The project is now organized for at least the first five years as an ordinary rental project with Section 236 financing. The owning entity is a limited partnership with the developer (in this case the tenant group) as a general partner. The limited partners (investors) are furnishing the equity money needed. The tenants of the buildings lease apartments from the owning entity, which they control. Since CATA controls business management, and sales, it effectively holds an option to buy the property (presumably at the end of five years of operation).

The organizational procedure for this limited-dividend partnership works as follows: the tenants' association becomes the tentatively designated developer for the project, i.e., obtains control of the properties; an equity sales prospectus is prepared to attract high-income investors who are entitled to returns primarily in the form of tax shelter in exchange for the purchase of equity shares. These investors buy into the limited-dividend partnership as limited partners.

The investors take full depreciation benefits in the form of tax shelter and, additionally, a percentage of the cash flow (surplus) limited by FHA to a maximum of 6 percent per year of 10 percent of development costs or 11 percent of the mortgage.

By now the Tenants Association, together with a larger community organization, has become "designated developers" by the BRA to rehabilitate the 105-unit apartment buildings.

In the summer of 1971, the working drawings were developed by architectural students paid through university "work-study" financing (a federal program) in the office of a local architect. In the meantime Section 236 financing has been obtained and commitments for equity funds from limited partners-investors have been made. In addition to the development funds generated by the sharing of benefits, aids such as job training, day care, and other community facilities will be incorporated, and possibly seed money for a second housing rehabilitation project controlled by an affiliated community group in the area.

The rehabilitation process will begin in 1972, and, hopefully, by the beginning of 1973, the people of Saranac-Newcastle Court will be in their newly rehabilitated, self-developed, and self-managed housing.

In this project the combined efforts of a tenant group with a technical assistance group worked out a method by which the autonomy of low-income people has been increased and by which a network of other professional resources has been tapped, under the control, and to the benefit of, the tenants. In addition, government programs and tax shelter provisions have been used in an innovative way, diverting the benefits from the developers to the low-income tenants as far as possible.

This experiment points to questions concerning traditional and new roles for professionals and their work relations with different types of clients. New work relationships between architect-planners and community groups are sometimes called advocacy planning or technical assistance–sometimes counterplanning–against city halls, planning agencies, highway planners, and speculative real estate developers.

We have to clarify some concepts and the social conditions under which this kind of work started in the U.S.

At the time when urban renewal and massive highway building through central cities was in full swing, it became clear that some people had to suffer disproportionately and pay the high price of losing their homes and neighborhoods for projects planned by various government agencies, along with their real estate, developer, and contractor allies interest for the so-called public or common good.

Urban renewal turned out to be good for some at a very high price to others. The Boston West End, described by Herbert Gans in *The Urban Villagers,* is a classic example. Critics like Gans and Jane Jacobs began to point out that areas labelled "blighted" or "decayed" by the official planners were in reality vital human communities.

At least some professionals began to perceive that a highly political and economic process was being disguised as technical decision-making, based on the officially proclaimed public need to upgrade the cities through improved transportation and modernized urban environments. But a fact which emerged from the federal highway program was that it facilitated communication between white middle-class suburbs and office jobs in downtown areas without doing anything at all for the poor and lower-middle classes in the cities except to destroy their homes and obliterate their neighborhoods.

Inherently the urban renewal system works according to the economic principle: least costs for city power groups and highest profits to private enterprise at the expense of those who have least power and who are seen as "undesirables."

Some architects and planners learned from the experience and began to step out of their collaborator role. They decided they did not want to work in a system which increased inequalities and forced the poor and lower-middle class to pay for the greater convenience and wealth of the middle and upper classes. As a result, they joined protesting groups threatened by highways and slum-clearance programs in order to resist government agencies or to prepare alternative proposals.

These renegade professionals acquired the name of "advocates." The term "advocate," which became current in the late 1950s, was coined by Paul Davidoff, a planner and lawyer. It was based on a pluralistic concept of planning in which different interest groups worked to produce alternative plans for the development of an area of the city. The official plans were for one group of interests—for the "haves." The advocate planners worked for the interest of the "have-nots."

The term is not ideal because it is derived from the legal profession and assumes that a professional presents the case of his non-professional clients to other professionals. But unlike the legal situation, the final arbiter is not the judge, the jury, or the law, but the political and administrative system of the community and the political power context.

Another problem with the term is that it has a certain caretaker implication—the advocate is another professional who knows what is good for the poor. With the increasing militancy and self-awareness of poor black and white groups on the local level, external or internal caretakers are not wanted.

This brings us to the problem of how a planner or an architect can work with local groups or with the disenfranchised. There are two broad alternatives. The professional can work:

A. *Directly with* local groups (*user clients*)—
—where he has the responsibility to let the community define the problem. He has to be prepared to learn a new lan-

guage and to accept human urgencies instead of design problems;

—where he has to articulate alternative routes to solve problems and deal with their impact on the poor within the frame of reference of the community, such as its life style and special needs as articulated and experienced by the community). Alternative programs have to be worked out which indicate a cost-benefit relation in favor of the poor. (An example is the above-described Saranac–Newcastle Court Project.)

B. *Indirectly as a professional advocate*—(advocacy with a *constituency* means interpretation of what the poor perceive to be in their own interests)

—outside the community in legislation or as a writer;

—inside government agencies or private industry as an "underground" professional, providing information to those advocates directly working with local groups or changing institutions from within;

—in universities or research organizations to clarify theoretically new roles and skills needed, and to develop in context with emerging practices new institutional settings for greater social justice.

The two roles can be and often are mutually supportive.

If the architect-planner decides to work directly with low-income groups, the professional-to-client relationship is different from the usual work relation with sponsor-clients. The traditional clients of architects and planners in the field of housing are sponsor-clients, rather than user-clients (except in custom-designed housing). Sponsors may be private or public institutions, industry, corporations, or government agencies; in other words, anonymous organizations. The planner works either with them, as a member of the organization, or for them, as their hired consultant.

The interests of the sponsors of housing are different from the interests of the users (unless the sponsor consists of community or tenant groups as in the Saranac–Newcastle Court example).

The sponsors may have social and/or financial interests (in order to make a profit or to secure their investment against risk). The users of housing, on the other hand, are interested in low rents, adequate maintenance, and good environmental quality. Both the interests of the sponsors and those of the users may be partially or totally in conflict. And in this conflict, the planners and architects have typically been allied with the sponsors.

The obvious explanation for this is that the planners and architects have been paid by sponsor clients. But this is not the only explanation. While they are anonymous in themselves, sponsor clients are made up of, and are represented by, middle- and upper-class people. Typical among them are high level civil servants and government appointees, influential entrepreneurs, university financial officers, members of church boards, and, of course, a host of lawyers.

The planner or architect, similarly, is of the middle or upper class, or has become so through his professional training and practice. When he deals with the representatives of sponsor clients, he is dealing with men and women of his own class who share his background, language, and values. The working relationship is one among professionals. Each has his special area of expertise (the architect, design; the financial officer, cost considerations; the lawyer, taxes and other legal and administrative complexities); yet all of them have in common the values and perceptions of the business culture, and they approach one another with a mutual respect for one another's credentials in their various professional fields.

The work they carry forward together, furthermore, is based on contractual arrangements, which represent a parity of bargaining power and a general consensus of interests. When they enter into binding agreements, they do so mostly on the presumption that, in the plurality of parties, all are legally and socially competent, are "rational" in the pursuit of their self-interest and in terms of what can be supplied, and will, in all cases, act by the implicit rules of the class and professional game.

It is no accident that the ultimate users of housing have been left out of this description of a working relationship between professionals because in the traditional setting the users do not participate. When their interests are represented at all, they are represented by one or more of the professional parties mentioned. Whether the housing in question is being designed for poor blacks or equally poor elderly whites, these people will not appear in the offices where their housing destinies are being decided. In terms of harmonious working relationships between architect and financial officer, or architect and tax lawyer, or planner and city zoning representative, low-income clients are, typically, bound to be viewed as the intrusion of an alien element.

Why?

First of all because they may press for facilities the professionals have agreed are impossible to provide. And even though, in the case of a profit-making venture, "impossible" may be a relative term, the team architect, because of his class and professional sympathies, and the source of his fee, will usually not intervene.

A second reason is that low-income users do not speak the language the architect and the sponsor representatives share. Users may have trouble expressing themselves in the professional jargon; they may express themselves in emotional terms related on a gut level to their experience, which is embarrassing to professionals and bureaucrats who have been trained to work in a climate supposedly free of emotions and of urgent expressions of need.

And a third reason is that many professionals cannot help assuming that low-income users are, in some sense, inferior to themselves. The professionals' relative affluence, social status, and sense of power seems to suggest to them that they must have some human qualities which have been denied to those for whom they are making critical life decisions. This sense of an innate difference between themselves and their ultimate clients projects them into the role of custodians looking after social orphans and incompetents who, presumably, could not be expected to speak responsibly on their own behalf.

To the difference in class, life style, and past experience is added the difference between professionals and nonprofessionals. This difference opens up a host of questions about the nature of professionalism, its self-conception, and its relationship to nonprofessional people.

Professional authority, based on credentials and expertise, is not automatically accepted by low-income users who have experienced institutionalized expertise as an oppressive, dominating force in their lives. Another most important difference is the legal and contractual relationship. Often the architect or planner is hired by some outside agency to serve minority groups, or he offers himself voluntarily to serve ghetto or low-income groups, without having a contractual relationship with them. This puts the professional into a paternal position where he can withdraw his services without legal consequences to himself, whereas the low-income community has no contract to monitor his services and cannot dismiss him in the event that his services are inadequate. Even worse, if the community wants to terminate cooperation for what it considers inadequate services, the threat exists that the work done and funds allocated by an outside agency will be lost.

The community-professional relationship is typically paternalistic, with the community in the inferior position, a position of "love it or leave it," whatever the "service" is, and the professional in the superior position, able to withdraw at his whim.

New professional-community relationships need to be built on something other than paternalism and elitist professionalisms, which have nothing but negative meaning and effect on users. The architect or planner has to earn the trust of the people he works with, and he has to be trusted to work *with* them, rather than *for* them. Mutual trust relationships have to be built on the basis of legally binding, contractual relations, on mutual appreciation, on mutual loyalties, and on mutual goals toward social change, with the understanding that both have to give and learn. The professional has to understand that he is a servant in a learning situation. Experts who have all the answers, and who insist on implementing them, cannot work in this relationship. The difference is that of authoritarian dominance and egalitarian cooperation, or that of oppression and liberation.

The new work relations require the development of a new self-conception on the part of the professional, since the traditional concept of professional autonomy is in question. Professions traditionally have defined themselves as occupations based on a unique, specialized, more-or-less scientific body of knowledge, and a societally sanctioned privilege of autonomy in the performance of their work. Another characteristic emphasized in all ethical statements of professional associations is an orientation toward service to society. Yet the issue of service to whom is not clear. These core features are interrelated; autonomy in work performance is granted by public acceptance of the professions' twin claims to expertise and altruism.

The autonomy or the power to determine what is best for the client depends on (or should depend on) the consent of the client. Most professionals work with sponsor-clients who have different problems and interests than user-clients. If the professional solves problems for powerful and financially strong sponsors, he may create greater problems for user-clients or low-income and minority groups. In this case the question of service to society is unbalanced in favor of stronger groups at the expense of weaker ones. If the disadvantaged groups do not consent and revolt against the professional's plans, then his autonomy and the political decision making context is challenged.

Marie Haug and Marion Sussman state:

> The idealized model of the professional is not now, if it ever was, isomorphic to reality. . . . Moreover professionals discovered that being other-oriented too much could be costly in relation to satisfaction of economic, status and power needs. Like others in competitive societies professionals have organized around a common interest in order to maintain and enlarge their privileged position in society.
>
> Furthermore, the meeting between professional and client now generally occurs in an organizational context which adds an entirely new dimension to the situation. The "free" professional with a private relationship to an individual in need of service is a vanishing breed. Given bureaucratic delivery systems for professional services, the client is faced not only with the authority of the professional as practitioner, but also as administrator, armed with the regulations and rules of the institutional setting."[5]

[5] Marie R. Haug and Marion B. Sussman, "Professional Autonomy and The Revolt of the Client" in *Social Problems,* vol. 17, no. 2 (Cleveland, Ohio: Case Western Reserve University, Fall 1971), p. 154.

This brings us to a point where a distinction can be made between two models of basically opposed work relationships and decision-making procedures: the technocratic caretaker model and the cooperative development model.

A. *The technocratic caretaker model* is authoritarian, often centrally controlled, and for the most part hierarchically structured. The relationship between professionals and their nonprofessional clients, particularly when the latter are low-income people, tends to be determined by this model, the more so if the professional is working in bureaucratic delivery systems such as planning agencies or private corporations. The professional will typically dominate his laymen clients with his credentials, his expertise, and the implied political and corporate power which stands behind him. Yet, we find more and more that with increased centralization and specialization, the professional is a captive of his tools, techniques, and jargon. *He defines the problems and orders solutions according to the techniques he has mastered, with minimal reference or no reference to those who are directly affected.*

B. An alternative can be described as the *cooperative developmental model* of work relations and decision-making. This model is based on mutual trust and radical democratic principles rather than on authority by status or credentials. To implement the model in architectural and community planning work, mutual trust has to be developed on the basis of legally binding contractual relations, on mutual loyalties and appreciations, and on mutual goals toward social change, with the understanding that both have to give and take.

Technocratic caretaker models are often built on centralized or coordinated activities of government agencies and business enterprises. Their goal, from the point of view of government and industry, is supposedly economic efficiency in the delivery of services or efficiency measured by political, bureaucratic, or corporate profit criteria, abstracted from the human context and devoid of personal responsibility. The methods are detached, impersonal, and the organizational forms are hierarchical and bureaucratic (see Turner, Chapter 7). Systematized and computerized information, which is closed to the public, flows toward the center, upwards, while decisions are made from the center, downwards. The model has a resemblance to military organizational forms and to fascist and authoritarian state organizations. It is often justified as an internal necessity in an increasingly technological and bureaucratized world.[6] Yet the questions remain: Who controls the technocratic and bureaucratic elites who command esoteric instruments for so-called value-free or unknown ends? What is the ultimate purpose of efficiency? Who benefits, and who has to pay?

Cooperative developmental models presume a decentralization of power and decision-making; also a cooperation between individual users and community groups in need of services with professionals or institutions capable of facilitating access to non-dominating outside resources, or of generating human and material resources within the community itself on the basis of local self-determination. The working methods in the context of local communities are personal, contractual, and based on democratic organizational forms which stimulate trust and the development of personal and group resources. The information flow is in an open network between equal units. *Decisions are made by those affected by them.* The goals are to decrease dependencies; to increase economic, social, and personal development and self-determination; to dismantle paternalistic and oppressive structures; to increase personal and community integrity; and to build democratic, developmental, liberating structures, based on the satisfaction of vital needs rather than on the maldistribution of basic goods and on the artificial creation of consumer wants.

The crisis situation in the professions and for many professionals has been brought to the attention of the general public by the revolts of unserved, underprivileged groups (both black and

[6] Hans H. Harms, "Towards a Theory of Democratic Administration." Unpublished paper, August 1967.

white), and by the rebellions of young professionals in their professional organizations. The Task Force on Social Responsibility within the American Institute of Architects was formed in 1969; Planners for Equal Opportunity constituted themselves at the annual meeting of the American Institute of Planners in 1967, and there are radical caucuses as well in the professional organizations of lawyers, doctors, sociologists, and economists. Last but not least, there are many socially concerned students in universities who want to do future professional work in a context of greater equality and social justice.

New professional roles are emerging in the field of social services directed to groups who have so far not been served or where services are provided in a totally inadequate way. The new roles are based on service to those in greatest need and on attitudes and values of cooperation and accountability to community groups and user clients, rather than on accountability to traditional employers and to peers in the profession. The aim is for greater self-determination and development of resources in disadvantaged client and community groups rather than for personal aggrandizement or professional advancement of the traditional kind.

The emerging institutional but not yet institutionalized settings for the new roles are nonprofit advocacy and service agencies in neighborhoods, i.e. neighborhood clinics; and for architects and planners, Community Design-Development Centers. The financial base of most of these enterprises is very shaky. Since user-clients are unable to pay the regular fees, some of the work is based on volunteerism (which is only possible as part-time professional work), or on the acceptance of extremely low payments or on funding other than client fees. Some foundations provide seed money for experimental programs, but this leads to the chronic problem of finding operating funds, and there is almost bound to be a discontinuity of work, even when experiments are going well.

Other more institutionalized settings, such as Legal Aid, funded by OEO, or certain special community service programs connected with Model Cities, or as adjuncts to other city agencies, may be financially more secure, but they are always open to political manipulation by the local or federal government, and staff or funds can easily be cut if conflicts of interests with more powerful groups arise.

Similar problems exist in university settings where community project-related learning and teaching programs, combined with a service provision for underprivileged groups, are always vulnerable to the charge of being nonacademic or politically controversial. At times of low university funding, they are often the first programs to be curtailed (e.g., Harvard Urban Field Service; Pittsburgh Carnegie Mellon Institute, Architectural Community Workshop; and recently M.I.T.'s Community Projects Laboratory).

Yet the American Collegiate Schools of Architecture do recognize the necessity for a new type of public service option in architectural curriculum development.[7] Their published guidelines (funded by HUD) strongly recommend community workshops and teaching programs which will heighten the social awareness and responsibility of architects. This official recognition of the necessity of university-community related programs is very important, since in the university, more than anywhere else, opportunity exists to coordinate three key elements: (1) action and service oriented projects with (2) mutual educational situations for students and community people with (3) identification of issues and problem areas for further research and development of theory.

The university context is also conducive to the development of new and innovative concepts of resource development (as shown by the Saranac–Newcastle Court experiment described at the beginning of this chapter), and to the exploration, development, and use of methods which allow a redistribution of benefits to community groups. The goal is to bring greater equity to the poor. In the case described, government programs were used for this redistribution, although they were not intended to be used in such a way. With the backing of a prestigious university, the

[7] American Collegiate Schools of Architecture, *Guidelines for a Public Service Option in Architectural Curricula*, May 1971.

leverage to get experimental projects of this kind off the ground is increased with relatively little risk to the university itself.

If there is to be a continuing development of new professional roles and skills to promote work *with* rather than *for* people and of new experimental institutional settings similar to the one described and others such as Community Development Corporations, which provide greater self-determination and development of human resources, then other financial bases have to be developed as well. One possibility at this time—economically, although not yet politically, feasible—would be a redistribution of favors from the wealthy and from the hardware supply side in the market to the poor and underprivileged through government support of a network of human services for those who need them most.

9

IAN DONALD TERNER

Technology and Autonomy[1]

MANY PEOPLE LOOK to industrialized or mass-manufactured housing systems as a way in which modern technology can serve unmet housing needs—especially of low-income families. Industrialization has led to immense increases in the production of almost all other material goods: clothing, vehicles, appliances, books, medicines, household wares, even food. Yet the one major area in which the demand for industrialization is still unsatisfied, even in high-income and highly developed countries, is the construction industry, especially in the production of houses.

It is difficult to think of any other field where a manufacturing "breakthrough" is so widely sought; industrialization schemes,

[1] Parts of this chapter have been adapted from Ian Donald Terner and John F. C. Turner, *Industrialized Housing: The Opportunity and the Problem in Developing Areas,* The Ideas and Methods Exchange (IME) Series, number 66, Department of Housing and Urban Development, Office of International Affairs (Washington, D.C.: U.S. Government Printing Office, July 1971). Distributed as Report Nr. PB206851 by the National Technical Information Service (NTIS), Department of Commerce, Springfield, Virginia, 22151.

ranging from Operation Breakthrough[2] in the U.S. to the importation of automated housing factories in the Third World nations, have virtually encircled the globe.

Nearly every society faces pressure to "do something" about improving the poor and at times inhuman housing conditions of some 20 to 30 percent of the world's population.[3] Furthermore, all indications are that this percentage continues to grow.[4]

An intense interest has been shown therefore in concepts of technology and industrialization as applied to housing. This chapter attempts to distinguish between the fashionable myths and platitudes which promise much but can deliver little, and the solid gains—including gains in dweller autonomy—which might in fact be attainable through industrialization and technological innovation. To this end, the chapter explores various strategies for industrializing and simplifying the construction process, and offers a tentative "innovations agenda," or a list of priority areas in which technological advances are most needed in order to increase dweller control of housing.

[2] Operation Breakthrough is a U.S. program, begun in May 1969, by the Department of Housing and Urban Development intended "to develop, test, and promote the best in technologically advanced systems for producing housing." See *Operation Breakthrough: Questions and Answers*, HUD-186-RT(2) (Washington, D.C.: U.S. Government Printing Office, March 1971); and *Housing Systems Proposals for Operation Breakthrough*, Department of Housing and Urban Development (Washington, D.C.: U.S. Government Printing Office, December 1970).

[3] United Nations, *Housing, Building, and Planning: Problems and Priorities in Human Settlements*, Report of the Secretary General (A/8037) (New York: August 21, 1970), p. 27 and pp. 52–54. The Report shows a 30 percent deficit for "Less Developed Areas" and a 21 percent deficit for the "World Total" in 1970. However, these widely used housing "deficit" figures are not generally of major value, since they are actually surrogates for poverty on the one hand, and functions of often arbitrary and inconsistent standards on the other. In Peru for example, in 1956, a government commission found that only 11 percent of the nation lived in "standard" or acceptable dwellings. Such an unrealistic figure not only loses its value as a policy instrument, but it also fails to discern the actual gap between supply and effective demand. In some areas, annual rents for urban dwellings have recently been found to exceed the full capital value of the housing unit itself—a much more important indicator of the failure of the market to respond to both actual need and ability to pay (see also Note 7).

[4] *Ibid.*

First, it is important to separate myth from reality in the area of industrialized housing systems. Failure to do so—particularly in developing areas, or in the industrialized nations in situations of poverty and scarcity—invites the danger that beleaguered housing officials will continue to build or import large, sophisticated, and costly manufacturing plants which have consistently failed to solve the problems of acute housing scarcities. Pursuit of the myth that industrially mass-produced housing modules can significantly lower costs, and can somehow reduce the deficit in the world's supply of safe and decent dwelling accommodations, has, in many instances, led directly to the opposite result—to a worsening of housing conditions.

The following case[5] is offered in some detail as paradigmatic of one of the most common kinds of effort undertaken by both the private and public sectors when they attempt to apply technology and industrialization to housing. The case points out the multitude of risks inherent in the introduction of a fully industrialized, high technology program into a less-developed economy, and underscores the cost-escalating contingencies that characteristically beset such efforts. The case, set in Latin America in the late 1960s, involves a group of private investors acting in concert with their government's Ministries of Housing and of Economic Development.

After an optimistic feasibility study conducted by a European industrialized housing manufacturer, negotiations were concluded for the importation of a highly sophisticated plant, valued at approximately $1 million. For this investment, which required considerably more than $1 million worth of local currency at the official exchange rate, plus ongoing royalty payments based on volume of production, the investment consortium purchased a

[5] The events presented in this case actually occurred, and are reported by the author from confidential firsthand observations. However, a number of facts have been changed to conceal the identity of the individuals, the company, and the country involved, and to make the case read more easily and illustratively. (The primary activity of the company in this case was the manufacture of materials for construction components.)

patent license, production equipment, and ongoing technical services from the European franchiser.

The down-time dilemma. From the moment of the initial payment to the franchiser, the company began a frantic race against "down-time" or periods without production. Once initial payments were made, the costs of interest and loss of liquidity on the capital investment became strictly a function of time, regardless of output quantities. The investors had to try to maximize production to offset the high fixed financial costs that continued to accrue every minute of every day. A series of initial mistakes and bad luck, however, conspired to handicap severely the company's race against time.

Start-up delays. First, the construction of the plant dragged beyond its scheduled nine-month period to fourteen months. Bureaucratic snarls delayed import permits. Last-minute problems developed with the owner of the land where the plant was to be built; and, in general, pre-start-up tasks and expenses exceeded time and cost estimates by nearly 50 percent.

Finally, when the plant was ready to begin production, the technical assistance team from the European franchiser was engaged in the opening of a plant on another continent because of the scheduling difficulties caused by the company's five-month construction delay. Thus nearly a month passed before the team arrived and test production could actually begin. When they did arrive, they could speak almost no Spanish and were unable to establish good working relationships with the plant management and personnel.

By this time, the delays were beginning to cause other problems. The construction project, which was to utilize the first output of the plant, had been halted after foundations had been readied; and the contractor was angrily calling the plant each day demanding components. The original plan had been to produce for a period before shipping components out to an actual job in order to assure high quality and uniform output. However, in view of the impatience of the contractor, who by this time had threatened a lawsuit, the trial production plan was abandoned and early components were shipped out, even though adequate production controls had not yet been established. The initially poor quality harmed the reputation of the company at least as much as the delay, and to this day complaints are still received from the occupants of the first buildings about leaks and unsightly joints and cracks.

Management problems. Early in the process, the firm also began to develop serious management problems. In a move that is not atypical in developing nations, the investor-owners of the plant hired engineers to fill the company's three critical operating positions—general manager, plant manager, and sales-technical service manager. *None* had had previous corporate management experience, although the three were generally well educated, and appeared to be technically competent and ambitious. Only the plant manager worked out well, and he effectively (although hesitantly, since all the engineering decisions and assumptions had been made by Europeans) applied his technical knowledge to the relatively successful operation of the plant. Nonetheless, when he became injured on the job and was out of work for two months, the plant lapsed into chaos because the position of assistant plant manager had never been filled. This was partially due to an ill-considered economy move combined with the fact that a good candidate for the job had not been found.

The general manager, the chief operating officer of the company, proved to be a total failure. Frustrated that he was not functioning as an engineer, inept and unsuccessful in matters of business, and possibly dishonest (although this was never proven), his performance prompted the owners of the plant to begin the search for a replacement after only six months of operation. They could find no one in the country who was competent and available, and even interviewed several foreigners, all of whom demanded outrageous salaries, and none of whom seemed to be particularly suited for the job. After a year, the desperate owners considered promoting the successful plant manager, but then decided against it based on the fact that he had become too valuable at the plant. Finally, one of the younger and more daring of the banker-owners assumed the job of general manager himself. Although he personally disliked the change and knew nothing of the housing or manufacturing operations, he felt an obligation to try to save the investment. The original general manager was fired, and the overall management of the company immediately improved from disastrous to mediocre.

The sales and technical service manager also felt disoriented and estranged from his traditional engineering practices, and was unable to deliver the absolutely critical volume and continuity of work needed to keep the plant producing at maximum efficiency. As a classically trained engineer, he was aloof and reserved, and found it difficult to relate to conventional builders. His cost analysis techniques were amateurish, and although the new general manager tried to school him, the sales manager resented the effort, was slow to learn, and failed to convince conventional construction companies to try to utilize the system on their projects. The new general manager, using his former banking contacts and his upper-class family and social connections, actually accounted for most project sales. In addition, he also assumed almost all public relations and advertising responsibilities.

The sales manager fared only slightly better in his technical assistance role of trouble shooting various site and erection difficulties. The owners sought to replace him as well, but they were unable to recruit a better prospect, and he lingered on in his job. He soon became the only man in the company who advocated reduced prices, arguing that that was the only way to improve sales. With the company at this point losing $500 per day, there was obvious reluctance to follow his suggestion, and in fact, prices were steadily raised.

Expanded repair facilities. Unfortunately, other problems also beset the embattled company. Normally minor repairs caused long periods of down-time. Weeks, and occasionally months, were involved in ordering critical spare parts from Europe or the United States. The owners diverted quantities of their already seriously depleted working capital to invest in a complete machine and metalworking shop at the plant, so that parts could be fabricated on the spot without crippling delays. A large inventory of other parts was also ordered from Europe in advance.

A similar problem developed with regard to the company's

vehicles. Normal maintenance and repair services were unsatisfactory, and after several commercial garages in the metropolitan area failed to perform adequately, and lack of vehicles began to bottleneck production, the machine shop was expanded to include an automotive shop which could accommodate and service the company's vehicles as well.

Ironically, immediately after the expanded maintenance facilities became operational, and it seemed that nearly all repairs could be made "in-house," a small fire damaged a large and important conveyor belt, and a custom-made replacement had to be ordered from the U.S. For two months, the plant limped along until the new belt and a costly back-up belt arrived.

Public works deficiencies. Gradually, however, the company was becoming a self-sufficient "island," attempting at great and unanticipated cost to reproduce in miniature the supporting elements of the society around it—most of which were found to be unacceptable or unreliable. Unavoidably these costs added to the corporate overhead and were directly reflected in increased prices.

The plant even installed emergency electric generators in order to continue production during the all-too-frequent power failures in the area. The plant also considered, but finally rejected, a plan to build its own dike along a nearby river after heavy rains and subsequent flooding closed the plant and caused serious damage, necessitating major repairs.

Thus, it was impossible for the plant to completely divorce or insulate itself from its general social setting. Even as the company began to service its own trucks and cranes, it quickly realized that the ten-mile road leading to the plant was a key problem, filled as it was with ruts, potholes, and cracks in the pavement. Furthermore, the route was indirect and tortuously curved. The management petitioned the metropolitan government to build a new road (which had been promised before the plant opened, and which already appeared in the metropolitan master plan); however, no response came back.

Finally, after the owners of the plant appealed to their highly placed friends in government, it was agreed that the company would pay a "special assessment," so that the road could be repaved—although not realigned. After nine more months without action, the company officials—frustrated and angry—decided to pave the road themselves, only to find that if they did not wait for the municipality to do the job, the standards they would have to meet would be absurdly high. Faced with the ruin of their new imported fleet of trucks, the company paved the road itself, with the government partially compromising the paving standards after the payment of another "special assessment."

Labor problems. Labor troubles also plagued the new plant. The workers were not unionized; and because management wanted to preserve this situation, wages paid were slightly higher than prevailing rates, partially off-setting the labor-saving features of the plant. Also, productivity appeared to be quite low, and it was later learned from one of the workers that they deliberately decided to work slowly because it was rumored that sales were poor and they feared layoffs—particularly when a series of expected government housing tenders failed to materialize.

Strikes among dockworkers and other related industries also caused delays and stoppages at the plant as various suppliers failed to meet commitments.

New office. Other minor irritants caused a complex of unanticipated problems. For example, telephone service to the suburban location of the plant was so bad that it became impossible to conduct business there. Thus a suite of administrative offices was rented downtown, which facilitated many business transactions but also further added to the company's overhead. Also, control over the operation was slightly diluted, since the plant and the office were now separated by a 45-minute auto trip. The special radio hookup between the plant and the downtown office was only slightly better than the telephone service, and both required furious shouting in order to be heard.

Deficient franchise service. Poor technical service from the European franchiser, who never seemed to overcome the language barrier (communication finally took place in English, which was native to neither group) led to numerous, costly cables and transatlantic phone calls, all of which added to the financial burdens of the company.

Extremely high-priced consulting fees were then paid to an American company in an attempt to acquire the services which the European franchiser failed to deliver, but for which it nonetheless received production royalties. Further aggravating the situation was the fact that both consulting fees and royalties were payable only in U.S. dollars, which had to be purchased at inflated rates with local currency. At this point the plant was losing $1,000 per day.

Devaluation and collapse. When the nation's currency was devalued, slashing the worth of the meager remaining capital reserves, the company was finally bankrupt, psychologically devastated, and had to sell its assets at a tremendous loss. Up to this point, the owners had clung to the hope that if only they could overcome the initial start-up hurdles, the plant would prove to be economically viable and could produce more and higher quality houses at competitive prices, if not absolute savings.

It is impossible to ascribe this chronicle of failure solely to the fact that the society around the ill-fated housing plant was not industrialized; but many of the obstacles encountered do appear to be endemic to less developed areas, particularly the management, down-time, and currency problems.

The tragedy of the failure is perhaps mitigated by the fact that a private investor, who acknowledged beforehand the risks of the venture and gambled on making a profit, bore the brunt of the financial loss. The loss of large amounts of public funds, of the type which have been committed to similar government enterprises in other countries, at least was minimized here.

However, even in this case, the government, the society, and particularly those in greatest need of housing also suffered—albeit indirectly. The government, in granting tax concessions to the venture, lost the potential revenues that might have been generated by an alternative investment of similar magnitude. It also had to contend with the loss of extremely scarce foreign exchange capital which, along with forgone tax revenues, limited the service options that could be provided by the public sector.

The society also suffered. The rising expectations, generated by the publicity that surrounded the initial stages of the project, were disappointed. Valuable resources, including raw materials, labor, management, and investment capital, were consumed or diverted. Housing shortages were not only unrelieved, but were aggravated by the unproductive use of these potential inputs. And, finally, the bankrupt assets of the company were purchased by a consortium of foreign investors at a small fraction of their original cost, hence delivering another element of the country's productive capacity into the hands of individuals who were generally less responsive to the national interest than native citizens.

However, it is important not to obscure the underlying theme of the case, which is that normal, industrialized operating problems can often be exacerbated in developing areas when the necessary economic and social supports are not available. When this happens, the venture, whether publicly or privately owned, is apt to defeat itself and its goals of reduced housing costs. It must often attempt—at great cost and effort—to become self-sufficient and independent of its surroundings. To do so, it must re-create in miniature many of the supporting services which industrialized producers in developed areas regularly take for granted.

Although this case may appear to be extreme, it is not unique. As Charles Abrams has noted with some sarcasm, industrialized housing techniques have

> been tried by less-developed nations with small success and sometimes near-disaster. In Ghana in 1952 precast concrete walls were hauled from Holland across the seas to Accra's promontory, lowered to rocking canoes, and paddled precariously by intrepid natives over pitching breakers to the distant shore, where they were set up miles away to compose a few lonely monuments to the industrial age. In Beersheba, where Elijah once sought refuge from Jezebel's vengeance, a Tourneau-layer crane shaped tons of cement in a huge iron maw; the hardened slab was then carried by crane to the site, only to demonstrate its high costs and imperfections. In Karachi small aluminum prefabs were expanded by additions of adobe and discarded wood to compose the first prefabricated slums.
>
> In the less-developed world, where labor is cheap and plentiful and where standards and materials are simple, the precast house is

unessential and premature. Despite the glib sales talk of prefab peddlers from abroad, the handicraft product is still cheaper, more expandable, and more realistic.[6]

There are three problems inherent in not recognizing the pattern of these failures:

1. The dramatic gesture of providing a large new housing plant may divert attention from the need for fundamental housing policy changes and reforms, particularly when answers are vague to such questions as: who shall be housed? on what land? with what services and infrastructure? and with what forms of credit and financing?

2. The provision of fully industrialized plants, which is often justified on the basis of exaggerated promotional claims, may continue to waste vast amounts of scarce material and human resources, promising great efficiencies and economies while ignoring the need for support from the society-at-large.

3. The provision of highly automated, sophisticated, and costly industrialized housing equipment may divert attention from a series of relatively simple, inexpensive, and highly productive steps toward housing industrialization which could be accomplished without such investment and promise equal or greater housing gains. Furthermore, the provision of large plants may serve to decrease, rather than increase, the autonomy and ability of low-income dwellers to provide their own housing.

This latter point demands some clarification, since, for many, the theme of dweller autonomy, or self-reliance in the provision of housing, is regarded as extreme, unnecessary, and unworkable. However, the traditional action sectors of the society, i.e., the private-commercial and the public-governmental sectors, have a record of consistently inadequate performance in this area.

The actions of the private-commercial sector have not been effective because the poor lack the ability to purchase or to obtain financing for unsubsidized profit-based housing. In the case of the lowest income renters, the activities of the private sector are

[6] Charles Abrams, *The Language of Cities, A Glossary of Terms* (New York: The Viking Press, 1971), p. 243.

particularly notorious, ranging from the well-known "rent-gougers" in U.S. urban areas to the unregulated commercial exploiters from Nairobi to Mexico City who often receive exorbitant rents for extremely depressed units. At times the *annual* rental income exceeds the *full* capital value of these units.[7]

The record for the public-governmental sector, with certain important exceptions, is not much better. Governments have typically lacked both the resources and the political will to be effective providers of housing. Qualified exceptions are those countries, such as the Soviet Union, Sweden, and Israel, where decent housing for all is not considered to be an economic privilege, but rather a high ideological priority of the state.

In these countries, the *practical* need for greater autonomy (although not necessarily the *theoretical* needs advanced in Chapter 7 of this book) applies somewhat less. However in the vast majority of the world's nations, the argument for autonomy is a pragmatic necessity, arrived at by default from the gross inactions of the private and public sectors. In the poorer countries, the basic problem is often an extreme scarcity of resources; in the wealthier nations such as the U.S., the resources clearly exist, although the political will to devote them to adequate housing for the poor is weak.

Where, then, does one look for improvements in housing? As has been suggested earlier, a fundamental premise of this book is that an important answer to the question lies in the autonomous actions of owner-builders, owner-rehabilitators, and dweller- or squatter-builders. Yet, to date, the relationship between the autonomous actions of these groups and the emerging technology of industrialized home building has been remote and limited, and all too often counterproductive, as in the above case study. In fact, current trends of industrialization would seem to indicate that the areas of industrialized housing and autonomous housing are *di*verging rather than *con*verging.

By far the most important and pervasive industrialization attempts at present are based on a general strategy of replacing rel-

[7] John F. C. Turner in an unpublished lecture at CIDOC (Cuernavaca, Mexico: September 1971).

atively costly and uncontrolled on-site labor with more controlled and more capitally intensified labor in a factory setting. The strategy is based on the model of other manufacturing industries in countries like the U.S., where factory workers have increased their productivity more rapidly than construction workers, while at the same time remaining lower paid than those in the construction trades (see Figures 11 and 12). As wages increase in developing areas, the same pressure to minimize on-site construction labor becomes increasingly important there.

A recent study[8] of eleven partially industrialized construction

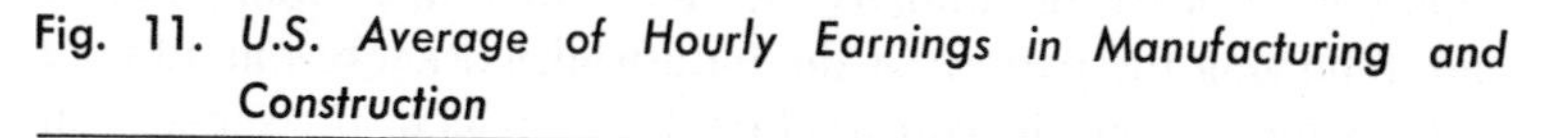

Fig. 11. *U.S. Average of Hourly Earnings in Manufacturing and Construction*

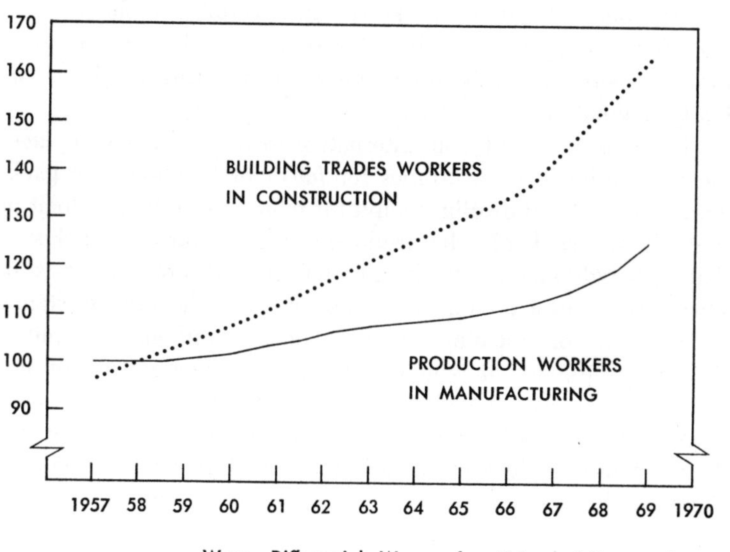

Wage Differential—Wages for U.S. building trades workers in construction, when compared with those of production workers in manufacturing, show an increasing tendency to be higher. (Wage index in constant dollars; 1957–59 equals 100.)

[8] Paul W. Strassmann, "Innovating and Employment in Building: The Experience of Peru," *The Oxford Economic Papers*, volume 22, July 1970,

innovations adopted in Peru indicates that all of them reduced total costs—mainly through on-site labor savings—despite the fact that eight of the eleven were simultaneously responsible for cost increases in materials. This is extremely significant, for although it might have been expected in the U.S. or Europe with their spiraling construction wages, it was less likely in Peru which is characterized by very low wages and chronic underemployment. Yet in eight out of eleven cases, net savings were realized even though materials costs rose, thus relying *exclusively* on labor cuts both to offset the materials increases, *and* to yield the net saving. Hence there is at least preliminary evidence that developing nations are following the pattern of the industrialized nations in attempting to reduce on-site construction labor—which, of course, runs directly counter to other stated goals, such as fuller employment.

Perhaps the epitome of the labor-saving trend is evidenced in the U.S. mobile home industry, where on-site work has been virtually eliminated.

This paper argues for an alternative to the continued replacement of onsite labor. It argues for *fewer* mobile-homelike packages, or completed dwellings, and for *more* on-site labor, albeit of a highly special kind. The argument is based on the conclusion that although factory production has indeed lowered costs in some cases (most notably of mobile homes) the process stands little chance of touching the lives of the millions of families throughout the world who are in most desperate need of improved dwellings. The alternative strategy proposed here may even hold promise for low-income families in the U.S., who for the moment must look exclusively to the mobile home as the *only* commercially available source of new low-cost housing.

---

pp. 244–259. The eleven innovations studied included: (1) vinyl tiles; (2) integral terrazzo; (3) metal ceiling forms; (4) prestressed ceiling beams; (5) tubular scaffolding; (6) metal wall forms; (7) prefabricated external panels; (8) sand-lime bricks; (9) lightweight, machine-made, clay bricks; (10) asbestos cement pipes; and (11) plastic P.V.C. pipes. Strassmann notes: "All eleven of the innovations here examined in detail reduced unit labour costs or the component in question between 20 and 90 percent, but usually by one-third . . . . On the other hand, only three of the innovations lowered material costs [vinyl tiles, cement-asbestos pipe, and plastic P.V.C. pipe], while eight increased them." P. 258.

Fig. 12. *U.S. Productivity in Manufacturing and Construction*

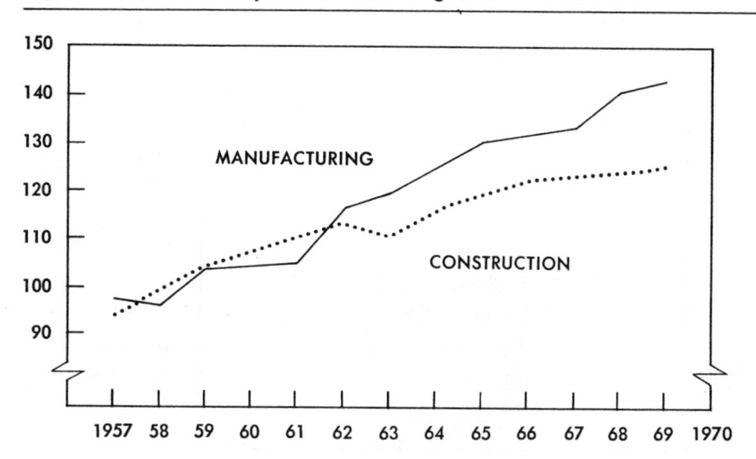

Productivity—From 1957 to 1962, productivity between construction and manufacturing workers was roughly comparable; however, from 1962 to the present, manufacturing productivity has increased more rapidly, despite lower wage levels. These trends are stimulating greater investment in the construction sector, and hence greater industrialization. (Productivity index in output per man-hour; 1957–59 equals 100). Source: Daniel Hodes[9]

An overall strategy for achieving these ends may be formulated by first distinguishing between *process* and *product*. As shown in Figure 13, the manufacturing *process* may be viewed as a continuum, ranging from hand-crafted to fully-industrialized techniques. In like manner, the technological output or *product* can be viewed as a continuum ranging from traditional to advanced. The schematic 9-cell table arbitrarily divides these continua into three segments each.

[9] Daniel A. Hodes, "The Modular Housing Industry," *Financial Analyst's Journal*, May–June 1970, p. 85, using the Manufacturing Index of the U.S. Bureau of Labor Statistics, and the Construction Index from the *Economics of the Construction Industry*, The Conference Board, 1969.

Fig. 13. ***Process and Product***

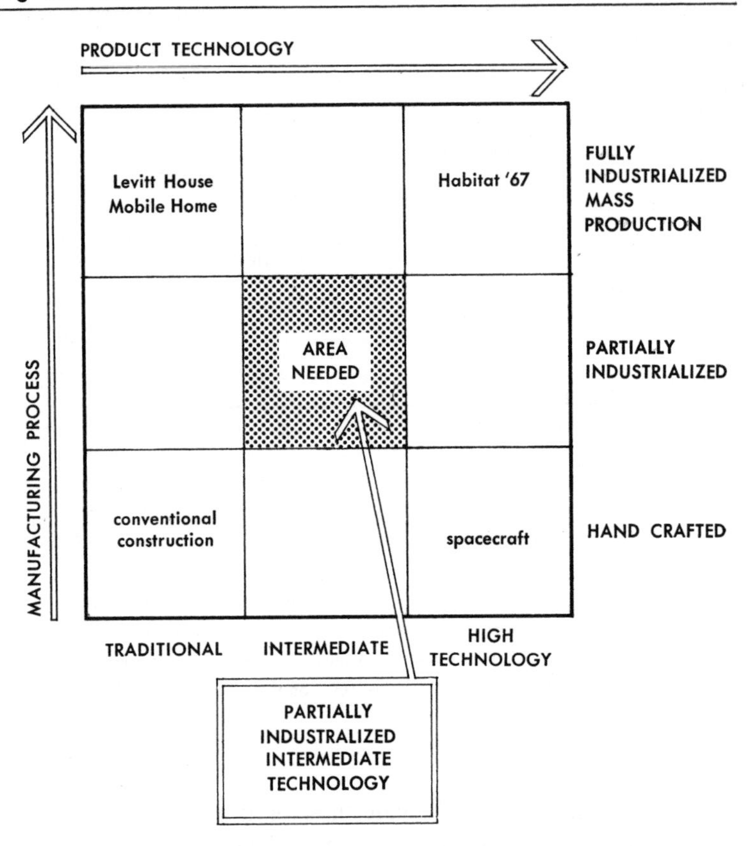

Target Area—In the schematic diagram above, the manufacturing process (vertical axis) has been divided into three production categories: hand crafted, partially industrialized, and fully industrialized. Similarly, product technology (the horizontal axis) has been divided into three parts: traditional, intermediate, and high technology. The center cell of the diagram indicates the product and process characteristics most needed in developing areas.[10]

[10] Source: Terner and Turner, *op. cit.*

In the first cell, the fully-industrialized yet traditional product may be typified by the famous mass-produced houses of William T. Levitt and Son, which were part of the U.S. response to its post-World War II housing shortage.

As a *product*, the house itself was extremely traditional, both in appearance and construction. The architecture was traditional American "Cape Cod," and the units utilized conventional, wood-stud, balloon-frame construction. Yet the construction *process* was highly industrialized. The final product was a standardized mass-produced item, even to the point of using assembly line techniques, although in the case of the Levitt houses, "the line," as it was known, involved moving workers, not products. The workers formed well-managed and highly organized teams which advanced from building to building with precise timing and coordination.

Skills were specialized as well, even to the point of subdividing traditional carpentry into many narrowly defined subtasks. Operations were concentrated; purchasing, construction, and marketing focused on entire town-sized projects—known as Levittowns—clustering together hundreds of houses.

Mechanization was perhaps the least-developed aspect of industrialization in the Levitt operation. The company's style of industrialized operations shunned the large, costly machine which stamps out heavy or complex components; instead it favored a myriad of smaller, power-driven hand tools to reduce and speed the large amount of routine hand labor.

In contrast to the highly industrialized yet traditional Levitt house, the last cell of the diagram describes a hand-crafted, high-technology product, epitomized perhaps by one of the most sophisticated types of dwelling yet produced—the spacecraft.

Since the demand for spacecraft is relatively slight, and spacecraft are constantly changing and evolving, mass-production techniques are almost totally irrelevant. Each craft is presently hand-built by master craftsmen and technicians.

The other cells in the diagram are representative of various mixes of process industrialization and product technology. The lower-left cell represents conventional construction methods producing traditional houses—typifying most residential construction in most countries of the world.

The upper-right cell represents both a high-technology product and a highly industrialized means of producing it. Habitat '67, the well-known industrialized housing exhibit at the 1967 Montreal World's Fair, is typical of this type of solution, as are some of the high-technology experiments in the current U.S. Operation Breakthrough Program, such as the filament-wound housing module and others.

This discussion posits that a reasonable and productive exploitation of modern science and technology designed to mitigate the housing problems of the poor should focus on the central cell of Figure 13—in the area of partially industrialized, intermediate technologies. To better define the characteristics of this cell, both the process and the product axes will be examined in greater detail.

Process—Toward Partial Industrialization

Industrialization may be viewed as a composite process. As noted in the example of the industrially produced Levitt house above, four aspects of the process are prominent: (1) systemization and standardization of products; (2) specialization of labor; (3) concentration of production and marketing; and (4) mechanization of production.

From the composite nature of industrialization, it follows that there can be different "degrees" or "types" of industrialization, depending upon which aspects are included and combined in any given scheme.

The primary thesis here is that certain of these combinations, which for our purposes can be labeled "partially industrialized technologies," can be immediately appropriate and useful, even in the economies of scarcity of the developing areas. This holds true both from the viewpoint of cost, *and* from the viewpoint of autonomy and freedom of action.

The concept of partial industrialization is based on a production strategy that selectively uses some aspects of industrialization while avoiding or postponing the use of others. It is specifically geared toward developing areas.

A combination of systems design and labor specialization is the foundation for a partial industrialization strategy because these two aspects incorporate the least risk of counter-productivity. The somewhat higher-risk aspect of concentrated, large-scale operations is then considered as a potential adjunct to the initial strategy; and finally, the highest-risk aspect of mechanization is considered (as used prematurely in the Latin American case), completing the cycle back to full industrialization.

SYSTEMS DESIGN AND LABOR SPECIALIZATION

Systems design, the first of the industrializing aspects considered here, is a broad and general term, but it directly involves the use of standardized components which interact with one another in a regularized and compatible fashion.

In developing areas of the world, systems design is clearly the most important and relevant single aspect of industrialization, since, as a design function, it depends on relatively little capital investment, no imported equipment or machinery, and virtually none of the institutionalized services and facilities that are often absent or unreliable in a less-developed economy. All that is required is a commitment of design time; and even if the higher-risk aspects of industrialization are not forthcoming or appropriate, the systems design process itself can yield significant benefits in the construction process. A case in point is the traditional and historic Japanese tatami house.[11] The tatami mat itself

[11] Bruce Martin, *Standards and Building* (London: RIBA Publications, Limited, 1971), p. 102. Martin notes:

> Possibly the most notable example in the history of building is the planning of Japanese houses on the bases of a standard double-square size of mat measuring approximately 900 mm x 1800 mm (approximately 36 in. x 72 in.) which is, in effect, a unit of area, and from which are derived the sizes and shapes of all rooms and the overall plan of the house. A similar method of planning was adopted in 1946 for the Hertfordshire County Council schools [England] when a standard plan unit 2515 mm (99 in.) square was chosen to determine the sizes and shapes of rooms and also to position the steel stanchions and the layout of beams. The method was further developed in 1950 with a plan unit 1016 mm (40 in.)

becomes the systemized component, and because it is standardized, the means of producing it become highly repetitive in nature. This may in turn encourage labor specialization, because the repetition involved in production often gives rise to a specialized expertise, which in turn may be reflected by increased production speed and quality. Historically the sustained repetition of fabricating a discrete component has also given rise to mechanization, since man has often invented ways to relieve his hands and mind of the endless monotony of highly repetitive work.

However, regardless of whether the design of standardized components ever leads to full and mechanized industrialization, the design serves as a crucial first step toward partial industrialization, and is particularly appropriate to less-developed regions, because little investment or risk is necessary for its execution. Furthermore, skill specialization, like the systems design aspect of industrialization, also requires relatively little investment or risk. Most of what little risk there is stems from the fact that once the number of employees and managers in an operation is expanded, with each performing a more narrowly defined and specialized task, then fixed costs, in terms of salary and a physical plant or facility to accommodate the workers, increase directly. Thus, unless production increases proportionally, unit costs will increase. The attraction of labor specialization, of course, is that production will increase *more* than proportionately, since it is likely that with more narrowly defined tasks, the repetitive na-

---

square, wall panels of a uniform thickness of 41 mm (1⅝ in.) and ceiling panels measuring 965 mm (38 in) square. . . .

The use of a standard unit of space in the design of buildings often recurs throughout the history of building, but it is not an accepted discipline today, perhaps because its implications have not yet been effectively studied and fully worked out. . . .

Many systems of building have been developed over the past twenty years on centre-line and tartan reference grids. But the use of such grids does not necessarily involve either the use of a repetitive unit of space or the use of related standard components such as floor mats, ceiling panels, and walling units. The reference grid may be simply a system of reference which neither determines the size and shape of components nor prescribes the rules which govern their position.

ture of the work will lead to greater expertise and speed which should yield both quantity and quality increases, and perhaps even innovations or improvements in the product design or the manufacturing process. The risk involved follows from the ever-present threat of bottlenecks, where a large number of workers may sit idle because of some contingency occurring during one of the production steps. But these risks can be partially mitigated by maintaining a flexible work force of part-time and overtime help which can be rapidly expanded or contracted.

The combination of both labor specialization and rationalized or systems design can become particularly powerful in defining a partial form of industrialization. It becomes important to recognize that the rationalized design process, in order to be truly beneficial, should not stop with the mere design of the component. Production design is also important, and when a component can be specifically designed with specialized labor techniques in mind, it stands an increased chance of achieving the efficiencies and benefits desired.

CONCENTRATION AND MECHANIZATION

The third and fourth steps on the path toward complete industrialization involve the concepts of concentrated and mechanized production. However, both of these aspects entail relatively greater investment and risk than systems design or skill specialization, and hence rely much more heavily on the full support of the institutions and facilities of an industrialized society.

Concentrated, as opposed to dispersed, production facilities are increasingly dependent upon a society's transportation and communications networks. Raw materials must continuously and reliably reach the plant; and the final product must leave the plant on schedule to reach markets.

Sheer size is another feature of centralization. A crippling contingency such as a flood or power failure that closes one plant having a thousand-unit capacity is much more severe than if it were to shut down only one of ten dispersed plants, each having a hundred-unit capacity. Dispersion spreads the risk; concentration accumulates it. As in the Latin American example, when risk and contingency factors are rooted in the facilities and services of the society in general, high-risk environments recommend a dispersion strategy of smaller-scale, individual operations to hedge against failure. On the other hand, lower-risk environments—those rich in reliable supporting services and facilities—may encourage a strategy of concentration designed to tap potential efficiencies and economies of scale.

Automated and mechanized production techniques are often closely related to concentration strategies, since large volumes of production are nearly always necessary to justify the acquisition and installation of costly machinery. It is usually not feasible to consider a high-investment item for each of many dispersed locations, not only because of diminished production requirements for each one, but also because of the absolute magnitude of the investment.

Since mechanization generally implies the highest cost-risk factor of the four aspects of industrialization, it emerges as the final stage of a strategic sequence ranging from partial to full industrialization. The other three aspects, particularly systems design and labor specialization—and to a lesser degree concentration—can be implemented with relatively little capital. A diagram can now be drawn schematically relating risk (which increases from bottom to top along the vertical axis), to the degree of economic development of a given region or society (which advances from left to right along the horizontal axis). Each element of industrialization can be plotted on the diagram as shown in Figure 14.

The horizontal progression from left to right is schematically indicative of increasing supportiveness in terms of the facilities and services of the economy or society. As this supporting infrastructure becomes more complete, the increasing risks of the higher-investment aspects of industrialization are mitigated.

Thus Figure 14 becomes a kind of "strategy map" for less-developed regions, indicating a sequence from partial to full industrialization geared to the growth of the supporting infrastructure of the society, and cautions against the premature adoption of modes which will require a simultaneous reproduction of indus-

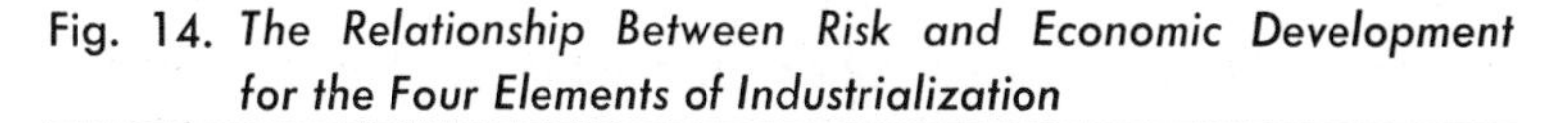

Fig. 14. *The Relationship Between Risk and Economic Development for the Four Elements of Industrialization*

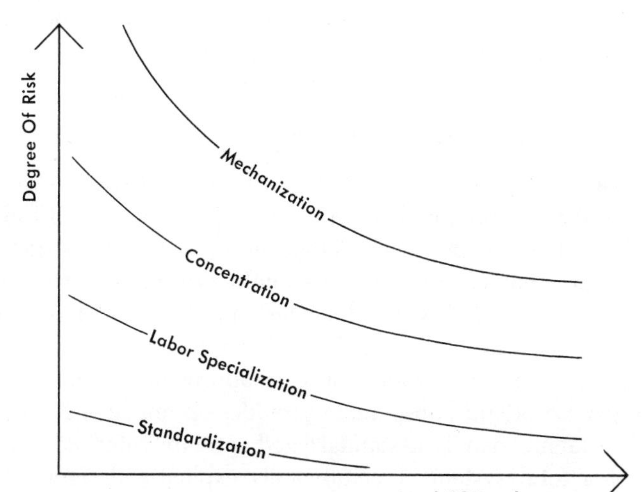

Development Decreases Risk—The diagram schematically relates risk (which increases from bottom to top along the vertical axis) to the degree of economic development (which advances from left to right along the horizontal axis) for each aspect of industrialization. Hence, the risk of counterproductivity for an investment in mechanization is greatest at all levels, although this risk drops as the supportiveness of a society grows with increasing economic development. On the other hand, the risk of standardization is always relatively low; although it too drops slightly with increasing development.[12]

trialized society in miniature for support. Thus, the argument has been advanced that industrialized manufacturing techniques need not be implemented on an either/or basis—forcing an unhappy choice between a high-risk fully industrialized housing factory and inaction. The former, as discussed earlier in the case

[12] Source: Terner and Turner, *op. cit.*

study, is perhaps one of the most flagrant and characteristic abuses to be perpetrated under the banner of "housing technology." In contrast, partial forms of industrialization have been identified which favor smaller decentralized operations while avoiding or postponing mechanization and automation.

Product—Toward Intermediate Technologies

However, the question still remains as to what kind of *product* these smaller operations should produce—or, in the case of fully industrialized economies, what kinds of products the larger and perhaps automated manufacturers might produce. Further, there is also the question of what effect these products will have on the housing process in general, and whether they will enhance or impair the cause of dweller autonomy. In addressing these questions, the Japanese tatami house again provides an analogy. As a product, the tatami mat is a standardized, prefabricated component, part of a total system of components explicitly designed to be compatible yet flexible in producing a wide variety of house types and sizes. The mat itself is predictable enough in size, shape, texture, and performance to be interchangeable with others; it is in such widespread use as to be readily available from a large number of specialized and competing suppliers. The tatami also became, and to some extent still remains, the basis for a degree of modular coordination among Japanese houses. Rooms and buildings often have been laid out in whole multiples of the tatami dimensions, thus avoiding the extra effort and waste involved in cutting and fitting fractions of the mats.

Although the tatami house could not be considered to be industrialized, it is an exceptional example of a rationalized product relying on the techniques of standardization and componentization. And it is this rationalized or systems design process which assumes special significance in the industrialization sequence since, as noted earlier, it can be undertaken with very little investment or risk. Basically what is required is a commitment of design time to produce a modular building component sensitive and appropriate to the needs of a given area. Although this is not by any means a simple or easy task, success can be immensely important, as in the case of the tatami, while failure can be relatively innocuous and at least will not consume or divert vast amounts of vitally needed housing resources.

Attempts at rationalized or systems design have embraced many product strategies, including various types of panel, framing, and volumetric systems. The size and complexity of the components involved have ranged from relatively small, simple, and standardized brick, block, and mat components, to rather large and complex room-sized and even house-sized modules.

TREND TOWARD PRODUCT PACKAGES

Unfortunately the trend in most areas shows an increasing infatuation with larger and more complex components and packaged modules, and diminished emphasis on new or incrementally improved small and simple components. Yet it is this latter type that can often be most critical, particularly in those areas where the traditions of self-help family construction are or may become strong. The U.N. emphasized this point in a recent report, noting that in some nations as much as 80 percent of all housing is self-built. The U.N. concluded that "public policy must, therefore, be directed toward preserving, encouraging and improving this type of production."[13] Thus, mass-produced components which are light, inexpensive, easy to handle—and which can be readily utilized by self-help builders—potentially have much greater impact than components which must be handled by experienced builders and contractors.

DISADVANTAGES OF PACKAGED COMPONENTS

It is also important to builder autonomy that components remain discrete, and that they not be extensively packaged or combined before reaching the user. This is a key consideration because packages, by their very nature, limit user options by precombining components. Yet most users, and particularly low-in-

[13] United Nations Technical Assistance Programme, "Housing in Ghana" (ST/TAA/K/GHANA/I) (New York: 1957), p. 4. The reporting team included Charles Abrams, Vladimir Bodiansky, and Otto Koenigsberger.

come users in less-developed regions, do not want fewer options. On the contrary, the very austerity of their lives demands a maximum of options in utilizing and combining whatever meager resources are available to them, so that their most critical needs are met as directly as possible. In addition, packages consume more resources than the sum of their combined components, for the process of preassembly itself demands labor and capital, and hence increased cost to the user. Thus, if components are designed so that their assembly is simple and fool-proof, packaging not only reduces options, but also increases cost.

Habitat. One of the most widely known examples of the packaged or highly-unitized approach to industrialized housing is the Habitat project which appeared in the 1967 World's fair at Montreal. In that project the basic package was a two-room, 90-ton, precast concrete module. Two or more of these modules formed a variety of dwelling units. As a prototype, Habitat was the subject of great controversy, winning high praise from many for its radically bold and dramatic design, while simultaneously drawing criticism from others for its cost (approximately $100,000 per module), social irrelevance, etc.[14]

However, apart from the controversy, Habitat, for purposes of this discussion, epitomizes a systems design commitment to a unitized or packaged strategy. It represents a bold and enduring design statement, but embodies little or no flexibility for change or individualized control of the dwelling environment. This type of design strategy may be valid for middle- or upper-income housing, but it loses its viability for low-income families for three reasons: First, a packaged or unitized housing module is by its very nature large and heavy, which inherently adds extra costs for special handling and transportation. Often, extremely costly, high-capacity cranes and trucks must be utilized in moving the modules to the site and into place, whereas smaller unassembled components can often avoid most of this type of cost.

Second, in purchasing room or house-sized packages, the buyer

[14] For a bibliography of periodical articles on Habitat '67, see *Habitat '67* (Ottawa, Canada: Queen's Printer, 1967). For the architect's own views see Moshe Safdie, *Beyond Habitat,* John Kettel, ed. (Cambridge, Mass., and London: The M.I.T. Press, 1970).

needs a relatively large bundle of savings, or at least access to credit, so that his payments may be made in relatively small increments over an extended time period. On the other hand, when purchasing small-scale components, savings and credit are certainly helpful, but without them the process does not stop—as is shown throughout the developing world where traditionally-built houses grow incrementally, using conventional components over the course of decades and generations.

The third, and perhaps most important, disadvantage of a packaged, as opposed to component housing, strategy is that packages are by nature predetermined and inclusive. The decisions that directly affect the living environment are often made by designers, engineers, entrepreneurs, and public officials with great social and economic distance between themselves and the lives ultimately affected by their decisions. The advantage of the simple component system is that a relatively small number of standardized building elements can be combined by individuals in a large number of ways to suit a great diversity of individual needs. Using this approach, a componentized system can be manipulated to conform to the user's living patterns; with preassembled packages, often the reverse is true.

Corollary to these three considerations is the fact that a critical performance requirement for low-income housing is the ability to easily accommodate and adjust to change. In most situations it is clear that the initial house, which often barely fulfills the most urgent, immediate needs, can hardly be counted upon to fill future needs as well. Hence the houses must be based on change, and an industrialized process which is to serve the needs of low-income families in developing regions must be at least as receptive to change as conventional construction, which is continuously expanded and upgraded by owner families. Thus the industrialized process must be able to provide an initially austere house, yet one that can grow and improve over time.

It is in this context that housing is most clearly seen as a dynamic process, rather than as a static product; the provision of incrementally additive components is crucial if the intermediate technology is to reflect this process properly. Where change is desired, indeed where it must become a way of life, a construction system must provide for alterations with minimal waste. This implies not only a componentized system, but a system in which components, once joined, remain individually discrete and replaceable.

Light bulb analogies. A typical light bulb provides an excellent example of this principle. When the bulb needs replacement, the only part of it which is no longer serviceable is a tiny strand of tungsten filament. All the other components of the package are still perfectly usable—the glass globe, the metal screw-in base, the internal wiring, etc. Yet because the bulb has been unitized or packaged, a discrete replacement is impossible, and the entire bulb must be discarded.

The packaged dwelling, like the light bulb, implies waste when there is change; and with the world's exploding population, and the still increasing gap between rich and poor, the luxury of wasteful discarding of usable components runs counter to both improving housing conditions and narrowing the income gap among people. The days may be numbered for reducing a wall or even an entire building to a heap of rubble when change is desired. If housing conditions are to be improved under the most austere circumstances, obsolete components must be recycled and reused with minimum destruction and waste.

On another analogical plane, the light bulb provides a model of a marvelously discrete component. When the bulb burns out, or when a change to a different kind of light is desired, the bulb can be neatly and easily separated from the fixture and the wiring of the building. The screw-in base is standardized, and interchangeable replacements are widely and competitively available with a large variety of performance, size, shape, and design. Thus, with a bulb, as with a simple componentized house, a user may start out with the lowest performance solution possible; but when he is ready, the initial component may be replaced, and if appropriate, enlarged and upgraded by the user himself, without dependence on an electrician or other skilled tradesman, and without the user being "locked in" to the first austere solution. Thus the component system can grow and evolve with the economic growth and evolution of the user.

In the absence of sweeping governmental change, dwellings of low-income families will probably continue to be extremely austere in the near future. If intermediate technologies are to make a truly significant contribution to the ability of low-income families to house themselves, they must yield easily assembled components which can be combined into an inexpensive dwelling. This dwelling, furthermore, must have the capacity to grow and improve in small increments into a fully matured home without waste of effort and destruction of materials.

The earlier chapters in this book by William Grindley on owner-builders and Rolf Goetze on owner-rehabilitators imply the need for this kind of technology in the U.S. as well as in developing areas. In fact a recent study of the U.S. Bureau of Census data indicated that "spending for home repairs and remodeling in which homeowners bought the building materials and provided all the labor" has increased 100 percent in the last four years.[15]

Yet, it can be argued that these increases are *in spite* of technology, not *because* of it. The fact remains that it is still very difficult for most people to undertake construction on their own. However, an example of a new technology which *has* indeed simplified one of the construction processes is found in the area of painting. Innovations in the form of quick-drying latex and water-based paints which can be cleaned up with soap and water—coupled with rollers and pans and small aerosol spray applicators—have reduced the skill-level necessary for home painting to the point where virtually anyone who can afford the materials can have an acceptable, even professional-looking, paint job.

These relatively simple innovations and applications of modern technology have liberated the dweller from reliance on the skilled journeyman painter. The homeowner or renter must still purchase materials, but the market serves him well, since it is extremely rich in competing brands, varieties, colors, and performance aspects of the paint.

The technological reduction of the skill-level needed to paint is

[15] Kenneth McKenna, "Money Pinch Helps Make Old Homes Look Like New," *Sunday News*, New York City, September 12, 1971, p. C-24. The author cites Seymour Kroll's study of U.S. Bureau of Census figures.

significant for another reason as well; for while it has increased the dweller's freedom to paint at his own initiative—without reliance on others—it has also increased his freedom *not* to paint. The dweller can now hire nonprofessionals (students and others) to do his painting for him at greatly reduced costs.[16] Furthermore, there is evidence that the journeyman painter himself has dropped prices, perhaps partly because he finds himself more productive using rollers (although painters' unions at first refused to permit them)[17] and partly from the pressures of increased competition by self-helpers and nonprofessionals.

From the painting example, one thing is clear: technology can significantly reduce the skill and experience requirements for participation in the building process. Technology can increase the individual's self-reliance by making construction easier. It can liberate the individual dweller from his present reliance on masons, carpenters, plumbers, and electricians in the same way that it has liberated him from the painter. And in some extreme cases, it may even mitigate the dweller's presently crucial dependence on the mortgage banker, land developer, or municipal utility network, all of whom have been known to make highly discriminatory service judgments based on a dweller's race, social status, or life style—as opposed to his economic potential, or their own public service obligations.

It is now possible to envision a technological, or "innovations" agenda designed to produce improvements in those areas of construction which are still difficult to undertake without special training or prior experience.

The innovations agenda may be organized under four broad headings: (1) structural-envelope systems, (2) water-waste systems, (3) power-energy systems, and (4) foundation-footing systems.

[16] In an informal experiment conducted in conjunction with the preparation of this chapter, estimates were solicited for painting the exterior of a single-family house in the area of Boston, Mass. Estimates for labor showed keen competition, ranging from $50 to $600, with the higher bids relating generally to greater experience and professionalism on the part of the painter.

[17] Interview with Wayne Horvitz, labor mediator and negotiator (Washington, D.C., September 1971).

STRUCTURAL-ENVELOPE SYSTEM

One of the most difficult construction tasks is to make a building stand up—straight, safely and securely. The easiest thing to build is a lean-to, a structure leaning against an object *already* straight, erect, and secure, be it a tree, a wall, an adjacent building, or whatever. A view of squatter areas in their early stages reveals an abundance of these appendagelike structures, simply because they are easier to build than free-standing structures.

In light of this, a persistent technological "dream" has been to create for adults what toymakers have succeeded in creating for children—simple sets of construction components with easy, virtually foolproof joining systems such as erector sets, Tinkertoys, Lincoln Logs, and Lego. Indeed, there have been a number of attempts at "erector-set technologies"[18] with commercial claims that two adults, with no special equipment nor prior construction experience or training, following a simple set of instructions, could build a wide variety of single and multistory structures, in much the same manner that a child builds with his toys. The structures were claimed to be safe, fireproof, wind and earthquake resistant, very inexpensive, and absolutely simple to build from a small number of standardized, lightweight components.[19]

Yet to date, this technological dream has not yet been fully realized—although there is little doubt in this writer's mind that it can be. Many attempts come very close, though they have usually been thwarted by cost.[20] Technological progress in the area of

[18] A small sample of four system descriptions of this sort may be found as follows: (1) Rita Reief, "Building Your Own House: 'Simple as an Erector Set,'" *The New York Times,* June 28, 1971, p. 26; (2) John Peter, "Tree House For Grownups," *Look* magazine, August 24, 1971, pp. 62-M to 63-M. (The house is typical in that it is described as designed "for step-by-step assembly by amateurs with ordinary hand tools" and with each part being "light enough to carry by hand."); (3) I. Terner and R. Herz, "Squatter Inspired," in *Architectural Design Magazine,* London, August 1968, vol. 38, pp. 367–70; (4) John Hoge, A. F. S. Group Brochure, Cincinnati, Ohio, mimeo, pp. 5.1–5.8.

[19] N. Mitchell and I. Terner, *Squatter Housing: Criteria for Development, Directions for Policy,* The United Nations Seminar on Prefabrication of Houses for Latin America, Information Document No. 19 (Copenhagen, Denmark, August–September, 1967), pp. 13–22.

[20] For a case example of one such attempt, see Terner and Turner, *op. cit.,* pp. III–11 to III–13.

cheaper, lighter, and stronger materials brings this dream closer to fruition. The implications of such a technology are potentially enormous, for they would enable dwellers to solve one of the most difficult aspects of self-construction—that of achieving structural integrity.

The task of enclosing or providing a weather-envelope around such a structure is a related problem. In some cases, when the building system incorporates structural panels, the weather envelope is combined with the structural solution. On the other hand, if the structure is only a frame, then various types of interior and exterior walls become a separate consideration, although their fabrication then becomes a function of various environmental requirements, but not structural requirements. Self-built walls, which need not be structural, are much simpler to build, as evidenced by the abundance of woven reed and thatch, mud block, and thin sheet material in use in developing areas. These walls can also be replaced or upgraded at the dwellers' initiative without jeopardizing the structural safety of the house when used in the context of a permanent and secure structural frame.

WATER-WASTE SYSTEMS

The second general item on an innovations agenda is water-waste systems. It is possible that through technology the skills required for installing plumbing systems and sanitary fixtures could be made no more difficult than hooking up a garden hose. The question must be asked: "Why should pipe be rigid?" If it were flexible, many costly fittings and joints could be eliminated entirely and those that remained could be designed for lay installation. The special and costly skills of the journeyman plumber may someday thus be challenged in the same way that the skills of the journeyman painter are being challenged at present.

Furthermore, not only in the United States but in all countries of the world, the dwellers' presently critical reliance on public water and sewage systems could be reduced through technological advances. It is not impossible to imagine a self-contained, recirculating, water-waste system in which a generally finite amount of water could be used, purified, and then reused. It is conceivable that such an appliance might not be larger nor more costly than, for example, a modern washing machine. The implications of such an appliance for developing areas could be enormous, particularly when one considers the millions of squatter and owner-built houses in those countries which *are* equipped with major electrical appliances, such as televisions and refrigerators, yet do not have running water. Nor are they likely *ever* to be individually serviced with water and sewage. There are three reasons for this: (1) the often-chaotic settlement patterns of these communities preclude the installation of major lineal service facilities, such as large water and sewer mains, without significant, and thus unacceptable, demolition and resettlement; (2) the land upon which the settlements occur is often so marginal with regard to slope and subsurface conditions that installation of water and sewer mains is prohibitively costly; and (3) the communities themselves often lack the political power to pressure the authorities to provide such systems.

In the United States, a recycling water-waste appliance could be equally important. As municipal utility systems are forced to expand in order to accommodate population growth, and as the dangers of pollution mount, the public sector faces major new investments in water treatment facilities. Thus an individual water-waste appliance could reduce the need for such investment, and could also reduce the costs of developing new land for settlement. Such an appliance would reduce the now critical dependence of a dweller upon a developer or a municipality to provide such services at the place where he wishes to live. Such technology might also imply more intense utilization of land already under settlement by replacing, in some areas, the need for individual land parcels to accommodate both a pure water well and a septic tank.[21]

[21] Several systems approaching the performance attributes described above are becoming commercially available in the U.S. For example, Advanced Waste Treatment Systems, Inc., (AWT), of Wilmington, Delaware, presently markets a "turnkey waste treatment and disposal plant" that can serve between 200 and 4,000 dwelling units. The cost per dwelling unit is between $250 and $375; and the cost per plant ranges from $50,000 to $1.5 million.

POWER-ENERGY SYSTEMS

Perhaps the closest analogy to the gradual shift that was observed in painting—the shift from journeyman to nonprofessional labor—exists in the wiring and electrical phases of construction. Vast numbers of squatter and owner-built houses in developing areas are electrified, often through illegal and clandestine "tapping in" to government or private power lines. Even in the U.S., where it is technically illegal and sometimes perilous, many nonprofessionals and homeowners wire houses in an attempt to bypass the high costs of the licensed electrician.

Modern technological innovations have played some role in liberating the dweller from a dependence on the electrician, but it is patently obvious that technology can go much further in making the electrification aspects of home building safer and far easier. For example, recent studies sponsored by the U.S. National Aeronautics and Space Administration (NASA) have led to the development of "scotch-tape-wiring," i.e., a wire with a profile as thin as a human hair which can be manufactured in an adhesive-backed strip much like a standard piece of cellophane tape.[22] This wiring can even be used with adhesive-backed switches, which resemble ordinary switches, but which do not penetrate the wall surface. Such "stick-on" wires and switches, and perhaps someday wall and ceiling fixtures as well, can be completely safe, simple to install, and can have virtually the same, or even improved appearance over conventional circuitry, which must now be laboriously buried inside walls, floors, and ceilings by highly skilled, licensed laborers. It is conceivable that in the future, technology may make "plugging in" the entire circuit system of a house as commonplace, easy, and safe as plugging in an electric clock or toaster.

The company states "that the not-too-distant future will see the introduction of many plants—with [lower] price tags to match—that could serve single family homes or even boats." See "Here's a Totally New Method of Sewage Treatment," *House and Home*, McGraw Hill Publishers, New York City, Volume 41, no. 2, February 1972, pp. 74–75.

[22] Anthony J. Yudis, "Cambridge Researchers Accept NASA Challenge, Space Age Technicians Envision Nail-free Fireproof Housing," *Boston Sunday Globe*, September 26, 1971, p. B-39.

Technology may also contribute to power and energy generation, as well as its internal distribution. Today, for example, deep sea buoys, and equipment for use in outer space, commonly generate their own electric power from solar energy cells. Whether it will ever be economical for individual dwellings to generate their own power (perhaps through solar cell roofing materials, fuel cells or tiny fission or fusion reactors) is beyond the scope of this book, but the question remains open.[23] It is yet another area wherein technical innovation embodies the potential to support an individual's autonomy and free him from reliance on often discriminatory or unresponsive government or private service networks.

FOUNDATION-FOOTING SYSTEMS

Finally, let us touch briefly upon a fourth potential area of technical contribution to dweller autonomy. One of the most difficult tasks for the inexperienced builder (and closely related to the problem of structure, discussed earlier) is the problem of joining the house to the ground. The problem of laying out and joining a regular and generally predictable building to the irregular and unpredictable earth is a major one for the owner-builder, and a major expense even for the conventional, professional builder. Variables such as slope, compaction, drainage, surface characteristics, and bearing capacity of the soil all can affect the success and safety of a building's roots, and catastrophes resulting in tragic loss of life, particularly in developing areas, have often been traced to improper foundations of dweller-built houses. In addition, the alignment and stability of foundations often affect how well and how easily the superstructure of the dwelling fits together. Various innovations yielding inexpensive, simple jacking and leveling devices, raft foundations, "screw-in" footings, structural pads, etc., would all be helpful. Technology might also

[23] *Business Week,* Feb. 26, 1972, "The Fuel Cell Goes to the Drug Store," pp. 20–21. The article describes experimental fuel cells operating in the U.S., noting that the electric power produced is "one-third more efficient than a typical central power station," thus making it one-quarter cent cheaper per kilowatt-hour. The energy derived is also noise- and pollution-free, since there is no combustion of the natural gas fuel.

be applied to improved "air-rights" platforms to utilize space above water, swamps, highways, etc. Increasing effective supplies of "buildable land" through technology can potentially benefit all dwellers—not only those of lowest income.

Unfortunately, a book of this scope permits only a brief indication of an innovations agenda; however, even in such an overview, a strong common theme runs throughout: all the innovations mentioned form parts of a "componentized" strategy of housing. None is dependent upon a "unitized" or "packaged" dwelling module. Like painting, much of the technology called for in the innovations agenda is labor intensive, and runs counter to the nearly universal trend to make construction more capital intensive, less reliant on labor, and more nearly akin to the high productivity format of other manufacturing industries. The component strategy advocated here *accepts* a high labor input, and in fact attempts wherever possible to trade *more* labor for reduced material costs—*so long as technological innovation can assure that that labor need not be experienced or skilled.* Indeed it is a fundamental assumption on the part of this author that if good houses could be gotten by trying—if the quality of a dwelling environment responded directly to effort—then the poor would be far better housed than they are now. Hence the present strategy looks in part toward technological innovation to mass produce simple and inexpensive components. These parts can then be assembled by dwellers in a wide variety of compositions and configurations, and can be directly responsive to needs not only at the time of construction, but also as needs change over time.

FINANCING

The componentized strategy described above has additional implications for another area of dweller dependency—the area of financing and credit. The strategy allows a dweller to pay as he builds; a packaged strategy demands an immediate lump sum —implying substantial savings or an ability to qualify for credit so that payments are "smoothed out" and extended over time. In the case of housing this is a crucial consideration, since a home is the largest single purchase that most families will make in their lifetimes, and accumulated savings are almost never sufficient to pay for a completed dwelling.

On the other hand, the vast majority of owner- and squatter-built dwellings in developing areas proceed without access to credit and without a dependency relationship with a mortgage banker. Family savings are typically used to construct a habitable but unfinished house which is then expanded and improved as the needs of the dwellers—and their ability to pay—dictate. Often over the course of years these houses evolve into fully finished and occasionally even elaborate multistory dwellings. (One unfortunate exception is the house is situated in a marginal neighborhood, as it often is, which may be totally up to "standard" in every other way, but may never be serviced by public water and sewage —another argument for an autonomous self-contained system.)

The fact that these dwellers can and will pay substantial sums for housing is underscored by the exorbitant rents that many are forced to pay simply because they have no access to land and/or accumulated savings with which merely to *start* the process of owner-building. In the developed nations, the process of owner-construction without mortgage credit is much more rare, mainly because land costs are higher, and squatting as a means to avoid this initial cost is vastly more difficult. Furthermore, owner-building an incomplete yet habitable house as a means of reducing first costs is much less frequent because of stricter construction regulations.

Although technology is limited in regard to increasing the effective supply of buildable land, the innovations on the agenda described above might well help in reducing the need for construction credit. By spreading the construction process itself into small increments over extended periods (which in fact is what credit is designed to do for construction cash outlays), owner-builders can afford to pay as they build.

Technology can also affect credit and financing in another way. It is well known that families who might never qualify for a home mortgage can often receive financing for televisions, automobiles, and even mobile homes. Why? Because when a product can be *moved*, it can be repossessed. In the case of mobile homes, this is significant, for even though they are rarely moved after their journey from factory to first site, the fact that they *can* be moved is enormously important, for it makes them a much more liquid asset. Hence a credit agency will qualify people of lower income as acceptable risks for mobile homes when they cannot obtain credit for conventional houses which are bound to the land, to a section of the city, and to a bundle of municipal services (or lack thereof, as is often the case for low-income households). In this context, again, a componentized technology—one where discrete building components can be returned, replaced, and even repossessed—can go far toward being as accessible to low-income families as major appliances or automobiles.

Conclusions

Several points emerge as critical in examining the impact of technology and industrialization on housing. First, the acquisition of large, high-technology, fully industrialized housing plants is often counterproductive. In the near future it is unlikely that they will touch the lives of those who most desperately need improved housing. This is particularly true in developing areas where the inadequacy of the economy's supporting services adds to the ultimate cost of the house. In the fully industrialized nations this point is mitigated, although even in these countries the houses thus produced rarely, if ever, reach the lowest-income families without massive government subsidy—thereby reinforcing rather than alleviating their dependency on a system that has thus far failed them.

In light of this, the author recommends the abandonment of heavy investment, high-risk strategies for full industrialization in developing areas, and a refocusing on the lower-risk concept of *partially* industrialized manufacturing processes, based primarily upon systemization and labor specialization.

Finally, regardless of the degree of industrialization, the trend toward packaged or preassembled modules must be reversed, and a highly componentized strategy must take its place. This recommendation spans Third World and fully industrialized nations. In both areas, short of a radical change in government and private sector views on housing, the concept of dweller autonomy—served and strengthened by new technology—appears to offer one of the few hopes for truly broad-based housing improvement. The challenge to technology is enormous. The job to be done is nothing less than to transform house building, which is now costly and difficult, into a process which is inexpensive and easy.

PART TWO

Increasing Autonomy in Housing: A Review and Conclusions

10

ROBERT FICHTER, JOHN F.C. TURNER, AND PETER GRENELL

The Meaning of Autonomy

The Hypothesis

OUR STARTING POINT for this discussion is the hypothesis that

> When dwellers control the major decisions and are free to make their own contributions in the design, construction, or management of their housing, both this process and the environment produced stimulate individual and social well-being. When people have no control over nor responsibility for key decisions in the housing process, on the other hand, dwelling environments may instead become a barrier to personal fulfillment and a burden on the economy.

The chapters in Part I substantially support this hypothesis. For example, both the legally sanctioned owner-builders of the United States and the squatter-builders of Peru described by Grindley and Turner achieve considerable economies and generate extraordinary equities in relation to their incomes through self-help.

In both cases, the self-helpers or owner-builders often manage to provide themselves with dwellings that would cost twice as much if built by a contractor. The Peruvian and United States owner-builders often create an investment in housing equivalent to four or five times their annual incomes, which is twice the normal maximum that can be obtained through mortgage borrowing on commercially built and sold property.

The nonquantifiable benefits of autonomous action are more difficult to document. Pride in achievement, the sense of competence and satisfaction stemming from direct personal action, is a subjective state not reducible to dollar terms. And the observations of Goetze, Grindley, and Turner suggest strongly that direct action in fulfilling housing needs can contribute as much to psychological well-being as it can to the physical improvement of inadequate housing conditions.

The Peruvian squatters are extremely poor by the material standards of the wealthy minority of the industrialized world. Nevertheless, they often make such good use of their meager resources that, over time, their poverty is significantly lessened. We suggest that this achievement is to a considerable extent a function of the squatters' relative freedom of action.

The fact that so many squatters and owner-builders do so much better for themselves than even well-intentioned government agencies or private organizations can do for them is, perhaps, the most persuasive argument for increased autonomy in housing. At the very least, it argues against the dependency relationship the poor fall into when they become wards of the state.

The poor can *be* wards of the state, however, only when they are a minority. When they are a majority, as they are in Peru or India, the state simply cannot afford the cost of distributing massive amounts of institutionalized goods and services which have the effect, as in the United States, of appropriating the autonomy of the poor. This explains the relative freedom of housing activity by the poor in a country such as Peru, and the almost total lack of such freedom for the urban poor in industrialized societies. Thanks to their autonomy, many of the Latin American urban poor make better use of their limited resources and sometimes are better housed, in absolute terms, than their wealthier North American counterparts.

We are not concerned here, however, with autonomy only as it relates to the poor. A lack or loss of autonomy, resulting in a dependency on other persons or institutions for those necessities one is willing and capable of providing for one's self, can be intolerably frustrating in any context. For physical and mental well-being, every man, woman, and child must be able to exercise his or her individual initiative; and housing, for the poor and the wealthy alike, is a major opportunity.

As Turner shows, autonomy enables the Peruvian squatter to maximize his scant resources. In the modern industrial setting, this quantitative increase may often be of secondary importance, as Grindley's data indicate. For the 50 percent of owner-builders in the United States whose incomes are above the national median, autonomy in housing may represent the desire to create something of uniqueness and personal significance (a feat increasingly difficult in a mass-production, mass-consumption society) as much as it is a way to get more housing for each housing dollar.

In the context of poverty, autonomy increases quantity: in any context, it increases meaning. And, of course, the converse is true as well. The Argentinian squatter, whose self-built house was about to be eradicated to make way for a high-rise apartment complex which he could not afford to live in, was suffering the worst of both worlds when he protested:

> It is not the discomfort of the physical situation the people of the *villas* feel most bitterly—it is the humiliation of being denied the opportunity of doing for themselves what they are quite able to do.[1]

Three Critical Assumptions

The first and most important assumption is that housing is to be understood as a verb. The word housing, therefore, ought to refer to *activities*—such as design, construction, and management—even before it refers to the specific physical entities designed,

[1] Albert Wilson, *The Voice of the Villas* (Washington, D.C.: Foundation for Cooperative Housing, Inc., 1965), p. 52.

constructed, and used. By virtue of the production *method,* the Peruvian squatter-builder and the North American owner-builder both get far more for their money and, quite possibly, far more existential meaning from their housing products.

A second assumption is that housing, far from being a "social overhead cost," can be a highly productive activity, whether measured in economic terms or evaluated by criteria of broad social benefit. The preceding case material and theoretical arguments suggest how and why appropriate forms of housing action, especially autonomous housing action, generate resources which cannot be coopted by public or corporate institutions. Conventionally built low-income housing is indeed a heavy social overhead, largely because it fails to utilize the users' own potential initiative and resources. The chronic humiliation and frustrations suffered by tenants in so many public housing projects, for instance, can result in hostilities directed against the projects themselves, with concomitantly high maintenance costs and blighted living environments.

Without doubt, the provision of housing for dependent sectors of the population does stimulate certain kinds of economic vitality. Developers, contractors, materials suppliers, skilled craftsmen, officials, and facilitators of all kinds thrive. But their well-being, based as it is on the provision of goods and services for those who, in a variety of ways, are not allowed to provide for themselves, implies an economy which must keep increasing the number of dependent poor to maintain artificially high levels of consumption in the interests of a parasitically dependent supply and service sector.

The third critical assumption, which emerges out of the second, is that our cherished notion of "development" in many cases signifies just the opposite—deterioration, both of the social fabric and of a rational economy. Development is a composite of two independent variables: quantity and quality. Both quantitative scarcity and quantitative excess preclude an acceptable quality of life. Therefore, while development in a poor country must include a quantitative increase in general levels of consumption, it may demand just the reverse in the wealthier countries of the world, in which excessive levels of consumption appear to threaten life itself.

Issues of Autonomy and Dependency

Thus far, autonomy in the housing process has been presented without much definition. This has been deliberate: the term covers a great deal of ground and emerges most usefully out of an overview of the terrain. We consider autonomy to be a good thing, and associate it with freedom of action in a variety of senses; we see it as a part of the life activity called "housing" which is to be distinguished from "housing products"; and we endorse autonomy as a pragmatic answer both to the shelter deficit and to the frequent mismatch of shelter and essential life needs.

Of course freedom to build cannot mean that every household must, literally, construct a dwelling in order to exercise autonomy. The villa squatter from Buenos Aires provides the existential definition of freedom (to be qualified in one major way) implicit throughout this book: *the opportunity to do for one's self what one is able to do.*

The physically or psychologically crippled are clearly incapable of successfully undertaking the task of building or contracting even a simple house. The traveling salesman, the transient student, and even many long-term, thoroughly competent residents cannot be bothered managing their dwelling environments; they either have no time or are preoccupied with other activities they consider to be of higher priority. Still others simply do not want the responsibility for designing, constructing, or managing their dwellings.

While the literal freedom to build, therefore, is imperative only for those who have acute unsatisfied shelter needs, and practicable only for those with the minimum material and physical resources necessary to become builders, in a broader sense dweller control in the housing market is important for everyone. The affluent dweller has this control over design, location, construction, and maintenance through his ability to pay for, and hence make a choice among, a wide variety of forms of shelter.

Yet as market forces become more concentrated on the supply side, even the relatively affluent experience a limiting of options. The $10,000-a-year household in the United States today, for instance, can be said to have little more real choice in housing than it does when it comes to choosing among spuriously individualized makes of cars, or brands of soap powder.

We have made a start toward a definition of autonomy, but the term must be further explained and in some ways qualified. Let us introduce a pair of key questions: When is dependency an unhealthy state? What is the relationship between autonomy and individualism?

We are all dependent, and in many ways. We are dependent on the planet as the source of our existence; we are dependent on the many complex arrangements which are our societies; and we are dependent on one another in all sorts of personal correspondences and exchanges. Dependency is a rule of life; there are no exceptions in the living world.

Dependency becomes destructive, however, when those in need do not enjoy a reciprocal relationship with those who supply their needs. In the housing situation, an undesirable dependency means that those who supply shelter are also the ones who decide how much shelter there should be, where it should be, and how it should function in the lives of essentially passive users.

In an open and healthy exchange, decisions are made on both sides: those with wants specify their wants; suppliers indicate how well they can provide for those wants according to considerations of cost; and by compromise on both sides, an exchange is effected.

This is clearly the case in the ideal free housing market. The two bartering parties depend on one another. It is in the interests of both to adjust their terms so as to facilitate an exchange. Each has an area of initiative, bargaining power, and control over his course of action.

In a situation of unhealthy dependency, however, the relationship becomes lopsided. The supplier has incentives and rewards other than satisfying his client; the client, meanwhile, has no effective way of enforcing his requests. In point of fact, what typically happens in housing arrangements for dependent populations is that the real exchange occurs at a distance from the ostensible clients. Politicians, bureaucrats, favored commercial interests, and the like negotiate among themselves, each to maximize his own benefits, while the dependent housing users exert little or no influence on the outcome of these transactions.

Some very simple tests can reveal the wholesomeness or unwholesomeness of a dependency relationship. Does the user have any effective bargaining power? Does he have alternative sources of supply? No matter what compromises he may have to make, are the critical life decisions still in his hands? Does the supplier invariably turn to him to check the acceptability of what is being supplied? Is there a mutual recognition of desirable goals?

These tests can be applied in the realm of education, legal services, and medical care as well as they can in housing; and predictably enough, the same or similar populations will be found in states of more-or-less helpless dependency in each of them.

Autonomy, therefore, entails the ability to enter into reciprocal relationships, to exercise both control over essential life needs and discretion in the trade-offs which establish priorities. Autonomy means the power to bargain, the ability to get what one needs, the capacity to pay, in one way or another, for what one gets. In sum, it is synonymous with substantial freedom of action.

But autonomy, as here understood, does *not* imply unqualified license. It signifies, rather, a freedom of action constrained by costs. Thus autonomy represents a measure of obligation and responsibility as well as the power to satisfy one's wants. In a simple bargaining situation, this simply tells us that goods cannot be supplied to a purchaser if he cannot or will not pay for them. On the open housing market—accepting our present distribution of wealth as it is for the moment—a man who would like a two-car garage and a swimming pool will have to do without them if he cannot afford them or will have to make unacceptable sacrifices to get them. In short, he must modify his wants to suit his pocketbook.

On another level, the millionaire who has a mansion built to suit his every desire may apparently enjoy unlimited freedom of action. He may well say that "cost is no object." But here our argument for autonomy in a special sense—freedom constrained by costs—tells us that the price of the millionaire's actions go far beyond the dollar value of stone and tile and mahogany. In other words, there are costs which he is not presently held accountable for. In building his mansion, he makes disproportionate demands on the allocation of labor, on the supply of energy, on the natural resources of the planet.

These demands will have consequences for everyone, hard as they are to calculate. Nevertheless, they *should* be calculated as far as possible, for while the affluent buyer may enjoy a freedom from the obvious kinds of constraint, his unconstraint—which amounts to irresponsibility—may limit the opportunities for an indeterminately great number of other human beings removed in time and space. On the international scale, this is precisely the relationship between the United States and a good part of the rest of the world at this time.

Another illustration may help to link the problem of dependency with that of insufficiently or irrationally calculated costs. Housing for low-income people is acknowledged, by everyone, to be anything but low-cost housing. The HUD 236 projects (government-supported projects designed to attract high-income investors in search of tax shelters), for instance, may cost two, three, four, or more times what comparable accommodations would cost on the open market.

On one hand, this means that the occupants are automatically denied effective control over the provision of housing, since their ability to pay is not a primary check on the supply side. But perhaps more serious than that—more serious even than the marginal role of the clients in the housing process—is the waste implied in housing actions which artificially inflate costs, support fictitious markets, and encourage housing products which promote production divorced from both near- and long-term cost consequences.

Autonomy, in the present context, implies a leveling out of consumption, a more uniform distribution of power, wealth, *and* responsibility. For the poor, autonomy signifies greater access to goods and services than is available to them at present, that this access should be determined by their individual needs, and that it should be obtainable through greater inputs of time, labor, and collective bargaining power on their part. For the affluent, autonomy entails access to goods and services priced to reflect, so far as we are able to determine them, the long-term costs to society of providing such goods and services. It is not enough to want everyone to satisfy his own needs according to his ability to pay. If autonomy is to increase and become a principle of action, there must be more than one kind of currency with which to pay, and there must be more than one kind of cost accounting.

Not the least of the costs to be taken into account, though among the most difficult to estimate exactly, are the cultural consequences of supply and consumption patterns, which minimize individual initiative in the name of the sacred cow called Gross National Product. Sapir noted the very negative effects of autonomy diminished in the guise of an allegedly higher good when he wrote that:

> It should be clearly understood that this ideal of a genuine culture has no necessary connection with what we call efficiency. A society may be admirably efficient in the sense that all its activities are carefully planned with reference to ends of maximum utility to the society as a whole, it may tolerate no lost motion, yet it may well be an inferior organism as a culture-bearer. It is not enough that the ends of activities be socially satisfactory, that each member of the community feel in some dim way that he is doing his bit toward the attainment of a social benefit. This is all very well so far as it goes, but a genuine culture refuses to consider the individual as a mere cog, as an entity whose sole *raison d'être* lies in his subservience to a collective purpose that he is not conscious of or that has only a remote relevancy to his interests and strivings. *The major activities of the individual must directly satisfy his own creative and emotional impulses, must always be something more than a means to an end.* The great cultural fallacy of industrialism, as developed up to the present time, is that in harnessing machines to our uses it has not known how to avoid the harnessing of the majority of mankind to its machines.[2] [Our emphasis]

The final irony, of course, is that our greatly increased tech-

[2] Edward Sapir, "Culture, Genuine and Spurious," in *The American Journal of Sociology,* Vol. XXIX, 1924. Reprinted in Edward Sapir, *Culture, Language, and Personality, Selected Essays,* David G. Mandelbaum, ed. (University of California Press, Berkeley, California, 1954), p. 91.

nological sophistication, whose "cumulative force . . . gives us the sense of what we call 'progress' "[3] has not even attained its own sanctified goal of ever more goods, ever more efficiently produced, as Terner suggests in regard to industrialized building systems.

The value inherent in the immediacy of experience which attaches to human actions done in and for themselves is thus a basic component of autonomy; the lack of such experience in housing, as in education, must be reckoned a heavy cost.

> The vast majority of us, deprived of any but an insignificant and culturally abortive share in the satisfaction of the immediate wants of mankind, are further deprived of both opportunity and stimulation to share in the production of non-utilitarian values. Part of the time we are drayhorses; the rest of the time we are listless consumers of goods which have received no least impress of our personality.[4]

Sapir may sound overwrought until one stops to think of the few areas of life in which one has done more than consume products in all essential ways prepared, preassembled, predetermined. The potential for greater autonomy in housing, we suggest, could restore in at least one sphere of activity a measure of spiritual satisfaction and "nonutilitarian value"—in addition to the minimization of near- and long-term costs which have been pointed out in Part I.

Networks and Hierarchies

Decision-making systems which provide for user control of an activity such as housing can be described as networks, while those which centralize control in corporate producers or in government hands can be described as hierarchies, or funnels, as Illich terms the institutionalized delivery systems in the areas of education and health care.[5]

As Turner points out in Chapter 7, the essential property of a

[3] *Ibid.*, p. 94.
[4] *Ibid.*, p. 101.
[5] Ivan Illich, *Deschooling Society*, Harper & Row, New York, 1970.

network is the multiplicity of routes it provides to the same end. The cash credit borrower, noted in Chapter 7, who was free to buy his own materials, had access to a network of suppliers and distributors among whom he could choose and with whom he could bargain to get the best mix of needed goods and the greatest financial advantage for himself. The materials credit borrower, on the other hand, found himself locked into the receiving end of a hierarchy or funnel through which the housing authority channeled the materials which *it* selected, bought, and distributed on behalf of the borrower.

The housing market network system was first observed and conceptualized by Grenell, Grindley, Schon, and Turner in their research into the success of owner-builders in the United States.[6] The OSTI team concluded that the extraordinary economies achieved by such a large proportion of owner-builders was mainly due to their multiple access to information and the basic resources for housing: land, materials, tools, skilled labor, and credit. Locally established residents who become owner-builders, whether in rural, small town, or suburban settings, have readily available to them market networks for all of these elements and are able, therefore, to assemble their own housing packages in their own individualized way, which is generally the most economical way possible.

Turner characterizes the present, supplier-favoring housing process as a hierarchic system. This is to say that as a dweller's economic, political, and social power decreases, he is more and more apt to be dependent on housing decisions made for him by increasingly centralized authorities according to criteria which will have little relevance to his personal life. In those areas of the world where centralized authorities and concentrated commercial interests are too little developed to intervene at will, the hierarchic model, of course, does not apply with maximum force.

However, the tendency is toward ever more centralized control influencing ever larger population blocs; and in the area of housing, there is a simultaneous tendency toward constantly increasing intervention—always in the name of higher living standards—throughout the world.

[6] See Chapter 1.

Need a hierarchic arrangement for the provision of housing always be a bad thing? To the extent that it limits choice, concentrates effective power on the supply side, undermines reciprocal exchange arrangements, and distorts and disguises costs, the answer is yes. But it cannot be a simple yes, No matter how much an outside observer judges users to have been robbed of their proper autonomy and the hierarchic system to be wasteful of human and natural resources, that system will not be really vulnerable until large numbers of users begin to *feel* a lack of autonomy.

In the United States, all of the many elements which go to make up a national housing mechanism have more and more clearly begun to appear monolithic and unresponsive to those at the lower end of the socioeconomic scale. But as long as they remain relatively accommodating, or *seem to be* relatively accommodating to the great majority of dwellers, the scale of change will perforce be modest.

The point to be made is that when a housing process begins to *feel* hierarchic to a sufficient number of users—when, in other words, their actual impotence is matched by their *sense* of impotence and frustration—and when the system is clearly delivering either an insufficient number of dwellings or dwellings of an inadequate kind to a critically large, critically aware population mass, hopes for radical alternatives can become real possibilities.

The housing network is such an alternative. In a supplier-oriented, bureaucratically dominated society, the network concept can be considered a response to mechanisms for producing shelter which seem both inadequate to the task itself and destructive of the kind of human integrity maintained when the housing task functions as a vehicle for individual human needs.

Like the term "autonomy," the term "network" is suggestive of congeries of attitudes and behavior patterns, of social and political and economic arrangements rather than a single, very specific solution to a problem. In broad outline, the network implies a maximum of individual initiative, discretion, and responsibility in the housing process. It implies a setting of priorities which reflect basic household needs; a spectrum of options within a framework of the minimum necessary rules; a variety of ways of supplying and obtaining the primary elements of shelter—land, materials and tools, labor, and credit.

Network arrangements can help to provide for all dwellers the autonomy which, through money, permits dwellers at the upper end of the income scale to participate in commercial markets as relatively self-sufficient, self-directing human beings.

To put it another way, well-to-do users of housing (and this may include a near-majority of dwellers in a country as affluent as the United States) still enjoy the benefits of a network. Many can make meaningful choices as to location, amenity, financing, and so on. By the standards of most of the world's people, they can bargain from a position of relative strength, they can make trade-offs without compromising basic needs, and they can have access to pools of advice and alternative sources of supply.

Many qualifications to this analysis could be offered. It might be pointed out, for instance, only the very rich get the full benefit of the tax structure in the United States. Just as autonomy tends to be a condition measured in degrees, so does the network. For some it functions so well, choices can be made down to the last detail of amenity; for others—about half the population in the United States—it functions sufficiently well so that apparently satisfactory choices can be made in all the essential housing decisions a household will face.

But a constellation of factors closes off the prevailing market network to an increasing proportion of the population in the United States. These factors include complex technologies which increase dependency on high-priced labor and thus raise housing costs, high minimum standards which derive, to a degree, from technological sophistication and also contribute to costs. Furthermore, racial discrimination which restricts income and dweller location exacerbates the problem for the poor.

To make explicit a point implied in our discussion of autonomy, the limitations are in some ways greatest for the *dependent* poor. Huge, impoverished population sectors of transitional economies may well enjoy more benefits, actual and potential, of supply and information networks than the urban poor or industrialized nations simply because they are beyond the influence of centralized authorities.

The extremely low material levels at which some autonomous networks function should not blind the observer to their essential value. It is just by virtue of such networks that the very poor can make best use of their meager resources. In Mexico City, by way of historical note, the freedom which the poorest had some decades ago has been lost, along with the networks which enabled earlier generations to erect their own rent-free shacks in the unused or unguarded interstices of the city. In Mexico City today, the poorest of the poor usually have to pay between one-quarter and one-third of their incomes for the now decayed and even more crowded shacks their predecessors lived in. In short, the submarket has been taken out of their hands by entrepreneurs, who now control the supply.

The fact that official policies unwittingly reinforce this sort of exploitation attests to the invisibility of the poor described by Grenell. In a sense, only the houses of the poor are seen, not the people themselves, so that the roles which their housing plays in their struggle to live are, of course, invisible. By condemning the symptoms of poverty, governments can destroy users' networks through the exercise of administrative and police powers; but when they cannot eradicate poverty itself, all such actions consolidate the exploitative power of those who buy up the increasingly scarce supply of slum dwellings—as in Mexico City. The same is true of Lima and probably the majority of cities in the rapidly urbanizing Third World.

11

The Necessity for Networks

The Problem Restated

HOUSING CONSTITUTES A PROBLEM when it acts as a barrier to personal fulfillment or as a burden on society as a whole according to our original hypothesis. Good housing, therefore, is that in which both the housing procedures and the dwelling environments produced act as vehicles for personal fulfillment and stimulate real social and economic development, or, to use Sapir's phrase, "genuine culture."

The problem contained within this problem, of course, is who is to say when housing acts as a personal barrier or a vehicle, and when it acts as a societal burden or a stimulus?

In recent times we have increasingly assumed that the definition of housing problems, both in their personal aspects and in their social aspects, is the job of the expert. Physical and social technicians analyze what the established authorities then take to be the various problematic conditions under which people are presently living. The technicians' proposals are generally debated with economic planners and, according to the political balance and political priorities of the day, greater or lesser appropriations are assigned to specific programs.

The authors of this book question and implicitly reject these generally unchallenged procedures for the definition and solution of housing problems. They regard the authoritarian presumption that experts understand housing problems and priorities better than dwellers themselves as absurd and often disastrous.

On the other hand, the authors emphasize the responsibility technical experts and political authorities have for understanding the general nature of the housing process, for appreciating the consequences of intervention in it, and for formulating alternative policies which respect both user autonomy and fully allocated costs. In other words, *an all-important distinction is made here between the local, small-scale problems of using available resources and the large-scale social and economic problems of the availability of those resources.*

If this vital distinction is not made and built into the system, local organizations and individual households cannot make their own decisions nor make best use of their own resources. Whether this matters or not depends on the variability of housing needs and people's adaptability to mismatches between their needs and the supply. Where housing needs are uniform or where people are able and willing to accept standardized solutions, authoritarian and hierarchic forms of organization may well be at least provisionally acceptable.

Where survival is at stake, we have to accept conditions which would otherwise be intolerable. Victims of disasters, for example, are indeed dependent on shelter provided for them. But when housing problems are regularly presented by agencies of the establishment as short-term crisis problems, one's suspicions should be aroused. Whether one has U.S. inner city ghetto dwellers in mind, or the Asian or Latin American urban poor, it is clear that the great majority suffer more from unemployment, low incomes, and the inaccessibility of resources with which to satisfy their own needs than they suffer from consequences such as physically poor housing.

The maintenance of a crisis image of the housing problem is

doubly advantageous to a repressive establishment. In the first place, it clothes the unacceptable nakedness of the underlying problems, and in the second, it is to the advantage of the political, commercial, and professional interests which profit from the dilemma of the poor.

In fact, this institutionalization of the housing crisis serves to reduce the freedom of the relatively affluent as well as to intensify the repression of the poor. To take a topical example, Operation Breakthrough, a U.S. government-sponsored industrialized housing experiment,[1] propagates the notion of a moderate-to-middle-income housing crisis which can best be solved—can *only* be solved, its proponents sometimes seem to say—through the mass production of complete shelter packages. Not one of the twenty-two proposals accepted for Breakthrough was designed to extend local network supply systems or to increase the availability of already highly industrialized building materials and components to local users.

In all the papers presented in this book, housing problems are associated with the predominance of hierarchic or the lack of network systems. Good housing, or the solution of housing problems (under nonemergency conditions), is seen as the product of people's freedom to build. Neither individual families nor local enterprises capable of serving individual needs *can* build, however, unless they have access to network systems.

A network system provides its users, both dwellers themselves and small-scale housing-related businesses, with (1) adequate resources, and (2) adequate access to those resources. Networks fail, or cannot come into existence, when there is a grave scarcity of resources or when access to sufficient resources is restricted.

Absolute scarcities of the basic resources needed for housing are rare. Hong Kong represents the exceptional case where land, one of the critical housing resources, exists in such short supply that new land can only be made available by dynamiting mountains and shoveling them into the sea. Other relatively exceptional cases are some African countries where there are absolute short-

[1] See Chapter 9, footnote 2, p. 200.

ages of building materials suitable for high-density urban development and situations such as that which prevailed in Europe, especially in Russia, after World War II, where there was an absolute shortage of building labor.

The solution to problems of scarcity, such as those cited above, should be the province of executives at a variety of levels, rather than legislators, whose province should be the rule-making which determines access to resources and upper limits on their use.

Here we must introduce a very important parenthesis. As implied or explicitly stated in the papers, networks and hierarchies are, in their theoretically pure form, the poles of a spectrum. At the left-hand (or network) end of the spectrum, there is a complete separation between the legislative (rule-making) function and the executive (game-playing) function. Parameters are centrally or consensually established, and within those parameters, the supplying of needs is left up to the users themselves, and to those charged with administering the laws. At the right-hand (or hierarchic) end of the spectrum, the legislative and the executive form one totalitarian whole. *What* should be done and *how* it should be done become lodged in the same agencies, so that there is a progressive loss of freedom from the bottom up and a progressive loss of judgment as to the appropriateness of laws and rules from the top down.

In the real world, legislative and executive activities obviously overlap. Many housing programs are formulated by legislators, and many individual executives and executive agencies may take the initiative in the institution of housing laws. Even so, the more decentralized decision-making is in terms of the *specifics* of housing action, the more adequate housing is liable to be for the dwellers themselves. The effectiveness of decision-making dispersed to the local level concomitantly depends on the appropriateness of centrally formulated laws.

To return to the main line of our argument, the most common housing problems have to do with the accessibility of resources rather than with their existence. Restrictions on the use of vacant buildable land, for instance, inhibits large population sectors and many smaller entrepreneurs. Another problem, particularly widespread and acute in countries with low per capita incomes and high rates of inflation, is the inaccessibility of credit for modest housing needs.

Yet even when an intending builder has obtained the land and credit or accumulated the savings sufficient for his needs, he may still be prevented from building because he cannot afford to provide shelter—however adequate it may be in his own eyes—up to the standards of housing law and other regulations imposed by rule-makers who presume to know what is best.

The economic behavior of land is largely a result of centralized rule-making. Thus, land suitable for urban housing in many of the so-called free market economies is often preempted by speculators profiting from the rules of the game. In metropolitan Boston, at the time of writing, suburban land prices are increasing about 10 percent per annum, and in metropolitan Mexico City, at about twice that inflationary rate.

As a result, the individual or small builder is as unfree in these free market economies as he would be in the most highly centralized state-capitalist countries, or even more so. It is ironic, in that regard, that in contemporary Warsaw single-family homes are being illegally owner-built, thanks to the survival of the now more-or-less clandestine networks[2] through which families can obtain land and building materials.

Conventionally defined housing problems, stated in terms of quantitative deficits, arrived at by applying physical standards, concentrate attention on end products and simultaneously divert attention from deficiencies in the housing process itself. It is hardly surprising, therefore, that conventional housing analyses rarely reveal the essential difference between problems of the existence or *availability* of resources and those of the *accessibility* of resources—when the issue of resources is raised at all.

Low-cost housing projects, a typical pseudo-solution to misstated housing problems, often ignore scarcities of financial or

[2] See Jan Minorski, "Architektura Samorzutna," in *Architektura No. 4*, Warsaw, 1963, pp. 113–124.

administrative resources or try to compensate for users' lack of access to submarkets, or both, as they attempt to impose ready-made housing products.

In countries with grossly inadequate financial and administrative resources, any serious attempt to eliminate quantitative housing deficits through massive direct construction by central agencies is absurd. The use of the centrally sponsored housing project as a way of overcoming the problem of users' and small builders' lack of access to resources is still absurd, if less obviously so.

The public or private housing corporation may well have available to it land and credit denied to users and local builders; yet their aggregated financial and managerial resources are often far greater than those of intrusive housing corporations, particularly in low-income, low-budget economies.

In sum, all that pseudo-solutions such as centrally conceived and produced housing projects do, apart from answering certain political and other nonhousing demands, is to provide largely inappropriate shelter for a minority of users while leaving the system responsible for the basic problem intact.

Network Preconditions and Goals

To some extent, network preconditions and network goals are one and the same. A housing network cannot exist without a modicum of access to resources, information, and tools; yet the existence of a network in the housing process facilitates the goal of such access for users and small-scale entrepreneurs.

Once again the "rules of the game" are all-important. If social and economic structures are such that land, labor, credit, building materials, and the knowledge of how these interrelated elements work are in the hands of a minority, it will be an exercise in futility or hypocrisy to talk about increasing self-reliance across the social spectrum. A housing policy, therefore, which has as its ostensible goals the satisfaction of individual needs, the most economical use of human and natural resources, and greater social equity *must* have the analogues of these goals built into the means by which they are to be achieved.

To put it another way, when the users of housing must rely on central authorities or favored supplier interests, or both, for the necessities of shelter, it is quite unrealistic to expect them to behave other than as passive or rebellious dependents. Denied a network which permits them to act in their own behalf, they are almost inevitably going to withhold the resources of individual energy and initiative which hierarchic institutions persist in expecting them to supply.

The preconditions outlined below are not offered as a blueprint to tap those human resources. They are, rather, a conceptual frame against which present and projected housing policies can be tried out. And while an apparent match will not guarantee the success of any particular program, a clear mismatch will guarantee failure in terms of the user needs this book is concerned with.

Decentralization of Control

A network of locally accessible housing services cannot develop, nor can there be real autonomy in housing, so long as control is concentrated in the hands of supralocal agencies. The illusion of power and choice is not enough. The consultative role sometimes given tenant groups in low-income housing projects in the United States, and the laborer role given to participants in aided self-help projects such as that described by Turner in Chapter 6, are examples merely of lip service paid to autonomy while they are, in fact, examples of attempts at cooptation. But fewer and fewer people are really fooled; the dependent poor, throughout the world, have begun to understand that if they had any choice or any power to speak of, they would not be living as they are.

Decentralization is a popular term. And it is much easier to recommend it than to specify its details. Any number of instances in the United States context, for instance, indicate that decentralized control would mean the restriction of opportunities for one group by the social imperatives of another group. Yet the Madisonian argument against the potential dangers of parochial interests should not have to leave us with the alternative of completely hierarchical control.

One of the reasons that ghettos *are* ghettos rather than communities is the relative lack of resources, of opportunities, and of scope for individual expression of needs. Strategies which presume to provide *for* the poor, either by dispersing them or supplying their necessities *in situ*, are equally unsatisfactory as preconditions for the goal of greater autonomy.

In this respect—and this is only one of the many aspects of decentralization of control in housing—much of the present debate about racial and class integration can be seen as a misstated issue. It is, in a sense, misleading and even hypocritical to locate the point of conflict in the resistance of white middle-class communities to poor blacks when the black population is essentially disenfranchised in its present location. To imply that they will be better off by being dispersed can be read as an unconscious effort to perpetuate dependency, to neutralize any real pressure to decentralize the resources available for housing and education, and to block the growth of political power.

Location is extremely important in this sense: the poor must have access to jobs and the chance to maintain or create or to be absorbed into a supportive community. A liberal authoritarian solution which would move them, school them, and house them without reference to employment opportunities, without reference to the need for a degree of cultural and community integrity, and without the option for individual control over the immediate living environment has, at best, simply shifted a social problem in space, and at worst may have prolonged it in time by diluting a potential political force.

Several ways in which power can be delegated by central authorities or generated at the local level are described in the chapters of Part I. The simplest and most effective—where it does not lead to violent retaliation on the part of the power structure—is for local groups to take action on their own behalf, even in defiance of laws which have excluded them from the housing market.

Large sectors of the Peruvian urban blue-collar and lower-middle white-collar class have done this, along with their counterparts in many other countries of Latin America. Most clearly in the Peruvian case, and to varying if generally lesser degrees in other countries, massive autonomous action by local groups has changed the law and led to policies which have eventually supported, instead of attempting to suppress, such action.

As early as 1961, a law was passed in Peru which legalized existing and improvable squatter settlements and provided for further low-income residential settlement on a rational basis. Not only were legal titles provided to the squatters—in itself a considerable stimulus to individual investment—but also the Peruvian administrators have proceeded with the installation of utilities and community facilities, and more recently, the central government has tied public works to the demands of the new neighborhoods.[3]

By 1971 the boot appeared to be on the squatter foot. When a major invasion of privately held open land took place early in the year, it was the minister responsible for sending in the police who was removed.

The proposed Housing Advisory Service described in Chapter 2 for the support and extension of local housing networks in the United States and the closely related supervised credit system tried out in Lima and described in Chapter 6 is one legal means for achieving a comparable decentralization in and through housing action. The latter began by putting the money into the hands of the user himself so that he could call the tune in regard to the way in which his house would be built, even if there were still considerable constraints on what he had to build. A more complete housing advisory service, which would help the user exploit the network to his own best advantage, should greatly increase his freedom to decide what and where he will build, as well as how. In Huascarán, the borrowers had no options in regard to location or major elements of design in the first floor of their dwellings—the part financed with the credit provided to them. Housing advisory service users, on the other hand, would ideally be assisted in the assembly of the whole package, from site selection to the scheduling of subcontractors. (Harms gives urban American example of this process in Chapter 8.)

We are not suggesting here that assisted self-help housing could

[3] This policy is administered by the *Oficina Nacional de Desarrollo de Pueblos Jóvenes* (lit., the National Office for the Development of Young Towns), created by Decree in December 1968.

lead to the withering away of the state, but rather that as the dwellers assume responsibilities and assume costs, the resources of the state could be made available to a far greater proportion of low-income people. Extended networks could eliminate the need for many of the centrally designed and administered programs funded to meet the chronic crises of dependent populations, but not entirely, for that would be an absurd inflation of such a program's probable success. However, it could carry a significant part of control over housing and responsibility for housing back where every bit of common sense says it belongs—in the hands of those who are to be housed.

The more thoroughly supervised system employed by Better Rochester Living (described in Chapter 3) could also be significant as a precursor of larger-scale decentralization in the housing process. Though limited to those able and willing to assume home ownership and to provide their own labor, such a program requires far less subsidy per unit than any publicly administered program the authors know of in the United States.

Furthermore, while a nonprofit sponsor of the BRL type operates within the present hierarchic system, in practice it achieves a significant degree of decentralization by contriving to have many of the most important decisions made by or in close consultation with the dwellers themselves.

THE REDISTRIBUTION OF WEALTH

As equalizers of access to resources, networks are also distributors of wealth. As long as a reasonable parity is guaranteed by the framework of custom or law, those who start with less can at least maximize their opportunities to increase their wealth. And in contexts where material resources are limited, or where their excessive use by a minority reduces their availability for others, a setting of maximum standards of consumption and possession will have to be imposed if the kind of autonomy defined here is to exist. This is true at the international as well as at the national and local levels.

Legislative and administrative measures for the redistribution of wealth—in the form of subsidized goods and services or of income maintenance—can only be practiced in ways which support network systems in countries where the poor are a minority or where the national purse is large enough to subsidize *all* those in need. Anything less will be productive of the sort of economic and racial caste system and dependency relationships prevailing in the United States today.

There are countries with very wealthy and powerful governments where the majority are poor—in the oil-rich states such as Kuwait, for example. Aside from such odd and exceptional cases, direct housing subsidies in countries with poor majorities are inevitably limited to a privileged few. In these cases—and almost all low-income countries have subsidized housing programs of one sort or other—available resources have to be allotted to an insignificant number of projects available to an equally insignificant number of those in need, sometimes selected by lottery, or to those already relatively secure, thanks to their status as government employees (see Grenell's study of Bhubaneswar, Chapter 5) or as workers in modern industrial enterprises which pay relatively high wages and provide social security and housing benefits.

The lesson is a simple one, however difficult it may be to implement: subsidies are not incompatible with network systems, but they must be given in cash or its equivalent directly to users wherever possible, they must be available to all those who need and request them, and they must not be subject to political fiat.

In a context of wealth, such as the United States, a considerable degree of pump-priming will be necessary to establish effective networks among the poor minority. In contexts of national poverty, resources are much better spent on land reform, materials supply systems, and community infrastructures to aid poor majorities whose lot will not be in the least bettered by a scattering of imitations of western housing projects which can benefit, at the most, a tiny fraction of those in need.

Access to Information

Access to networks and the goods and services they can provide, along with the ability to use those resources, depends, of course, on information. The viability of the rules governing networks and their resources also depends on information. Users must have access to knowledge; planners, legislators, and administrators of norms and plans must know what users do with their laws and plans. Thus information resources and information feedback are complementary aspects of a key network precondition.

These imperatives raise issues already familiar to readers of the preceding chapters of this book. To the extent that local network users depend on professional and specialist knowledge (though often rather less than most experts would willingly admit), their expertise must be readily available. The difference between the professional mystery man (whether architect, lawyer, doctor, or teacher) who enjoys power through his monopoly of knowledge and the specialist who enjoys a creative life through sharing his knowledge is, of course, crucial in this context. Networks demand the support of specialists committed to increasing user autonomy; networks are destroyed by the professional monopolists.

The necessity for adequate feedback once again raises the issue of authority and authoritarianism. Authoritarian systems promote and to a degree are the product of massive collections of data. Data collection, as we are all well aware, has become an extremely sophisticated technique; yet in areas such as housing and education the knowledge gleaned has as often served to confuse or obscure as it has to clarify needs.

This should not raise the spectre of 1984. Information gathering has its legitimate place, but it does not permit a dialogue between the researcher and those researched. Statistical summaries, consumer surveys, and voter polls are all characteristic of hierarchic modes where the initiative lies in the hands of the few. While needs may in theory be satisfied on the basis of such research, a primary imperative of the subjects of such research to act on their own behalf, to evolve their own solutions, and to keep open an indeterminate sphere of life where needs can be expressed as they develop rather than being anticipated is left out of account.

The kind of feedback which emerges out of networks implies a parity of initiative between users on one hand and legislators and administrators on the other. It implies a dialectic in which rule-makers and those who are governed by the rules make mutual accommodations based on the constantly evolving context of their relationships.

In his study of Bhubaneswar, Grenell describes a classic denial of mutuality between rule-makers and those who must live under rules. Housing facilities were planned, at the outset, as if the planners knew all they needed to know or ever would need to know. It was only the undeniable evidence of certain failures which forced the providers to open a kind of dialogue (and that reluctantly) with those provided for. Similarly in the United States today, the planners of housing projects for low-income people have time and time again been forced to concede the failure of their plans, but how seldom, if ever, do they concede the failure of the fundamental relationship between themselves and those planned for.

It is not enough, therefore, to calculate a theoretical deficit of units and set out to make up that deficit by production strategies which leave out of account the dwellers themselves. At its worst, such strategies can produce projects like Pruett-Igoe, in St. Louis, an instant slum of such notoriously impacted social problems that the place has now been partly demolished. (See Plate 5.)

Pruett-Igoe is not a unique case. Other projects dedicated with great fanfare and optimistic forecasts have deteriorated as quickly; and it must be taken as a sign of the general blindness to how housing *works* that the failure of one federally sponsored experiment after another elicits only chagrin, dismay, and even disbelief on the part of officialdom.

There is an element of tragic humor in such reactions. Our technocracy has made us masters in the monitoring and adjusting of machines. Our space explorations are a triumph of electronic feedback used to produce exactly the desired results. But comparable if cruder methods applied to human engineering have failed miserably, for the basically simple reason that in housing, as in many other areas of life, the information sought has been the wrong information and the goals set have been the wrong goals.

Feedback is a topical term; it is often used casually and indiscriminately. But in housing it has a very real significance: it describes, or ought to describe, a constant reordering of perceptions, a constant process of bargaining and compromise between users of housing and those who set the rules under which housing is supplied. The kind of highly disciplined, single-minded effort which carried men to the moon is quite inappropriate in the area of housing. Housing does not represent one common objective agreed upon by all the actors involved nor is it facilitated by uniform procedures. Defects in its production cannot be corrected by information systems which report quantitative deficits of arbitrarily standardized units.

What central authorities do need to know, and what they have typically been unable or unwilling to inquire into, are such things as how dweller priorities are actually ordered, how dwellers' own resources might be used to achieve those priorities, and how existing constraints might be relaxed or removed so as to create varieties of housing types, which would be feasible in terms of their users' life interests rather than desirable according to supplier interests and criteria of often irrelevant or destructive dominant class values.

The Need for Simplified Technologies

Autonomy in housing depends to a large extent on the ease with which the elements of housing can be purchased and manipulated. There is a striking dichotomy here between the furnishings of a house and the house itself. The former can be purchased piecemeal over time and very much according to perceived and evolving needs; the latter is usually a discrete package which requires either a considerable cash accumulation or dependency on a lending institution. The poor may well be able to buy furnishings of some expensiveness, but the massive outlay for a house or the credit standing required for a mortgage loan to buy the house is out of the question.

As Donald Terner points out, a house is typically an indivisible product. Because of its complexity and the fact that it is attached to a particular piece of ground, it is removed from the effective demand of vast numbers of people who nevertheless have the need and the desire to become homeowners. And even for those who can buy this peculiarly expensive product, its complex subsystems often require the homeowner to become dependent on extremely expensive labor specialists.

The imperative here is conspicuous: if home ownership (and this includes cooperative ownership of apartment-type structures) is to be extended to the many families presently excluded from the market, the components which make up a dwelling must be made simpler, must be made cheaper, and must be made in such a way that they can be assembled incrementally.

This would not only allow more families either to build for themselves or to hire relatively unskilled labor to build for them, but it would also loosen credit (since the components would be easily repossessable), which is presently and understandably extended with great caution by lending institutions, whose policies are now so much determined by the fact that housing is a single package, virtually fastened to a single plot of land.

Performance Standards vs. Specification Standards

Among the most influential regulators of access to networks are the standards to which housing products must conform.

As Turner points out in Chapter 7, there is an important distinction between conventional building standards which prescribe the specifications of particular components (even determining dimensions and materials) and those which specify the physical *performance* of the component or product.

There is a world of difference between being told to build a wall of brick, so many inches thick, and being told that a wall must be capable of bearing such-and-such a load and that it must insulate to a given degree. In the first case, the user may be tied down to one path or combination of suppliers and contractors, but in the second case, he is free to use his imagination and skill and may find many alternative paths, any of which would meet the performance standard.

This vital distinction between specification and performance standards applies to architectural design as well as to building construction. Architects are often required to build certain specifications into their designs: a room must have a minimum window area, for example, irrespective of the fact that the shape and location of that window in relation to the exterior orientation and the interior surfaces will make enormous differences to the amount of daylight it admits. A smaller window may provide more daylight than a larger one if placed in a different position or if differently shaped.

Design standards, which include construction standards, go much further than purely physical considerations, of course. The combined effect of construction requirements and architectural or physical planning forms impose patterns of social relationships and are major determinants of household (and neighborhood) economies. Zoning and density requirements, house design and construction standards, together with licensing and financing regulations, may determine all but the most superficial characteristics of a residential environment.

Design performance standards, on the other hand, would establish parameters of a different kind. Just as physical performance standards for the technical aspects of building liberate the imagination and initiative for maximizing resources and encourage the discovery of new solutions without endangering people's safety and health, so would social and economic performance standards liberate us from the tyranny of socioeconomic homogenization.

Instead of being forced to build at a given density, for example, the promoter or owner would be obliged to generate tax returns which would pay the public costs of the density of occupation that he actually creates. Or, instead of insisting that any new construction be of a standard acceptable to the family of median (or an even higher) income level, any physically tolerable and safe shelter would be allowed as long as the price charged to the user maintained a reasonable (maximum) ratio to its cost. These particular examples may not be the best or most practical in all contexts, but they serve to illustrate the point. Strict rules of this kind, which would tend to emphasize *maxima* as much as, or even more than, *minima*, would be powerful instruments for the redistribution of wealth and political power.

Properly designed performance standards, for the physical, economic, and social components of housing, would revolutionize the role and impact of housing standards generally. The contemporary emphasis on what is minimally *desirable* in the view of authorities with power to impose specific forms would give way to standards which would define what is minimally *feasible*. That is, instead of exacerbating the gap between the poor and the better-off by insisting that low-income people build or rent what they "ought" to have or, if they cannot, to stay in their deteriorating slums, low-income people would be encouraged to make the best of what they have and to do so in ways that do not lock them, or future generations, into new slums.

While many, if not most, low-income urban families are necessarily renters rather than homeowners, this should not mean that they are powerless and passive recipients of housing supplied by public or private landlords. Their present powerlessness is reinforced by and is partly a consequence of unrealistically high minimum standards. These, of course, raise construction and rehabilitation costs to levels the unaided poor cannot afford and, therefore, increase their dependency. But if entrepreneurs were legally free to supply housing of standards the poor *could* afford, then both the poor and the authorities would have more control over the supply.

Unrealistic minimum standards contribute to premature obsolescence and deterioration, and inhibit progressive development. This point is illustrated by the diagrams contrasting two building-life cycles. In the worst of all cases, a dwelling, in its obsolescence, deteriorates rapidly as a result of factors such as tax laws penalizing improvements, housing codes which greatly increase the cost of repairs, and the tax-sheltered exploitation of deteriorated housing by speculators. In the second and ideal case—more common perhaps in poorer than in rich countries—the dwelling starts life at a low level. It improves rapidly at first, reaching an acceptable standard at an early stage; subsequent improvements continue to increase its value, and obsolescence and deterioration are delayed. In addition to tax legislation designed to maximize the life and usefulness of property and to curb speculation, performance housing standards and codes would slow deterioration as well as permit progressive development.

In the first case, the dwelling is accessible to low-income house-

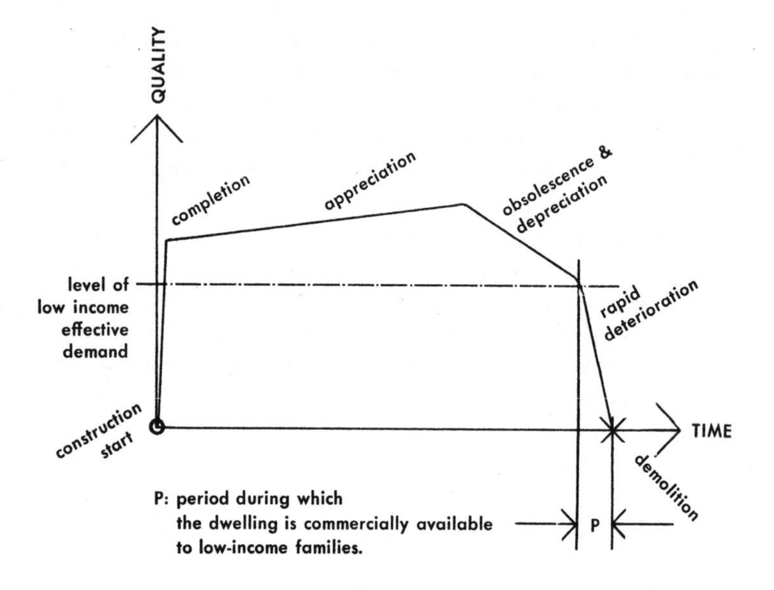

holds only for the short period of deterioration. In the second case, it is at least accessible to low-income users in the initial stage of progressive development as well as the much longer period of deterioration, which may even lead to a cycle of renewal. When continuously occupied by the original owner-builder's family, the progressively developed (or, as in the United States, the rapidly owner-built) dwelling may remain in the hands of relatively low-income users, thanks to the great economies they can achieve when free to build for themselves.

The justification for, or the necessity of, performance standards does not rest on the needs of low-income people alone. As Grindley shows, people of all income levels demand the freedom which

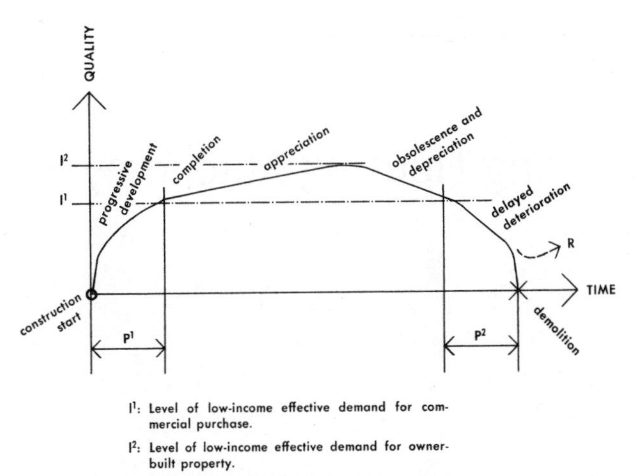

I^1: Level of low-income effective demand for commercial purchase.

I^2: Level of low-income effective demand for owner-built property.

$P^1 + P^2$: Periods during which the dwelling is commercially available to low-income household (entire period if owner-built and maintained).

R: Rehabilitation is faciltated if deterioration is checked.

only network systems can provide and which can only be protected and extended through the institution of performance standards. The fact that specification standards greatly limit freedom of action and starve network organizations means that they reinforce powers of central authorities and corporate organizations. The strong and often emotional resistance to the substitution of proscriptive for prescriptive norms and, especially, resistance to the acceptance of feasible standards instead of arbitrarily defined standards of desirability, suggests that these ideas are threatening to some. Those who fear them should ask themselves, or they should be asked, to what extent their reactions are due to a fear of losing power and authority to which they should have only limited rights anyway. Or, to what extent do they fear their own ignorance of the systems they manipulate and, therefore, their inability to formulate rules that would give people freedom instead of specifications which deprive them of it?

12

Increasing Housing Autonomy

THE PRINCIPLES AND ISSUES raised in this book have a universal relevance, but specific housing problems vary considerably with their cultural, political, and economic contexts. Since this book is written for those who are best acquainted with a highly industrialized and institutionalized world, it is reasonable, therefore, to limit the concluding discussion to that context. There is another reason for this narrowing of scope: the dominant and rich countries of the world provide the models and goals for the governments and dominant classes of the poorer part of the world. Until those models change, genuine and world-wide development is politically improbable and perhaps materially impossible.[1]

This is more often realized in industrialized than in transitional countries of the world, a situation which puts the disaffected but still very rich revolutionaries in an invidious position. It seems

[1] Typical of the more authoritative exponents of the necessity for limiting and redistributing economic growth are Herman E. Daley (viz. "Towards a Stationary-State Economy" in *The Patient Earth,* John Harte and Robert Socolow, eds., Holt, Rinehart and Winston, New York, 1971) and Robert Heilbroner (viz. "Ecological Armageddon" in *The New York Review of Books,* April 23, 1970).

more appropriate that they should give first priority to setting the house they live in in order and to changing the corporate-industrial model from within. It is up to their colleagues in the exploited, poorer countries of the world to reject the colonialist's self-serving definition of "development" and to evolve their own alternatives.

Who Practices Autonomy Now?

It may have come as a surprise to some readers of this book that each year in the United States as many as 160,000 families build or manage the building of their first (as distinct from their second or vacation) homes. This figure does not include those who make major alterations to their existing homes or who buy and rehabilitate older dwellings—both of which activities represent significant contributions to the national housing stock and to the social and economic sum of national fixed capital.

Since there must be as many people who significantly enlarge, improve, or rehabilitate existing structures as there are who build entirely new ones, we can say that approximately 300,000 U.S. families annually exercise a very considerable measure of autonomy in housing construction and reconstruction.

It is important to stress that the exercise of autonomy crosses a spectrum. At one extreme there are those who clear the land, gather the materials, and perform most or all of the actual building tasks themselves. Then there are those who act as their own general contractors, hiring out construction tasks. And then there are those who buy complete housing packages, but in a market situation which gives them a great latitude to fit available products to their perceived needs and ability to pay. Beyond this point, autonomy decreases sharply. In constrained markets purchasers may have to settle for considerable mismatches between what they want and what they can afford, and the poor and powerless must take what governments and protected suppliers assume they need or deserve.

From what Grindley, Goetze, and Harms have observed, however, many more families are capable and desirous of assuming responsibility for the provision of housing than our present situation permits. This is especially true for families with young children where resources needlessly diverted into cost-inflated, high-standard housing packages could much better be used in other ways.

What Are the Constraints on Autonomous Housing Action?

Those who literally build or who manage the building of their own homes without help from sponsoring and technical assistance organizations, such as Better Rochester Living, succeed by virtue of networks of locally available supplies of land, materials, tools, labor, and credit. As we have noted, it follows that the most common constraints are blockages in, breakdowns of, or absence of network access to one or more of these critical elements.

Lack of access to land and to credit are by far the most typical problems and the most difficult to overcome. With land prices rising at twice the general rate of inflation in many urban and metropolitan areas, this is certainly the major constraint, both on owner-builders themselves and on the small entrepreneurs who might act for them.

In addition to the inflationary increase in the price of buildable land (noted by Harms in Chapter 4), local banks are often unwilling to provide mortgage loans for owner-builders and even less willing, it seems, to service those who would be willing to rehabilitate deteriorated structures. This reluctance on the part of commercial credit institutions is exacerbated by the discriminatory practices of the FHA, noted by both Grindley and Goetze. And here one cannot help pointing out an irony in terms of our national ethic: that those who best exemplify the traditional American virtues of initiative and self-reliance should be denied privileges granted to those who have less or no need of public support should be seen as a cause for wonder, as well as an injustice that needs to be better understood and energetically protested.

Although we know less about owner-rehabilitators than we do about owner-builders, it has been noted (in the discussion of housing codes and their administration on pages 148–151) that they too are often severely hampered by regulations which demand an "all-or-nothing" approach to improvement. While many rural and even small town owner-builders are allowed or can get away with incremental construction (the unfinished but habitable home which may be nothing more than a semibasement in the first stage), this is impossible for owner-builders in city and suburban areas, and at best must be carried on clandestinely in the case of occupant rehabilitation.

Information is, of course, an essential ingredient in any market or submarket. Grindley finds that owner-builders are generally long-term residents of their neighborhoods and therefore know and are known by the suppliers of goods and services they need in order to build. Newcomers to an area, or those isolated because of race or class, are seriously handicapped. Even when such people persist in wanting to take advantage of existing networks and find means to obtain credit and land, or credit to buy a salvageable building, they are often at a loss to discover which supplies and services they really require, or from whom they can get them without being cheated.

In addition to the constraints imposed by land speculation, the reluctance of mortgagors, inhibiting housing codes and standards, the discriminatory administration of public programs, and the lack of information, Terner anticipates the negative consequences of mass-produced housing packages. There is a real danger that the fast-growing mobile home and so-called modular construction industry will corner the U.S. housing market. Even if these generally short-lived, difficult-to-maintain, and expensive or impossible-to-alter construction systems become absolutely cheaper than conventional methods, they would practically eliminate the self-help or owner-built options. It is extremely unlikely that even the most highly standardized, mass-produced units, of reasonable quality, could achieve the economies that the owner-builder can commonly obtain. Housing units prepackaged and mass-produced like automobiles will never have the flexibility or responsiveness of either traditional or modern component systems.

Changes that Must Be Made to Increase Autonomy in Housing

In highly institutionalized and industrialized countries, the measure of freedom people have to do what they are capable of doing for themselves in housing, and the ability of professionals and nonprofit organizations to assist them, depends on housing, building and planning law, government policies and programs, and the organization and trends of the construction industry.

The conclusions already pointed to in this book can be briefly summarized as follows: housing law should be rebuilt around performance standards which recognize the fact that housing is a process; government housing policies should be restructured on the basis of actions that generate support for networks of open housing services and, thereby, deal with the systems that produce houses rather than with the production of houses; and, finally, the building industry must modernize through the mass-production of compatible components which people (and small entrepreneurs) can use and assemble in their own ways.

The details of the change-over from project-based to service-based policies have yet to be spelled out. This change, from public entrepreneurship to the role, essentially more legislative than executive, of ensuring the just operation of a network of submarkets, can be simply described if three levels of government action are recognized. In between the "packages" of housing projects and the "elements" provided by the submarkets (defined by Turner in Chapter 7 as land, building materials and tools, labor and management skills, and financial credit), there is the intermediate level of "components."

A component is a part of a complete system. A housing project is a complete system or set of components, commonly consisting of a series of communications and utility networks (roads and sidewalks, water mains, sewers, electric light and power lines, etc.), a series of public, semipublic, and private spaces, and, of course, a series of structures including shops, schools, and so forth, as well as houses. Each of these more or less independently variable components can be built or installed and even owned and managed separately. There are markets for the basic elements from which all components can be assembled; there are markets, or at least different and independent supply, distribution, and management systems for most components; and finally, there are markets for different types or classes of complete systems or packages.

These levels can be arranged on a spectrum which runs from one extreme where the risks taken with public expenditures are very high and the potential material and human returns from

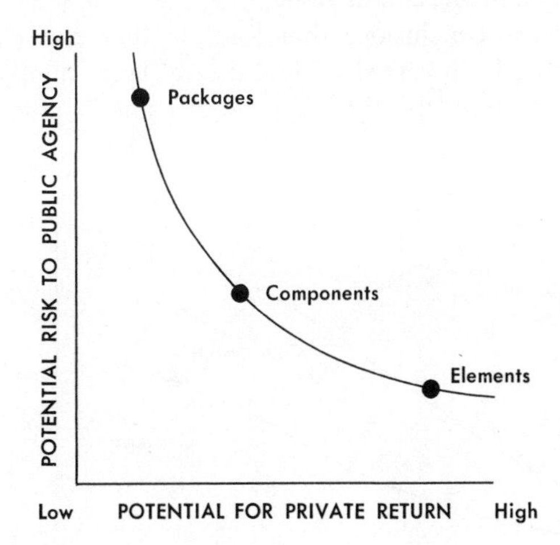

those expenditures are very low, to the opposite extreme where the financial risks are low and the potential returns are very high.

At the most risky and uneconomic end of the spectrum is the most common form of public housing program—that of the complete housing project or "package" of components. At the intermediate level are the projects in which a particular component is (or a few complementary components are) installed. A road and public transportation system, for instance, or a water supply and sewer system would be component levels of action. The risks of decapitalization in such programs are, of course, much less than in the conventional housing program; at the same time, the probability of considerable private investment resulting from such action is far greater. The third, least risky, and potentially most productive level is that of the basic elements of housing. These elements, common both to components and complete packages of systems, are: land, building materials, tools, labor and management, and, finally, finance and credit with which to obtain them. Effective action on the submarkets for these essential elements can have enormous repercussions, and these effects can often be achieved through legislation alone.[2]

The obvious conclusion, therefore, is that the conventional priorities must be reversed if significantly large numbers of people are to be served by the public sector and if government ac-

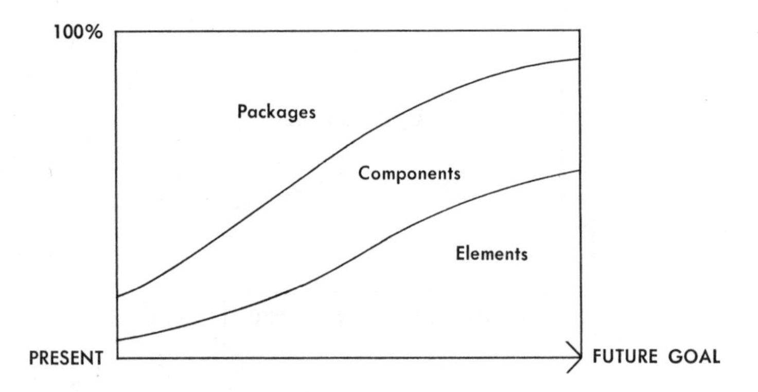

tion is to generate any significant increase in housing investment without driving the public authority into bankruptcy.

If public action were limited to controls over the basic markets and the provision of guidelines for the investments made, then public investments in housing and urban development would be minimal. Public utilities and many other services, however, are

[2] When unused urban land is free from property or capital gains taxes, speculative buying can force prices up so high that half the cost of a modest dwelling is absorbed by the unimproved land alone. In Mexico City, for example, tens of thousands of families are prevented from investing in improved dwellings because land costs are three or four times as high as they are in, for example, Tel Aviv, where speculation is minimized through taxation.

necessarily installed and managed by public or semipublic organizations. It is also a fact that in some emergencies even the most agile housing market is unable to respond to legitimate demands. In a less than perfect market, and in contemporary political reality, a minimum of public expenditure at the least economic and productive level is unavoidable and even necessary. The recommendation, therefore, is that all new investments in housing should be concentrated at the component and element levels. If these actions are taken in cognizance of the nature of the housing

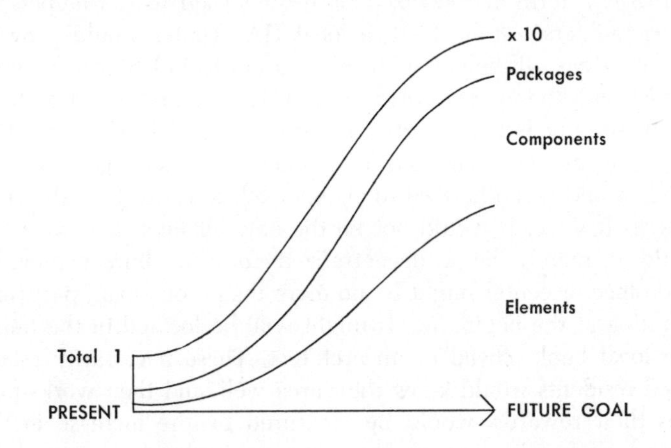

systems and their roles in the urban process, then the increase in private investment and in the proportion of the population served will be very large, even with only a modest increase in the national or state budgets for housing.

This policy assumes that the major problem in housing is inaccessibility of the principal resources or elements and the consequent loss to the housing sector of the investments that would be made by commercial entrepreneurs, by nonprofit groups, and by individual families if they had access to resources they are quite capable of using.

This brings us back to the practical problem of increasing access where it already exists, and of generating networks of services where they are needed but do not exist.

The Housing Advisory Service (HAS) is one solution to this problem. HAS was inspired in part by a highly successful service instituted in Australia after the Second World War[3] (and partly from the present proposers' previous experience in Latin America). OSTI first made the proposal to HUD in 1970[4] as one of a series of proposals for federal support to self-help builders in the U.S. More recently, the idea has been developed by Spohn, Grenell, and Grindley. Their proposed legislation is included in Chapter 2 (see pp. 22–52).

HAS is a form of socialized professional aid to self-helpers or owner-builders. At the least, a local HAS center would provide the intending self-helper with information to aid him in making contact with the network. At the most, HAS would act as a channel for state or federal mortgage insurances to local lenders. The service would be analogous to a telephone exchange, but one which would be authorized to channel subsidies for long distance calls, as it were. It would not be the only channel, however, nor would it merely be a decentralized form of bureaucracy. A local office or center might be no more than a one-man, part-time operation at the beginning. It might well be located in the home of a local bank official or an architect. These necessarily established residents would know their area well, and their work—perhaps their rewards—would be measured by the increase in the number of families served from sectors previously unserved by the local housing market.

In the case of the Architects Housing Service of Melbourne, Australia, the service was set up on the initiative of the regional chapter of the Royal Australian Institute of Architects and a local newspaper in response to the huge and sudden increase in the need for new homes by returning servicemen and their growing families.

The established building industry was either unable to supply

[3] The authors are indebted to Professor John Brine of the University of Edinburgh for this information.

[4] See *Organization for Social and Technical Innovation, Owner-Built Housing in the United States,* Report No. 8 prepared for the U.S. Department of Housing and Urban Development, Washington, D.C., 1970.

enough new homes, or to supply them (as in the contemporary U.S. case) at the prices which those most in need of them could afford. The architects developed componentized plans, specifications, quantities, and cost estimates, which provided an immense range of alternative solutions capable of meeting all but the most peculiar conditions and individual needs. The newspaper set aside space for directories of real estate agents, banks, materials suppliers, specialist contractors; for reports on current prices; for articles of practical interest, and so forth. Between the two, an extremely effective network-supporting service was created. It aided a large proportion of all home construction in the postwar years and continues, on a reduced scale, to this day.

As the Australian HAS demonstrates, the private sector in general embodies the potential for encouraging greater autonomy in housing; the young professionals generated an effective demand for their services and the commercial newspaper greatly increased its circulation.

The private sector has, however, been more often cited for its profit orientation and alleged irresponsibility than for its potential as a force for increasing individual freedom—at least in recent years. This trend has had its effect: to underestimate the impact of consumer advocates such as Ralph Nader on contemporary corporate management in the U.S. is to fail to appreciate what many executives have come to view as a significant threat to the perpetuation of their institutions. Hence some corporations have tentatively ventured into "limited profit" activities—trading off "normal" levels of return on investment for the sake of an improved image.

Yet these activities, often undertaken because of the pressure of public opinion or the threat of legal action, and paid for out of corporate profits, are unlikely to reduce housing costs or to do anything to improve the housing situation of the poor.

It is more than likely that such "altruistic" programs will continue on into the future; and while some may prove to be worthwhile, the majority will operate on a token scale and will be aimed more at good press than at good housing. This is not merely to indict the executives of the private commercial sector as cynical or unconcerned. The indictment is far broader; for these executives reflect the priorities of the much more broadly based population of corporate shareholders to whom they are ultimately responsible. Hence, short of radical social change, corporations will probably continue to exist primarily as creatures of profit.

How, then, can private-commercial sector interests respond within the profit framework? First, they must fully recognize the magnitude of the world's unmet housing needs, and understand that this need, although not presently backed by the resources of money that guarantee huge profits with no risk, *is* backed by *some* money—and tremendous reserves of energy, ingenuity, resourcefulness, and competence on the part of the people.

Should the executives of the building materials portion of the private sector doubt that there is cash, that there is potential effective demand, that, indeed, there is profit to be made through service to the low-income segments of the world's markets, then they ought to take note of the successes of those who have marketed consumer durables to low-income users. Those who are in the shelter market should count the number of items such as television sets, refrigerators, and automobiles in the ghettos, slums, *favelas, barriadas,* and *bidonvilles* of the world.

This is not to suggest that the problems of marketing shelter and durable goods are the same. They are not. But what this does suggest is that a significant, effective demand does exist among low-income populations, and in the case of shelter, enormous, pent-up demand. Those who are potentially capable of tapping the market must understand that in order to do so they have to follow the lead of other consumer suppliers by totally reexamining such things as methods of credit and levels of risk, and product design, use, and life. With regard to the latter, monolithic "packages of housing" must be dismantled and disaggregated into discrete and manipulable components that respond to the energies and capabilities of low-income dwellers. The private commercial sector must recognize that its present array of prepackaged products does not meet the needs of this segment of the market. To participate, the private sector will have to concentrate its research and product development efforts on the kinds of housing components described by Terner in his innovations agenda

(Chapter 9). Furthermore, these components should ideally be thought of as "tools" for improved shelter in the hands of those in need.

Such components must possess at least two crucial characteristics which demand industry-wide cooperation or regulation. First, they must be dimensionally coordinated, and second, they must join and connect easily and compatibly. Additional desirable characteristics, as discussed in Chapter 9, should include a network of highly disaggregated components, which can be combined according to preference and without special skills into a very large variety of compositions. If this can be accomplished, then the private commercial sector may well find its involvement in improved housing not to be a token altruistic gesture, but a needed and viable extension of its present market.

Simultaneously, the private sector can use its considerable lobbying expertise to seek removal of government obstacles and red tape that hinder autonomous housing actions, while pressing for demand-side subsidies to improve the direct purchasing power of low-income families. The overriding goal of the private sector ought to be to assure that all families—but especially low-income families—attain maximum leverage with their housing expenditures by having access to products better designed to respond to a range of goals, abilities, and levels of direct participation.

The Role of Professionals in the Increase of Autonomy in Housing

Those of us who are professionals should remind ourselves, at the outset, that our actions will be determined by the stand we take on the basic issue raised in this book. That issue is user control versus authoritarian control of the housing process. As professionals, either we can help people to make their own decision, or we can try to make decisions for them.

It goes without saying that we reject the second alternative in all but crisis situations, and we further reject the institutionalization of the housing crisis as an excuse for institutionalized values and professionalized decision-making.

Those who would like to direct their skills to the increase rather than to the decrease of control on the part of user-clients need a conceptual framework which will help to identify the various professional roles. Donald Terner developed such a framework during the seminar sessions held by the authors of this book and others at CIDOC in September 1971.

It was agreed that the key considerations are *who pays for* and *who receives* the professional's services. The situation schematically described by the first cell in the diagram (upper left) is obvious and very common. It could indicate, for example, the case

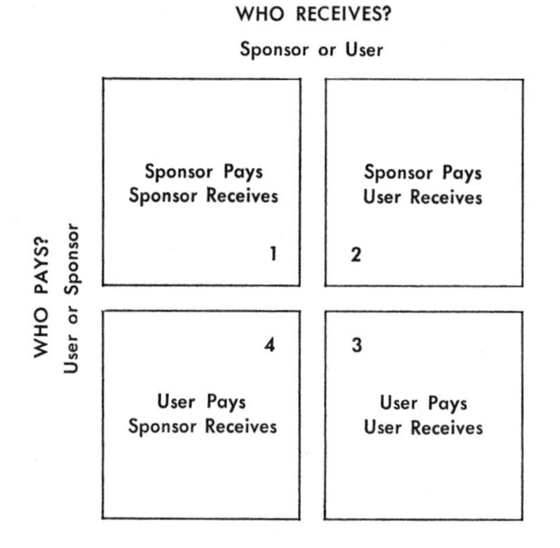

of a professional employed by a government to study housing conditions and perhaps to recommend to that government a series of program priorities and alternatives.

The basic distinction implied in the diagram (and explored by Harms in the area of architectural design in Chapter 8) is that between sponsor-clients and user-clients. Thus an architect or planner working for HUD or for a municipal urban renewal agency, for instance, clearly belongs in Cell 1. His services are bought by and directed to a nonuser client.

Although it is not the rule, when a professional working within this cell senses that his recommendations are at odds with the sponsor-client's prejudices and interests, and therefore are being ignored or perverted, he may deal with this dissonance either by doing careless and superficial work or by assuming a fifth-column role.

An example outside the role of housing is the case of Dr. Daniel Ellsberg and the now famous "Pentagon Papers." Ellsberg was initially located in Cell 1 of the diagram, but after resigning in frustration (and incidentally finding himself another sponsor) offered the results of his Cell 1 research to the public at large.

In terms of our schematization, Ellsberg has moved from Cell 1 to Cell 2 (upper right), and in the course of that move has, to say the least, incurred the displeasure of his original sponsors.

A less dramatic case is that in which the sponsor-client pays the professional's salary knowing that the latter's work will be directed to user-clients. This is an intrinsically unstable situation, since the sponsor obviously expects conformance to its values and goals, in spite of the great likelihood that basic user needs will conflict with those values and goals.

Let us give some examples. A physically expanding university has run into conflict with the surrounding community. Its expansionist policies have driven up land values and are beginning to force local residents out of the area. Since it is sensitive to its image as a humane institution, the university appoints a community relations officer. Yet if the community relations officer construes his role as an advocate for the community rather than as a spokesman for his sponsor, he will very quickly find himself in an untenable position and will probably be fired.

A classic national instance of this conflict can be found in the nation-wide legal assistance offices funded by the Office of Economic Opportunity (OEO). Young lawyers were in theory hired to protect the rights of the poor. Some of those lawyers took the mandate seriously and found themselves pressing class action suits against the government. With a chagrin hardly surprising, the government treated these too-committed professionals as troublemakers and renegades who were "biting the hand that fed them."[5]

[5] See, for example, Jack Rosenthal, "Agnew Questions U.S. Aid for Poor to Sue Officials," *The New York Times*, February 3, 1972, p. 1.

Some of them, when they were fired, continued in their jobs, fighting the same battles but drawing their salaries from more neutral sponsors or directly from the users themselves. In the latter case, the professionals have moved into Cell 3 of our diagram (lower right). In present circumstances, this is a situation which requires a rare commitment on the part of professionals, who must often accept financial and status rewards far below those offered to peers who have contributed their services to munificent institutional and governmental clients.

Cell 3 illustrates the case of many advocate planners; yet communities are not the only beneficiaries of their work. Alternative plans and proposals have frequently been presented to government and other agencies, and thus we move toward Cell 4 (lower left), where users or local sponsors pay for services which are per-

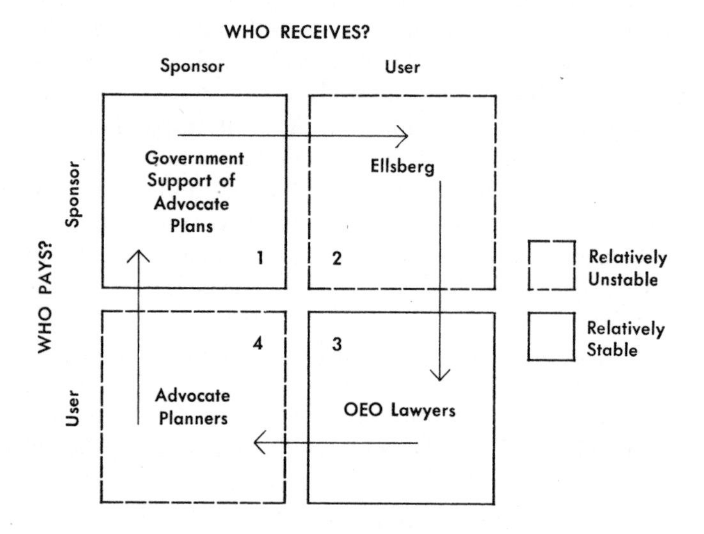

formed in lieu of inadequate or irresponsible central planning. But when this is the case, the question inevitably arises: "Why shouldn't the government or central authority foot the bill?"

The professional who is, in effect, using the initiative and investments of his local user-clients to demonstrate new techniques or to introduce solutions to the problems of society at large *should* be paid by the public. He will naturally seek and will probably be encouraged by his clients to move into Square 1.

This cyclic movement is not necessarily followed, however, even by the professional committed to the users' interests and autonomy. The appropriateness and relative stability of one professional situation over another depends, as the following paragraphs explain, on a third dimension that may now be added to the paradigm.

In any of the four situations, the professional will either be working on the regulations governing actions or on specific actions—either as a rule-maker or as a game-player, to use Turner's chess analogy. If the goal is to satisfy needs in ways which increase rather than decrease the autonomy of the users of housing, then the administrative separation of these crucially different rule-making and game-playing functions is essential. As we have seen, the fusion or confusion of these roles generates hierarchic and authoritarian forms of organization, the antithesis of network forms and autonomy.

Unless a distinction is made between setting the limits to what people may build on the one hand and telling them what to build on the other, there is no way of knowing whether the professional is likely to be contributing to the increase or decrease of user autonomy. If the model is to serve as a guide for those concerned with this issue, then a rule-game or norm-specification dimension must be added.

In Square 1, where the professional is employed by a sponsor—which we can assume to be a supralocal or central organization with powers to regulate and program the activities it sponsors—he may have either a normative or an executive role. That is, he may be formulating the rules and regulations governing the sponsors' activities, or he may be preparing or carrying out specific actions within the framework of existing rules. In the first case, the professional's activity may support local autonomy. In the second case, however, it is likely that he will be destroying or frustrating it.

A professional architect who designs housing projects for a

public housing agency, for example, is part and parcel of an authoritarian system, no matter how liberal and well-meaning he or she may be. For so long as the agency designs and delivers the housing package, it maintains the user in positions of dependency, and therefore reduces the value of the process to the material value of its physical product. With the partial exception provided by the subsequent freedom of housing project tenants to modify, or simply to redecorate and furnish, their assigned dwellings, the actual processes of sponsorship, construction, and management are of no interest or value to the users since they have no responsible part in them.

The number of professionals and administrators aware of the problems of nonparticipation and uneasy about its significance has grown enormously during the 1960s, especially in the wealthy and highly institutionalized contexts to which we now refer. This is shown by well-meant but often counterproductive efforts to build "participation" into housing legislation and in the rapidly growing interest in and demand for studies on behavioral effects of the built environment (sometimes called "socio-physical technology).

There is less tension, however, in the situation of the socially conscious or concerned professional (Cell 1 of the diagram) who is working on the rules rather than on specific games. For the professional committed to the increase of autonomy, the opportunity to work with legislators sympathetic to the antiauthoritarian goals of network organization and local autonomy is ideal. If he cannot, or if his character and skills are more suited to the carrying out of specific works, the professional's ideal situation will be the opposite and complementary situation of Cell 3 in which his paying clients are the users themselves.

If the professional's user-clients require him to formulate rules and regulations, however, he will again be in a tense situation. Local groups who presume to create their own laws only for local use isolate themselves from the rest of society even if the local lawmakers do not end up by exploiting those who become dependent on them. The common cases of local communities which adopt their own zoning codes, or of towns which pass their own housing and building regulations, clearly show how these can become instruments of oppression directed toward ethnic or class minorities as well as weapons of self-defense against exploitation by superior commercial market forces. Local bodies should have no need for such legislation, and if they do, it is owing to deficiencies in state or national law or its administration.

Whether the professional concerned with the development of network systems and autonomy finds himself working for would-be local lawgivers or with local builders frustrated by supralocal regulations, he will tend to move into Cell 4 where, though paid by the local user-clients, his interest will be to effect changes in the state or national law. And from that situation he will, of course, tend to move into the more appropriate situation of Cell 1 in which the legislative authority is his direct client.

In addition to knowing who pays for and who gets his services, it is also essential for the professional to recognize the difference between the complementary skills of designing norms and normalizing designs. Those who fail to make this distinction and who cannot clearly define their roles are much more likely to be decreasing than increasing autonomy.

The well-intentioned professional, schooled in the liberal authoritarian tradition of presumed superiority of the institutionally educated, is undoubtedly the most successful builder of hell-on-earth. The more the liberal or radical authoritarians persuade themselves (and their subjects) of the power of their pseudo-knowledge, the more power they have in political fact. By building "citizen participation" into legislation and through increasingly sophisticated "socio-physical technology," those who have great financial and institutional resources may indeed impose the designed city on man.

The physically preplanned city, designed in detail and even built by the socio-physical technocrats, is an Orwellian antiutopia for the authors of this book—and anyone else for whom real life lies in the relationships between man and man, between men and the things they make, and between human life and the living universe.

"... people do not only need to obtain things. I think they need, above all, the freedom to make things —things among which they can live. To give shape to them, according to their own feelings, their own tastes, their own imagination. And to put them to use in caring for each other and about each other. Prisoners often have access to more things and services than other members of their families. But they have no say in how things are to be made and cannot decide what to do with them. Their punishment consists exactly in being deprived not of things but of what I call conviviality. Not of products, but of intercourse—real live intercourse. I choose the term 'conviviality' to designate precisely the contrary of productivity. I want it to mean autonomous and creative intercourse among persons, and of intercourse of persons with their environment. In this sense I oppose conviviality to the conditioned and efficient response which persons give to the demands made on them by others."

From "The Destruction of Conviviality," a conversation between Ivan Illich and Richard Wollheim, recorded at a conference of philosophers in Cyprus (*The Listener*, Vol. 86, No. 2229, December 16, 1971, p. 827).

PLATE 1. *Saranac-Newcastle Court buildings, Boston, 1971.* Through parties and a music group, a tenant organization was formed in order to save the buildings from destruction, purchase them and rehabilitate them (see Chapter 8).
DAVID JUDELSON.

"Planners want 'social change'; they deal in words, drawings, programs and buildings, not guns and napalm. But the kind of 'social change' they usually find themselves dealing with, whether or not they recognize it, is organizing the oppressed into a system incapable of providing them with a humane

PLATE 2. *Publicly subsidized and built "low-cost" housing in the Philippines, 1970.* PATRICK W. CROOKE

PLATE 4. *Publicly subsidized and built "urban renewal" housing in Korea, 1970.* In the foreground, a squatter family's dwelling reerected among the ruins of a former home destroyed in order to relocate the occupants in the new apartment block in the background. Another block, in a similar relocation program, had collapsed weeks before the photograph was taken, killing thirty-two occupants, and other blocks in that project were promptly evacuated and demolished. PATRICK W. CROOKE

existence, pacifying them with the meager welfare offerings that help maintain the status quo. At best we help ameliorate the condition produced by the status quo; at worst we engage in outright destruction." *From After the Planners by Robert Goodman, Simon & Schuster, 1971.*

PLATE 3. *Publicly subsidized and built "low-cost" housing in Brazil, 1968-69.*
COHAB, RIO DE JANEIRO

PLATE 5. *Publicly subsidized and built "urban renewal" housing in the USA, 1972.* Pruitt-Igoe, St. Louis, Missouri. An international architectural award-winning project, occupied in 1954. In 1972, after years of uncontrollable vandalism, violence and semi-vacancy, a number of the buildings in the project were demolished and others rehabilitated. The latter were reduced from eleven to four stories in order to achieve a more human scale in the project.
UNITED PRESS INTERNATIONAL

PLATE 6. *A bachelor-worker's dwelling in Delhi, India.* Suspended from a public utilities pole during the day.
YASHWANT DAS

PLATE 7. *Very poor squatters in Ahmedad, India.* Note the middle-class neighborhood in the background—this provides the squatters with their market.
PATRICK W. CROOKE

PLATE 8. *A public housing project in an Indian city.* These two-room apartments have to be heavily subsidized, and, even then, only better-paid workers and government employees can afford to live in them.
PATRICK W. CROOKE

PLATE 9. A barriada, *or squatter settlement of the poorer sort, in Lima, Peru.* Note the middle-class neighborhood in the background—which provides many of the settlement's inhabitants with job market. JOHN F. C. TURNER

PLATE 10. A bustee, *or squatter settlement of the poorer sort, in Delhi, India.* This settlement is also located near the city center and adjacent to middle-class residential neighborhoods. PATRICK W. CROOKE

Both settlements occupy inner-city land of high and rising commercial value. In neither do the squatters have secure tenure. Little or no physical improvement takes place in these conditions, partly because of their insecurity, partly because an increasing proportion of the people rent from the original squatters, and partly because of the high and rising population density.

HANS H. HARMS

PLATES 11–13. *Direct action: A squatter demonstration, Boston, 1968.*
The purpose of the Tent City demonstration was to protest the Boston Redevelopment Authority's neglect of poor people's housing and to demand control by residents over local housing action. The site of the demonstration was (and still is) a parking lot belonging to the then City Fire Commissioner. The site was previously occupied by deteriorating, low-rental tenements. Although the BRA was carrying out a federally supported program for the rehabilitation of some 4,000 units, very few of these were available to those who lost their homes through demolitions, and no new units were built for them. Tent City was organized by the Community Assembly for a United South End (CAUSE), created in February, 1967. CAUSE organized its first demonstration, picketing the BRA's local office, on April 23rd, 1968. As this brought no official response, the building was occupied by the demonstrators. After ejection by the police it was decided that the Fitzgerald parking lot should be picketed. An incident provoked by an impatient car owner led to the arrest of 23 persons; it was then decided that the parking lot should be occupied. Tent City was established at 7 A.M. on April 27th and was held until 1.30 P.M. on the 29th. As an immediate result, the city council passed a resolution to institute a local urban renewal committee to be elected by local residents.

PEOPLE
NEED
HOMES

PLATE 14. *Direct action: Squatters take land in Chile, 1971.*
If inflated land prices or snob planning and building codes prevent people from housing themselves, then they must either continue to live in overcrowded and overpriced slums or they must squat. This is the only choice for most people in the cities of rapidly urbanizing, low-income countries where governments attempt to solve problems created by poverty, speculation, and subsidized programs for the rich. But where annual budgets for housing amount to a few dollars (or even cents) per capita, and where most peoples' housing needs are unsatisfied, subsidies can reach only a privileged few—even in socialist or "planned" economies. The banner reads: "[The] 'Che Guevara Encampment–[The] Homeless Citizens' Movement–(a) House or Death, We Will Win." This is not empty rhetoric. In many countries squatters have been killed resisting eviction by the police or armed forces. JAMES GOODSELL, THE CHRISTIAN SCIENCE MONITOR.

AMPAMENTO
"CHE
GUEVARA"
MOVIMIENTO
POBLADORES SIN CASA
CASA O
MUERTE
VENCEREMOS

The progressive development of a Pueblo Jóven *in Lima, Peru*
Three contemporaneous photographs from similar *pueblos jóvenes* (as the perjoratively termed *barriadas* are now officially designated) showing three typical stages of autonomous development.

PLATE 15. *Squatters consolidate their tenure by building a wall around their lot.*
The family may continue to live in the woven cane matting shack for several years while saving to build their permanent home. In the mild and rainless climate of Lima, domestic life in the enclosed lot is far healthier and more comfortable than in the overcrowded tenements—and, with no mortgage payments, they live rent-free. WILLIAM P. MANGIN

CHILCA
CEMENTO
CEMENTO

PLATE 16. *Little by little, the squatters build the first floor of their permanent house.* A reinforced concrete roof capable of supporting a second storey must be built in one major effort, however. After years of savings, or, as in this case, (Pampa de Comas, 1963), with a short-term credit from a government agency, the owner-builder hires a neighboring contractor to do the work.
EVA LEWITUS, FOTO ART, LIMA.

PLATE 17. *As the houses are completed and as second storeys are built for siblings or for renting, utilities and sidewalks are installed.* In this case (san Martin de Porres, 1965) the utilities were installed by a government agency and the sidewalks and planting by self-organized block and street associations. JOHN F. C. TURNER

PLATES 18–20. *When commercially valueless hillsides are located conveniently near central city areas, they are often preempted by squatters.* When they have reasonably secure de facto tenure, the squatters invest as rapidly as they can, whether it is in Seoul, Korea (18) or Lima, Peru (19). Autonomous urban settlements, whether developing at the margin of a technological society or in the mainstream of a preindustrial society, as in Mykonos, Greece (20), a genuine vernacular and culture emerges.

PATRICK W. CROOKE

JOHN F. C. TURNER

JOHN F. C. TURNER

PLATE 22. *The first stage of an unaided self-help or owner-built home in rural South Dakota.* Only the habitable semi-basement and garage had been built at the time the photograph was taken (March 1969). The main structure will be added when the family can afford (or obtain credit for) the extension—hopefully before it has more than one or two children. JOHN F. C. TURNER

PLATE 21. Mexican American participants in an aided and mutual self-help home-building program, originated, co-sponsored, and directed by Self Help Enterprises Inc. (SHE), of Visalia, California. During the first seven years of operation, SHE participants have built over 1,000 (mostly 3-bedroom) units for average mortgage loans of $8,500 and 1,250 hours of labor. GEORGE BALLIS

PLATE 23. *A home built by unemployed coal miners in the first mutual and self-help housing project in the United States.* Westmorelands Homesteads, Norveld, Pa., based on cooperative poultry farming, was initiated in 1933 with 100 families; 250 units had been completed by 1940. The original community flourishes today (1972).
PAUL M. CAMPBELL, C. 1935.

PLATE 24. *An owner-built home in Beverly, Massachusetts (a North Shore suburb of Boston).* Initially a four-room "cape cod" built for $6,000 in 1955 by the owner, a 25-year-old machinist, this enlarged eleven-room house was worth more than twice the total cost to the owner-builder, an engineer when the photograph was taken in March, 1969.
JOHN F. C. TURNER

KING-BISON CO., BOST

PLATES 25 and 26. Even though the cost of rehabilitating structurally sound older buildings suffering the effects of deferred maintenance need be no more than half the cost of new buildings, many more inner-city and inner-ring dwellings continue to be destroyed than new ones erected. In Boston (upper photo) 1⅓ units were demolished during the 1960s for every unit of new contsruction. Most of the demolished dwellings were occupied by low and moderate income families but few of the new units built in the same period were for lower income families. Large-scale demolitions and inadequate replacements also displace those unable or unwilling to accept the generally homogenized renewal housing—often of the kind shown in the background of the lower photograph of the Bronx, New York City. The displaced poor create critical concentrations in already blighted areas, precipitating wholesale abandonment and therefore leading to further demolition.

JOHN LITTLEWOOD

MFRS. of
HOTELS,

PLATE 27. In 1965, Better Rochester Living, Inc., a private nonprofit enterprise in New York State, initiated a highly promising way of rehabilitating homes and of protecting neighborhoods from premature decay and destruction. In this program, which had served over 300 families by 1972, the future owners select their own homes, decide on the improvements to be made and carry out many of the tasks themselves. Few middlemen are involved in the process, the overhead costs are low and the participants, highly motivated by the expectation of homeownership, contribute and learn all they can. Another nonprofit program for the rehabilitation of the same kinds of houses in the same neighborhoods and for the same kinds of people failed after providing only 30 dwellings at an average unit cost 80 percent higher than those of BRL. This program followed procedures encouraged by the FHA; many intermediaries were involved, the construction was contracted and the heavily subsidized units were for rental. BETTER ROCHESTER LIVING INC., ROCHESTER, NEW YORK.

PLATES 28 and 29. Before and after photographs of a sub-dividable unit typical of the larger homes rehabilitated through the BRL program. The average purchase construction and administrative cost of all BRL units was approximately $11,500 in 1970. WELTON MYERS.

PLATES 30–35. *Erector set technology.* A persistent technological dream has been to create for adults what toymakers have succeeded in creating for children—simple sets of construction components with easy, virtually fool-proof joining systems such as Erector Sets, Tinkertoys, Lego, etc. Two such attempts are illustrated here. The one on these two pages utilizes a lightweight, precast concrete frame with bolted joints; the one on the following two pages, a precut and predrilled wooden frame with bolted joints. Both systems were designed for use by people with no prior construction training or experience, and no access to power tools or equipment. Both also include complete step-by-step assembly instructions.

IAN DONALD TERNER

IAN DONALD TERNER

IAN DONALD TERNER

SHELTER KIT INC., FRANKLIN, N.H.

SHELTER KIT INC., FRANKLIN, N.H.

SHELTER KIT INC., FRANKLIN, N.H.

PLATE 36. *Kit houses.* One of the techniques which can be employed to reduce the skill levels required for construction is to combine prepared building materials and components with complete sets of assembly instructions. In this manner, construction kits can save the inexperienced builder considerable efforts, including design, phasing, sequencing, measurement, cutting, drilling, and selecting and purchasing materials. Kits are not a new idea; the advertisements shown above are from the 1908, 1912, and 1918 Sears, Roebuck Catalogues. SEARS, ROEBUCK AND CO. CATALOG, SPRING 1908, SPRING 1912, SPRING 1918

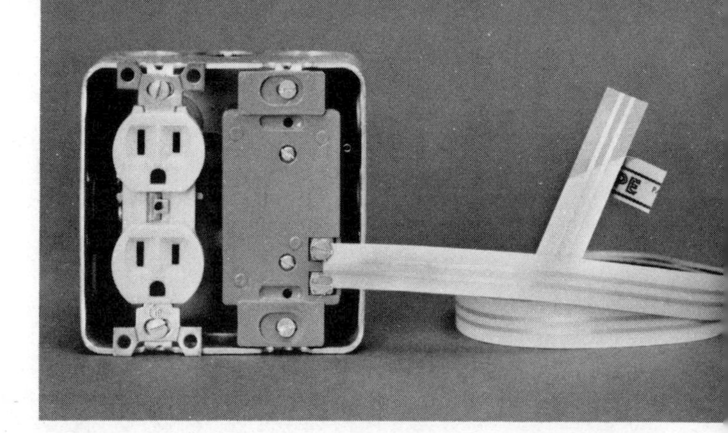

PLATE 37. *Scotch Tape wiring.* For the layman, one of the most difficult aspects of wiring or rewiring a home centers on the wires being "buried" inside walls, floors, and ceilings. Often the wiring is difficult or impossible to reach without considerable experience and unsightly cuts into wall surfaces which are time consuming and costly to repair. Surface-mounted wiring, with a profile as thin as a human hair, can now be manufactured in adhesive-backed strips much like a standard piece of cellophane tape. This wiring can even be used with "stick-on" switches which do not penetrate the wall surface, or with conventional electric boxes as shown in the photograph. The wiring can be installed or moved easily and safely by self-helpers without reliance on skilled electricians. ABT ASSOCIATES INC., CAMBRIDGE, MASS.

PLATE 38. With a model made of movable pieces similar to the one shown in the photograph, architect Diego Robles discusses alternative house plans with participants in an aided and mutual self-help housing project in Peru, 1959. EMIL WILLIMETZ.

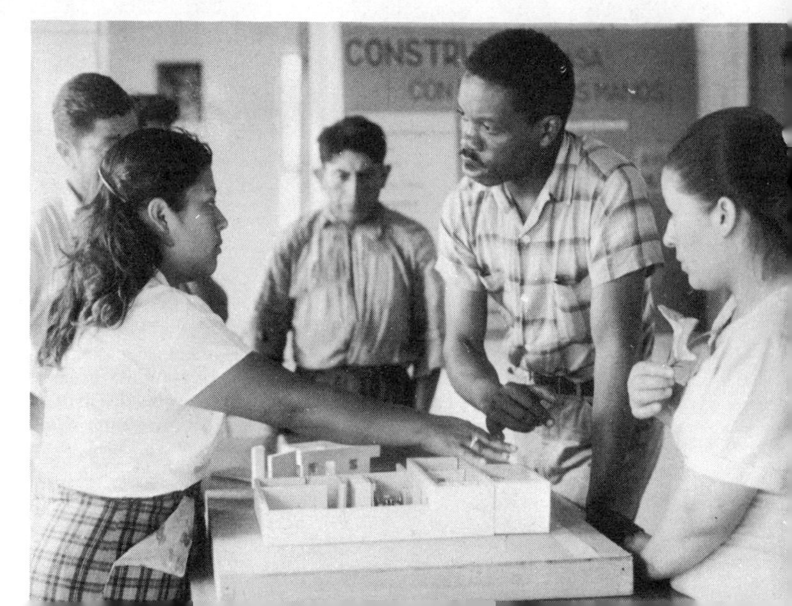

PLATE 39. Student architect Robert Yelton, of the Community Projects Laboratory of MIT, helps members of the Saranac and Newcastle Court tenants' association (see PLATE 1) plan the remodelling of their own apartments. Boston, 1969. DAVID JUDLESON.

Index